Sport, Media and Society

Sport, Media and Society

Eileen Kennedy and Laura Hills

Oxford • New York

English edition
First published in 2009 by
Berg
Editorial offices:
First Floor, Angel Court, 81 St Clements Street, Oxford, OX4 1AW, UK
175 Fifth Avenue, New York, NY 10010, USA

Berg is the imprint of Oxford International Publishers Ltd.

Library of Congress Cataloguing-in-Publication Data

A catalogue record for this book is available from the Library of Congress.

British Library Cataloguing-in-Publication Data

A catalogue record for this book is available from the British Library.

ISBN 978 1 84520 686 4 (Cloth)
ISBN 978 1 84520 687 1 (Paper)

Typeset by Apex Publishing, LLC, Madison, WI, USA
Printed in Great Britain by the MPG Books Group, Bodmin and King's Lynn

www.bergpublishers.com

To the Hills: Richard, Mary, David and Stephen
and the Bates: Bridget, Carla, Ellie and Jack

Contents

Acknowledgments

We would like to thank everyone who has helped us write this book. In particular, our colleagues and students who have been unreservedly supportive and have read and commented on drafts of chapters: Helen Pussard, Andrew Thornton, Miyoung Oh, Evdokia Pappa, Lacey Wismer, Ellen Manning. Thanks go to Laura Green for helping us with the index. We would like to thank Ashley Jones of the Wimbledon Lawn Tennis Museum for providing the cover image. We would also like to thank the following for the use of photographs in chapters 3, 7 and 8: Frank Platt Electrical Ltd, National Football Museum and Jack, Daniel and Marie Wilcockson. Thanks for the sabbatical leave provided by The School of Human and Life Sciences, Roehampton University, which enabled great progress to be made on the book, and to students on the Sport, Media and Visual Culture module at Roehampton University who have provided valuable feedback over the years. Finally, we would like to thank our family and friends, especially Phil and Andrea for their tireless encouragement and enthusiasm for media sport.

Introduction: Interacting with Media Sport

The 2008 Beijing Olympics attracted an audience of 4.7 billion over the seventeen days that the event was staged, equivalent to 70 per cent of the world's population, making it the 'Most Watched Games ever' (Nielsen Media Research 2008: 1). The Games cost China £20 million to host and involved 10,708 athletes, 400,000 Chinese volunteers and 100,000 members of the army and police force (Elmer 2008). This global media spectacle merged the worlds of popular cinema and sport to create a breathtaking opening ceremony codirected by the acclaimed Chinese film-maker Zhang Yimou with a cast of 10,000 people. The resulting extravaganza used choreographed bodies, music and visual effects to construct an image of Chinese culture interwoven with the symbolism of sport for consumption by a global television audience. To begin to unpack the ways that events like the Olympics frame our understanding of bodies, nations, identities and values requires us to step back from the spectacle and analyse how it produces its effects in us. Sport has become such a powerful vehicle for mediating meanings and feelings that this is not a simple task. Every image of sport in the media evokes a wealth of associations, constructing a lens through which to view society. Inevitably, the picture we see conveys all the complexities of contemporary cultural politics.

In the build-up to the Beijing Olympics, another film director, Steven Spielberg, publicly withdrew from his appointment as artistic adviser to the opening ceremony by informing Hu Jintao, the President of the People's Republic of China, that his commitment to overcoming 'intolerance, bigotry, and the suffering they cause' (Spielberg 2007: 1) was incompatible with China's support for the Sudanese government, accused of genocide in Darfur. This was not the first time that the Olympic Games had been the stage for political protest. The spotlight of the world's media on one sporting event provides a forum for political activists to convey their message to huge audiences. The photographs of the Black Power salute given by the African American athletes Tommie Smith and John Carlos on the winner's podium at the 1968 Olympics in Mexico City present an example of the enduring nature of media records of Olympic protests. Similarly, pro-Tibet campaigners who used the Olympics in China to draw attention to their cause took advantage of the close connections between sport and the media. In March 2008, a member of the campaign group Reporters Without Borders disrupted the speech being given by the president of the Beijing Olympic Committee to the world's assembled media at the lighting of the Olympic flame in Greece. In addition, developments in communication technology have meant that protesters no longer need to rely on official media channels to voice their concerns as they can upload their own footage to YouTube and other video sharing Web sites.

Media protests at sport events illuminate the constant interaction between sport, media and society. Sport is a product of society and bears its imprint in every aspect of its manifestation. The international sporting events that attract the world's media are intrinsically connected to the global political and economic organisation of society. Sport is enmeshed in the networks of global capitalism. Sport spectacles provide platforms for cities to attract international investment and garner tourist trade. Success on the sporting field is used to symbolise national success and to promote government policies. The bodies of sports people are branded with the logos of global corporations, transferring the qualities of the athletes onto consumer goods for mass consumption. The communication and media networks enable these connections to be made and broadcast around the world. Olympic protests reveal the overt political content of mediated sport, but there is implicit political content encoded into every sport broadcast. As Frey and Eitzen (1991: 507) observed, the media representation of sport 'can influence our ideas about sport, our perceptions of gender, race, social relations, and proper behaviours, and our adherence to certain values'. These are the everyday politics that are equally inseparable from media sport.

The academic discipline of sociology of sport has addressed itself to unravelling the social and political dimensions of sport in both their explicit and implicit forms. Investigations of the sport media have been intrinsic to this aim. The way that sport is represented in the media can illuminate central themes in the relationship between sport and society. For example, the values of society, along with its heroes and villains, are constructed in the sport media. The media is also central to sociology of sport's long-standing interest in the commercialisation of sport and the construction of social identity through sport. Interrogation of the media also enables an exploration of the cultural politics of embodiment in sport. The sport media provide a rich terrain for analysis through the critical perspectives offered by sociology of sport, and our approach in this book is to show how these connections can be made.

This book will provide a theoretical and methodological framework for analysing sport in the media. It will demonstrate how to analyse the sport media and provide examples of analyses as original, researched case studies. At the background of our analysis is an understanding of the themes of scholarship in sociology of sport. To make sense of sport in the media, it is necessary to engage with the wealth of literature that the discipline has produced. Some central preoccupations with the media in the work of sociologists of sport are described in the following section. We hope this section will provide a useful guide to making links between the construction of sport in the media and its significance within the wider society. As indicated previously, important themes that reoccur in sociology of sport include the relationship between sport, media and the values of society; sport, media and commercialisation; sport, media and social identity; and sport, media and embodiment. We will discuss each of these in turn and provide a guide to further reading at the end of the chapter.

Sport, Media and the Values of Society

The connections between sport and values have been of interest to sociologists of sport with reference to the assumed characteristics and qualities of sport participants, particularly young people and celebrities. The 'fair play' ethos at the heart of modern sport has been critically examined as reinforcing dominant values and social cohesion (Jarvie and Maguire 1994). Sport stars are often expected to serve as role models and to behave in socially approved ways according to the demands of an assumed and imagined community (Eitzen 2000). In addition, the behaviour of athletes with endorsements may be further scrutinised by advertisers, sponsors, managers and administrators with little tolerance for negative publicity (Whannel 2002). The mediation of the character of sport stars, therefore, involves linking particular significations to an image that may appeal to media consumers. For example, MacDonald and Andrews (2001: 21) discussed the ways that '[Michael] Jordan's celebrity sign is also incredibly malleable, highly mobile and the carrier of shifting, but important cultural meanings.' Jordon's positioning as a transnational superstar and a commodity was linked to his perceived ability to transcend race and signify multiple desirable qualities, including hard work, achievement, family orientation, trustworthiness and affability. Whannel (2002: 215) observed that 'the public identities and images of such figures are a product of the social relations of moral contestation rather than an expressive product of their own actions.' Of particular interest in analysing celebrities and values, then, are the characteristics of the layers of mediation surrounding sports stars as well as public engagement with these images and discourses.

The capacity of sport to reinforce the social order has also emerged as a persistent theme of sport broadcasts and dramas. The sport media in all its forms regularly accentuates attributes of fair play, impartiality and meritocracy and deemphasises interconnections to broader social issues, problems and challenges. Hillyard (1994) referred to the presence of an (anti) sociological imagination to capture how sporting controversies and scandals were reported in ways that protected the interests of those in power and deflected attention away from political and social issues. For example, stories about performance-enhancing drug use tend to emphasise the bad behaviour of the individual, deflecting responsibility or culpability away from organisations, clubs and coaches (Padwe 1989).

Sport, Media and Commercialisation

Some of the earliest scholarship on sport and society focussed on the way commercialisation has shaped the experience of sport. In his now classic text, Huizinga

(1949) lamented the loss of the play element of modern sport in the face of increasing professionalisation. From a neo-Marxist perspective, Rigauer (1981) argued that sport has become the mirror image of work, so that achievement is the motivating principle for both top-level sportspeople and the labour force. Brohm (1978) echoed this view of sport, suggesting that an athlete is prepared for competition like a racehorse, creating monsters and machines that had internalised the principle of maximum productivity. As a result, the athlete is as much alienated from sport as the worker is from his labour: 'even his body no longer belongs to him: it belongs to science' (Brohm 1978: 107). Brohm (1978) charged the sport media with assaulting the hearts and minds of the masses with ideology that functions as an opiate to distract the people from social change.

The sport media can be seen as an expression of the commercialisation of sport in its entertainment style, its emphasis on goals and spectacles and its construction of performers as celebrities. Sport and its audience are sold as commodities to advertisers—the high price of the advertising slots during major sport events is based on the capacity of sport to reach millions of potential consumers for any number of products. Associations with sport can add the 'fun factor' (Kellner 2003: 3) to any aspect of the economy, even banks and insurance companies. The sport media is part of the commercialisation of sport, but it can also make commercialisation its subject matter. Hollywood films such as *North Dallas Forty* (1979), *Jerry Maguire* (1996) and *Any Given Sunday* (1999) contain scenes which depict the ravages of commercialised, professional sport on the bodies and souls of the athletes. These films remain products of the entertainment industry they ostensibly critique, however, so that the narrative resolution presents little challenge to the established order of sport.

Sport, Media and Social Identity

A great deal of research has focused on the way sport, and in many cases, mediated sport, contributes to collective and personal identity formation. The gendering of the sport media—the way that men's sport dominates and women's sport is sidelined—has attracted much attention from scholars. Critics have argued that this inequitable coverage has the effect of symbolically annihilating women's sporting accomplishments. In addition, when women's sport is shown, it is often trivialised and sexualised, undermining its power (Kane and Greendorfer 1994). However, gender is not just constructed in the mediation of women's sport—the sport media can be understood as a powerful site for the reproduction of masculinity. The sport media does not simply reflect gender difference, but constructs differences by engaging the audience in terms of what Hargreaves (1994) called masculine- and feminine-appropriate sports. As Whannel (2007: 16) observed, an image of a sport star, such as David Beckham, involves 'a range of audience expectations and mobilises and speaks to a range of identities'. Whannel (2007: 16) considered that the film *Bend It Like Beckham* (2002) was successful because it drew on tensions between the masculine and the feminine, 'between femininity and sport, between Britishness and Asianness, between parent and child'. National identity is also encoded into the sport media. Research, such as Blain and O'Donnell's (1998) interrogation of the representation of football in the European media, has suggested that the way a nation mediates sport can be understood as a signifier of that nation's identity. Certain sports become more associated with national identity than others. In the United Kingdom, the dominance of football in the media is connected with that sport's particular capacity to inspire the nation—one of the reasons why many of our examples in this book reference football.

Tolvhed (2007: 1) argued that while 'sport, and especially the Olympic arena, is very much focused upon the nation and competition between nations', the sport media also 'puts the body in focus—how bodily capabilities and limitations are constructed in different ways'. As a result, scholars have increasingly sought to highlight the intersecting dimensions of social identity in the sport media. Wensing and Bruce (2003), for example, analysed the representation of Cathy Freeman during the Sydney 2000 Olympics and argued that Freeman's importance as a symbol of national conciliation resulted in a disruption to the media's usual emphasis on the gender of female athletes. The case of Cathy Freeman was shown to highlight the way that national identity intersects with gender, class, race and sexuality in the sport media, constructing a complex and shifting set of identity codes. The analysis of mediated sport is a way of exploring the changing formations of power and social identity.

Sport, Media and Embodiment

The sporting body has become an object of 'contemplation and improvement, in the spectacular discourses of the mass media' (Horne 2006: 2). Much of the work on sporting embodiment has drawn on the work Bourdieu and Foucault. Bourdieu (1979) theorised the interrelationships between the social order, particularly class, and embodiment. Bodies develop, acquire meaning and attain value with respect to socially constructed 'tastes' and individuals' desire for social distinction. For Bourdieu (1979), the slender, healthy body valued by the dominant classes was a reflection of their investment of time and money, while the more instrumental relationship to the body preferred by members of the working class was linked to their limited leisure time and financial resources. The mediation of bodies may link particular sports with lifestyle and the impetus towards defining and maintaining class-based distinctions. An important objective for analysts of the sport media is to unpack the ways that meanings are constituted through the address to an imagined audience with an assumption of particular tastes, interests and embodied subjectivities.

Foucault's work has been widely used within the sociology of sport to explore 'knowledge formations and systems of power that regulate corporeal practices' (Rail and Harvey 1995: 165). Power and the disciplining of bodies operate through the normalisation of particular forms of embodiment and practices of self-regulation.

Duncan's (1994: 50) analysis of *Shape* magazine employed Foucault's frameworks to understand the ways that media discourses served to encourage women to define and discipline their bodies according to normative frameworks of an idealised female physicality. Foucault's work, however, can also be used to illuminate the potential for changing discourses of sporting femininity by pointing to the shifting and conflicting significations of the female body. Media analysis provides an opportunity to interrogate the coding of bodies and their associations with practices of self-monitoring, social aspirations and lifestyle choices.

How to Use This Book

This book is about ways of unravelling the connections between sport, media and society. Our experience of sport is inevitably informed by the sport media, and an understanding of the way the media constructs meanings around sport and identities among its audience is central to a critical engagement with sport. As a phenomenon, however, media sport is forever moving, constantly reconfiguring sport in relation to changing social contexts and values. Our aim here is to present students and researchers with a conceptual toolkit to begin to unpack the richness of the sport media in its emergent manifestations. This book will provide, in one place, the analytical concepts and methodological approaches used in studying the sport media, along with a demonstration of these approaches applied to original case studies. It avoids an artificial separation of media sport analysis into dominant themes, which can result in a flattening out of the dynamism of the sport media. Instead, this book encourages readers to interact critically with media sport by drawing out the complex intersections of social issues within a variety of sport media. In doing so, the book aims to transform the experience of consuming media sport into an analysis of this fascinating facet of culture.

This book should be read in conjunction with research in the sociology of sport. While some classic studies have already been discussed, current research from around the world is published in academic journals such as *Sociology of Sport Journal, International Review for the Sociology of Sport, Sport and Social Issues Journal* and *Sport and Society.* Some excellent literature is already available on media sport. For example, David Rowe's (2004a) *Sport, Culture and the Media: the Unholy Trinity* presents the social context of media sport and discusses issues in media text analysis, pointing to a range of examples from existing literature. Rod Brookes's (2002) *Representing Sport* and Boyle and Haynes's (1999) *Power Play: Sport, the Media and Popular Culture* introduce a range of issues relating to sport media such as globalisation, national identity, race and gender. There are several edited collections which bring together research articles on aspects of media sport, for example, Rowe's (2004b) *Critical Readings: Sport, Culture and the Media,* Blain and Bernstein's (2002) *Sport, Media, Culture: Global and Local Dimensions,* Birrell and McDonald's (2000)

Reading Sport: Critical Essays on Power and Representation and Wenner's (1998) *MediaSport*. These texts will help introduce those new to studying the sport media to the wealth of existing research, providing resources to complement the analytic approaches developed here. The unique contribution of this book lies in its development of a 'sociological imagination' around the sport media by critically reflecting on the many aspects of the audio-visual culture of sport. It encourages an approach to analysis that takes account of the specificity of the many facets of the sport media. It considers the sport media as inherently interactive. Mediated sport interacts with the politics of society; it interacts with its audience; it interacts with the wider visual culture in which it is embedded; and it is interactive through developments in new technologies. In using the book, students and researchers are encouraged to interact with its content to frame their own independent analysis of media sport. In this way, the book provides a means to explore the dynamic interplay of power politics in media sport by working through original case studies, making connections and demonstrating the steps of analysis. As such, it will provide the basis for launching an independent enquiry into the sport media.

At the heart of the book is a conceptualisation of the relationship between sport, media and society as a series of interactions: interactions between the audience and the content of media sport; interactions between sport, media and social identities; and interactions made increasingly possible through new technologies. The book focuses on the diverse forms of media sport—film, TV, newspapers, magazines, advertisements, three-dimensional media environments and the Internet—developing skills of analysis appropriate to each one. Each chapter builds on the theoretical and methodological insights of the previous chapters, resulting in a complete toolkit for analysing the sport media. Extended case studies, drawn from both the United Kingdom and the United States, are featured in every chapter. The case studies, based on original research, demonstrate a detailed application of concepts and analytical techniques. The focus on worked examples enables students to appreciate the complex interplay of cultural politics within the sport media, showing how gender, race, class and national identity are encoded into the fabric of media sport, often in shifting and ambiguous ways.

The first chapter, 'Analysing Media Sport', takes the reader through a range of techniques for the analysis of media sport, explaining their theoretical contexts and the contributions of key thinkers such as Ferdinand de Saussure, Roland Barthes, Michel Foucault and Stuart Hall. The chapter considers the sport media as collections of *signs,* as *discourses* and as *affects.* A semiotic approach to making sense of words and images in the sport media is demonstrated as a series of steps of analysis. Discourse analysis is presented as the utilisation of a series of concepts—the statement, discursive formation, intertextuality—to illuminate meaning in media sport. Finally, the power of mediated sport to move us bodily is explored through the concept of affect, which is introduced as way of analysing the nonrepresentational impact of media sport.

The remaining chapters consider the different facets of the sport media, showing how these analytic approaches can be developed in relation to specific media forms. Chapter 2 explores approaches to the analysis of sport films. The first part of the chapter explores the signifying systems of film (camera, lighting, editing, sound and mise en scène) to consider how sport films communicate their meaning. Particular attention is paid to the importance of sound for rendering the power of sport through film. The concept of narrative is introduced as a way of knowing sport through film, and the second part of the chapter discusses genre in relation to sport films. The first of the case studies in this chapter looks at *Raging Bull* (1980), analysing three fight scenes from the film to show how camera, lighting, sound and editing render the perspective of the boxer, Jake La Motta. Baseball movies are the focus of the second case study, which unpacks the formulaic aspects of these films and questions whether they compose their own genre.

Chapter 3 builds on the identification of the importance of signifying systems, narrative and genre in making sport meaningful in film by extending these concepts to the analysis of sport on television. Televised sport is understood as comprised of five channels of communication, graphics, image, voice, sound effects and music, simultaneously constructing a narrative or way of knowing sport. Approaches to the analysis of the five channels of communication are demonstrated, and, as the only programme type that globally attracts more male than female viewers, televised sport is considered as a gendered genre, containing features which draw in masculine audiences. The first of two case studies for this chapter focuses on men's and women's televised football on British television. The other explores the spectacularisation of televised sport by analysing the opening ceremony of the 2002 Winter Olympics held in Salt Lake City, Utah, in the United States.

The fourth chapter pays attention to the interaction between images and words in the ways that newspapers construct discourses of sport. The particular combinations of codes that are specific to newspapers are explored, and the meanings of sport news stories are considered as effects of connotation and intertextuality. The chapter demonstrates how newspapers use codes in their selection of words and pictures that stand in place of their readers, constructing subject positions for readers to occupy and points of identification on the basis of class, nation, ethnicity and gender. These subject positions are considered to vary according to the type of newspaper, the decisions about which sports to include or exclude in the coverage and the way of reporting those sports. Newspapers are thus shown to use sport to engage in a dialogue with readers, constructing mythic communities based on assumptions of shared values. The two case studies for this chapter explore discourses of nation, gender and ethnicity in British newspaper reports and photographs of Kelly Holmes's double Olympic victory in 2004 and discourses of deviance in the coverage of doping scandals in the US sport press.

The way that media sport addresses its differing audiences is further explored in Chapter 5. Sport and fitness magazines are shown to use direct and indirect address to interpellate their prospective readers, and the close analysis of magazine covers shows how images, layout, typeface and sell lines combine to hail readers to step into the subject positions offered. By choosing which sport magazines to consume, the identities of readers are shown to be constructed in interaction with the sport media. The two case studies for this chapter focus on the address of two specialist sport magazines, the British-based magazine *Climber,* and *Crush,* an official publication of the Ladies Professional Golf Association.

Chapter 6 explores ways of making sense of sport-related advertising. Sport advertisements sell us something more than the product advertised—they sell us ourselves by creating a structure in which we and the consumer goods associated with sport become interchangeable. The chapter demonstrates how the power of sport advertisement lies in the gaps between what is shown and the meanings the audience supplies to complete the picture. The importance of difference for advertisers to sell their product is explored in relation to the way audiences seek social distinction through their consumption of advertising imagery. Advertisements are often created specifically to tie into major televised sport spectacles. The case studies for the chapter consider two examples of this—US commercials created for the Super Bowl and Peugeot advertisements broadcast in the United Kingdom during the 2007 Rugby World Cup.

Meanings, discourses and mythologies constructed in the sport media and through advertising campaigns are not simply layered on top of the real world, but rather are built into the fabric of objects and spaces. Chapter 7 shows that the study of media sport should not be confined to the two-dimensional imagery of films, television and the print media, but rather needs to embrace three-dimensional objects and spaces to fully comprehend the interaction between sport, media and society. Objects are reflections of the wider lives of communities and individuals, and many objects—cars, balls, trainers, toys, replica football shirts, mobile phones—have been imprinted with meaning through the sport media and advertising campaigns. This chapter discusses approaches to the analysis of the interaction between sport, media and the wider visual culture of which it is a part. It looks at the way media sport informs and is informed by developments in art and architecture. Sport museums are understood as mediating meanings of sport, constructing perspectives on what is valuable and interesting about sport through the display of artefacts. The work of Foucault and de Certeau are applied to the analysis of space to explore the ways people navigate through parks, leisure centres, gyms, museums, shops and stadia, interacting with media sport and advertising as they go. The case studies for this chapter focus on the interaction between media and sport in the space of the National Football Museum in Preston, UK, and the Boston Red Sox baseball stadium, Fenway Park, in the United States.

Chapter 8 focuses on branding and the Internet to explore the emergence of new media sportscapes. The sports brand is understood as a new media object, capable of organising the exchange of meaning between producers and consumers (Lury

2004). Interactivity is central to the new media experience of sport. Developments in digital television, mobile phone technology and the Internet have expanded the potential for consumers to tailor media sport to their own requirements. The chapter draws attention to the ways that new technology might shift the power dynamics of media sport. The chapter considers interactive sport media as requiring consumers to navigate through virtual spaces, and thus builds on the previous chapters to present an approach to analysing Internet sport sites. The case study explores the interaction between sport advertising, sport spaces and the audio-visual culture of sport on the global Web site http://www.adidas.com.

The concluding chapter focuses on a case study of the Wimbledon Lawn Tennis Championships to bring together the concepts, themes and approaches used in the book to demonstrate the many levels of interaction between sport, media and society. Wimbledon is analysed as both a space and a media representation, and the chapter shows how the Wimbledon brand is embedded into the fabric of the buildings. The chapter compares the televising of the space of Wimbledon in the United States and the United Kingdom to show how the virtual space of Wimbledon is communicated via the media. The chapter shows how this process shifts the ties of meaning to place, offering the potential to disrupt the established hierarchies of class, gender and nation at Wimbledon. The chapter ends by encouraging researchers and students to engage in two- and three-dimensional analyses of sport, media and visual culture to produce their own independent explorations of the interactions between sport, media and society.

Analysing Sport in the Media

Each chapter encourages readers to begin their own analysis. To model the steps of analysis appropriate to each of the sport media forms covered by the book, each chapter includes a section explaining the practical aspects of analysing one of the chapter's case studies. Researchers and students can follow the approach taken to applying the concepts from the chapter to the investigation of, for example, *Raging Bull,* Fenway Park or http://www.adidas.com. In addition, Chapter 1, "Analysing Media Sport', contains a step-by-step guide to analysis that provides the foundations for researching all forms of media sport. At the end of each chapter, the suggestions for analysis present ideas for pursuing original investigations, and the guide to further reading points to publications readers can use as a starting point to frame their analyses.

Further Reading

Bourdieu, P. (1979), *Distinction: A Social Critique of the Judgement of Taste,* London: Routledge.

Brohm, J.-M. (1978), *Sport: a Prison of Measured Time,* London: Ink Links.

Duncan, M. C. (1994), 'The Politics of Women's Body Images and Practices: Foucault, the Panopticon, and "Shape" magazine', *Journal of Sport and Social Issues,* 18: 40–65.

Hargreaves, J. (1994), *Sporting Females: Critical Issues in the History and Sociology of Women's Sports,* London: Routledge.

Huizinga, J. (1949), *Homo Ludens: A Study of the Play Element in Contemporary Civilization,* London: Routledge and Kegan Paul.

Kane, M. J., and Greendorfer, S. (1994), 'The Media's Role in Accommodating and Resisting Stereotyped Images of Women in Sport', in P. Creedon, ed., *Women, Media and Sport,* London: Sage.

Kellner, D. (2003), *Media Spectacle,* London: Routledge.

Rigauer, B. (1981), *Sport and Work: European Perspectives,* tr. A. Guttmann, New York: Columbia University Press.

Wensing, E., & Bruce, T. (2003), 'Bending the Rules: Media Representations of Gender during an International Sporting Event', *International Review for the Sociology of Sport,* 38: 387–96.

Whannel, G. (1992), *Fields in Vision: Television Sport and Cultural Transformation,* London: Routledge.

–1–

Analysing Media Sport

KEY CONCEPTS

Semiotics	Discourse analysis
Signifier & signified	Discourses & statements
Denotation & connotation	Discursive formation
Myth & ideology	The gaze
Encoding & decoding	Affect
Intertextuality	Autoethnography

This chapter introduces techniques for the analysis of media sport and explains their theoretical context using the work of key thinkers such as Saussure, Barthes and Hall. Media sport is conceptualised in three ways within the chapter, as *signs,* as *discourses* and as *affects,* and corresponding analytical toolkits are presented. Firstly, a semiotic approach to analysing media sport is demonstrated, using newspaper coverage of footballer Paul Gascoigne. The second approach presented is discourse analysis, which involves the utilisation of a series of concepts—the statement, discursive formation, intertextuality—that can illuminate meaning in media sport. This form of analysis is explored with reference to the media's portrayal of celebrity footballers. Finally, the power of media sport to move us bodily is explored through the concept of affect, and reflexive techniques are presented as a means of analysing the nonrepresentational impact of media sport. Used alone or in combination with each other, these approaches provide a basis for understanding the multiple forms of mediated sport. Subsequent chapters build on the foundations of analysis presented here, drawing out the specific characteristics associated with different media.

Sport as Signs: Semiotic Analysis of Media Sport

The study of signs, otherwise known as 'semiotics' or 'semiology', originates with the Swiss linguist Ferdinand de Saussure (1857–1913) and the American philosopher Charles Saunders Peirce (1839–1914). Both theorists had their work published posthumously: in the case of Saussure, as lecture notes, and in Peirce's case, as successive reworkings of his thesis.

Saussure developed his ideas regarding language in response to dominant trends among his contemporaries, who thought of language as a naming process asserted the existence of an intrinsic link between a word and the thing it denotes. Saussure challenged this conceptualisation of language, and instead saw language as a system of signs that express ideas—a network of elements that have meaning only in relation to each other. For Saussure, a sign was composed of two parts: the signified and the signifier. In language, this would mean that the letters *F-O-O-T-B-A-L-L* are the *signifier* of a concept 'football'—a round, air-filled object used in the sport of football—which is the *signified.* Together the signifier and the signified make up the *sign:* football. The two parts of the sign have an arbitrary connection with each other—there is no direct or inherent relationship between the word and the object it designates: we could use another arrangement of letters (in another language, for example) to signify the same concept. In fact, in the United States, the letters *S-O-C-C-E-R* signify what *F-O-O-T-B-A-L-L* refers to in the United Kingdom, and *F-O-O-T-B-A-L-L* signifies an oblong-shaped ball used in a different game—known as *American* football in the United Kingdom and elsewhere. What makes it seem like the two parts of the sign are intimately connected is simply that everyone in the United Kingdom has agreed that *F-O-O-T-B-A-L-L* signifies 'football'. It is a socially determined, consensual relationship.

For Saussure, the identity of any signifier or signified is established through the ways in which it differs from all the other signifiers and signifieds to which it can be compared. The meaning of a sign, therefore, resides not in what it is, but in what it could be and is not. Saussure said that signs enter into two kinds of relationship with each other: paradigmatic relationships and syntagmatic relationships. A paradigm is a group of signs whose relationship to each other is one of similarity or comparability. Paradigmatic relationships can be illustrated by words that are synonyms or antonyms—for example, advertisements for opticians might use the term *eyewear* to give their products a distinctive meaning which is reliant on this term being chosen from a range of more mundane but similar terms like *glasses* or *spectacles.* A syntagm, on the other hand, is a rule-governed combination of signs in a determined, chain-like sequence. Syntagmatic relationships can be seen in the rules governing the order of words in a sentence, a series of shots in a film, garments of clothing worn together, or a combination of dishes in a meal. Every syntagm is the result of a series of paradigmatic choices. As Seiter (1992) observed,

> in a given syntagm, the individual signs are 'united in absentia' with others of the paradigm that were not selected. The meaning of a given syntagm derives in part from the absence of other possible paradigmatic choices. (p. 46)

We can think about the various signs of sport in these ways. There is a range of physical movements people can do—they can jump, run, catch, dodge, hit, carry or throw objects. A particular sport, such as basketball or tennis, involves a paradigmatic choice: out of the range of possible movements—the *paradigm* of sport moves—only some are selected. For example, tennis involves hitting a ball with an object, but not passing to a team member. Basketball involves throwing a ball at a target, but not hitting a ball with an object. During a game, certain movements follow others—a whistle is blown, and a body moves, catches or jumps. The series of events in the game can be seen as a syntagm. The rules of the game connect the combination of movements in a particular formation.

This example makes it clear that there may be other kinds of signs beyond words. For Peirce, a sign was to be understood as something that stands for something, its object. Peirce identified three types of signs which allow the semiotic domain to extend beyond language. Visual or iconic signs, such as photographs, paintings, cinematic images and graphs, signify by resembling something in the world. The connection between the sign and its source is something we can directly see. Indexical signs have a causal connection to the thing that they stand for, for example, the way a symptom (red spots) stands for a disease (measles). There is a conceptual link, but we must still figure out the meaning of the sign. Convention is all that connects symbolic signs, such as words, numbers and flags, to the things that they signify, and to decode them, we need to learn the system. There is no obvious connection in a symbolic sign like a flag, and we must learn that particular patterns of shapes and colours can represent nations or that a wave of a chequered flag in motor racing means that the race has been won.

What is important is the realisation that all signifiers, even the most iconic or indexical, can become conventionalised, and are given added meaning in the process. Silverman (1983: 23) used the example of the kind of lighting used to accentuate the female face in Hollywood films of the 1930s or 1940s: 'The standardization of this effect permits it to signify more than "look here" to suggest values such as "star" and "ideal female beauty."' As a result, we need to be schooled in systems of representation before certain signifiers will reveal their iconicity to us. Road signs mean nothing to the uninitiated, for example, and we have to learn that something that may look like a man opening an umbrella is meant to stand for 'road works taking place ahead'.

Meaning, Myth and Ideology

The work of Roland Barthes (1915–1980) provides the bridge between the ideas outlined so far and the semiotic analysis of media sport. In his essay 'Myth Today', Barthes (1993) described a second-order signifying system which he referred to as myth, a kind of message found not just in oral speech, but in a range of things such as photography, cinema and sport. *Mythology*—part semiology and part ideology—is the term he gave to the process of understanding these messages. In myth, two semiological systems operate: language itself (which he broadened to include cinema, written discourse and photography) and the metalanguage of myth.

Barthes illustrated the operation of myth using a photograph of a young black soldier saluting the French flag on the cover of an issue of the French magazine *Paris-Match*. Barthes described the photograph as an iconic sign at the first level, a picture of a soldier saluting a flag. Barthes also found the image of the black soldier to have a mythical significance, that of 'harmony in the French empire'. He suggested that the effectiveness of myth is that it does not need to be deciphered or interpreted to be understood—for myth to have power, it must seem entirely natural, and if the ideological message is evident, it ceases to work as myth.

There are two stages of meaning operating within Barthes's magazine cover. Firstly, there is the literal, descriptive meaning of the image, which we can call 'denotation'. The viewer decodes the signifiers (soldier, arm raised, eyes uplifted) and arrives at the denotative meaning: a black soldier is giving the French flag a salute. The second level of meaning is the connotation of the image, meanings that the image of the soldier evokes; that France is a great empire and this soldier is typical of all her subjects in his zealous support of his so-called oppressors. Connotation refers to the social meaning of an image. In this case, referring explicitly to a patriotic, black soldier might have been deeply controversial. At the time that Barthes saw the magazine, there were anticolonial struggles in Algeria, and the crisis was widely reported in the French press. Yet the power of this simple image lies in the way it indicates support for the empire without requiring assent or disagreement.

There are, therefore, two processes of analysis that are necessary in attempting to capture the meanings of media sport. To arrive at the denotative meanings of an image or television programme or advertisement, the first stage of analysis must be performed. We must decode the signifiers to describe what is going on in the image. Only then can we proceed to the second stage of analysis, which involves considering its connotations or social and cultural implications. As we have seen, myth works by making these two stages of signification blur into one. Analysts must halt this process and take account of what each signifier is being made to signify. The careful, detailed description of all the signifying elements in media sport is crucial to enable their connotations to be examined.

Analysing the Spectacle of Sport I: Semiotics of Sport Celebrity

The Observer is a British Sunday newspaper that carries a glossy magazine called *Sport Monthly* as a Sunday supplement. Owned by the Guardian Media Group, *The Observer* has a liberal political orientation and is one of the British newspapers 'designed to sell to the richer social classes' (Richardson 2007: 80). According to its own readers' editor, 'Observer readers are generally assumed to be middle-aged, middle-class, university educated and relatively affluent' (Pritchard 2002: para. 1). The cover images of *Sport Monthly* tend to be photographic portraits of sportsmen and, less regularly, sportswomen. The sports stars are drawn from a range of sports, but football is arguably the national game in England, and football stars are frequently shown on the *Sport Monthly* covers (Bower 2007). Traditionally, football has been associated with working-class culture in the United Kingdom because of its historical development (Walvin 1975), which contrasts sharply with the class profile of *Observer* readers. Class connotations form part of the richness of the imagery of *Sport Monthly* covers, which can be unpacked using the tools of semiotic analysis.

The cover of *Sport Monthly* from February 2003 featured the celebrity football player Paul Gascoigne. Paul Gascoigne is a white, working-class footballer from the north-east of England. At the time of the magazine's publication, Gascoigne was at the end of his career, which included playing for a number of high-profile clubs, including Newcastle, Tottenham Hotspur, Lazio, Rangers and the England national team. Gascoigne was as famous for his indulgent, often obscene behaviour off (and on) the pitch as he was for his magnificent feats of football. Gascoigne's physicality—his drinking, his belching, his sobbing, his football—has been the subject of a great deal of media interest throughout his career. He has also been associated with criminal behaviour linked to domestic violence and fighting.

The first stage in conducting a semiotic analysis of a media text such as this is to identify the signifiers on the cover. In Barthes's (1967) terms, this is to describe the cover at the level of denotation—to give its literal meaning. The process of describing the media at this level is an important part of the analysis and is not as simple as it appears. When we 'read' the media informally, we comprehend the message without needing to go through this stage. In contrast, a semiotician focuses on how the meaning is being made, rather than on what the meaning is. As a result, it is necessary to account for all of the signifiers before we can make the link to what they signify. For example, we can

- describe the people and objects
- describe the colours
- describe the shapes
- describe the lighting

Gascoigne was depicted leaning against a breeze block wall, thumbs in the belt hooks of his jeans, wearing heavy gold chains around his neck and right wrist, displaying an expensive-looking watch on his left wrist and looking down into the camera with a set expression on his face. He was also naked to the waist. The headline next to the image read 'Gazza Laid Bare: the Broken Dreams of Britain's Greatest Footballer', using a nickname for the player regularly deployed by the British tabloids ('Gazza Laid Bare' 2003).

Once we have described the magazine cover, we can then consider what the arrangement of words and image connotes. The absence of clothing revealed Gascoigne's body. There are many cultural associations of naked bodies in the media, including pornographic, aspirational or vulnerable. The display of naked flesh has traditionally been associated with women; however, sport is one arena where men's bodies are regularly shown. As Miller (2000: 97) observed, 'sports allow spectators to watch and dissect men's bodies. It provides a legitimate space for gazing at the male form.' This creates some inconsistencies: while sport can carry connotations of hegemonic masculinity, this can be undermined by the associations of bodies on display. Gascoigne's body as shown on the cover of the magazine was noticeably thinner than it had been at other times during his career, yet it was not the athletic, hard body associated with sportspeople at the peak of their careers. In fact, his stomach appeared concave beneath his prominent ribcage, giving the impression that he was sucking it in. Altogether, these signifiers created a picture of vulnerable masculinity, a body sensitised to the media's appraising gaze. It was a body laid bare, as the headline says, for the inspection of *The Observer*'s readership. The unglamorous associations of Gascoigne's environment (the concrete block wall) compounded the impression of failure. Gascoigne looked less like a professional, celebrity sportsman than a typical working-class member of the public. Horrocks (1995) has observed an underlying tension within the gender and class identities of players like Gascoigne:

the body/spirit split is mapped onto dualities within class and gender. The working-class male is seen as corporeal, gross, eructating: the middle class is more spiritual, more refined but looks with envy and a certain excitement at the physical carnival enacted by men such as Gazza. Gazza's body and personality become a text which is alienated from him, in fact becomes public property, upon which can be inscribed various messages. (p. 163)

The magazine cover image evoked both sadness and inevitability in the ordinariness of the image, perhaps confirming the feelings of class superiority among the readership, which might have been challenged by the capacity of seemingly undisciplined footballers such as Gascoigne to display such immense sporting talent in a desirable and lucrative profession. However, to understand further the cultural politics of media imagery, it is necessary to go beyond the analysis of what is being represented to the way those representations position the viewing subject. To do this, we need to consider how the sport media is constructed as discourse.

Sport as Discourses

There is a connection between the systems of meaning Barthes (1993) described as 'myths' and Foucault's (1972, 1977, 1978) analysis of the operation of discourse. Foucault understood discourse not so much as a set of signs constituting a text, but as practices, institutions and spaces through which regulatory power operates to enable what can be said, what (social, moral, political) positions can be adopted and what meanings can be ascribed to events, texts and objects. Discourses can be detected in the repeated ways in which an event is framed and the effect of that framing on individuals' behaviour, thoughts and opinions. An example might be the discourse of fair play in competitive sport. The media repeatedly invoke the spirit of fairness when constructing stories about sport. The notion of fair play has effects on players' behaviour and frames the way the action is perceived by the audience and participants. However, there is a great deal of complexity and contradiction inherent in discourse. Discourse is powerful because it absorbs contradiction, enabling multiple positions or arguments to be made within its terms. For example, the notion of fair play appears to exist unproblematically alongside evidence of glaring inequalities in resources available to different teams or players, and professional imperatives to win at all costs (hence the acceptance of the professional foul).

Discourse is, therefore, a way of knowing—one that has an effect in the world. The connections between truth, power and knowledge are critical to understanding the effects of discourse. The power of discourse lies in its assumptions and claims that the knowledge it constructs is the truth. Knowledge and power, therefore, are intimately connected: 'all knowledge is discursive and all discourse is saturated with power' (Rose 2001: 138). The intersection of discourses of gender and sport make this clear. The apparently self-evident 'truth' of sport as a masculine enterprise is repeatedly illustrated by the absence of gender marking. For example, in professional basketball in the United States, the women's professional league is gender marked as the Women's National Basketball Association and stands in contrast to the unmarked National Basketball Association, indicating the obviousness of men's association with the sport. The social effect of this truth-claim is to grant men's sport greater legitimacy, reinforcing their access to greater resources and media airtime as a matter of course. This becomes understood as common sense and, as such, appears impossible to question. These gaps or silences indicate that what is left out can have as powerful an effect as what is present.

Foucault (1972) considered discourse to be made up of groups of 'statements'. Statements can be thought of as those 'utterances which have some institutional force and which are thus validated by some form of authority' (Mills 1997: 55) and which thereby claim to speak the truth. Thus it is possible to differentiate between discourse as a whole and individual discourses or groups of statements. The valorisation of 'playing hurt' could be thought of as a statement that forms a part of the broader discourse of sporting masculinity. Putting one's body at risk is celebrated and rewarded as appropriate, tough, masculine behaviour in sport.

Discourses and statements incorporate spoken and written words, images, gestures and practices. Analysis of all of these elements is necessary to understand the discourses underpinning media sport. The concept of intertextuality is useful for capturing the accumulation of meaning across different texts or images. Any individual utterance (a word, an image, a gesture) always evokes previous associations with that utterance. When we see an image of a snowboarder in an advertisement for a dry, financial product, for example, instances of similar images we have encountered are inevitably recalled, affording the bank or lending company some of the fun and youthfulness associated with these so-called lifestyle sports.

Patterns of representation, where images or words are positioned in similar ways again and again, can be understood as discursive formations. The way champion athletes are repeatedly pictured kissing their medal or trophy can be thought of as a discursive formation. Discursive formations can be identified whenever 'one can define a regularity (an order, correlations, positions and functionings, transformations)' (Foucault 1972: 38). These discursive formations also serve as a focus of intertextuality in that meanings are constructed in relationship with a host of previous associations of a text.

An understanding of the media as discursive was central to Hall's (1980) influential encoding–decoding model of media communication. Van Zoonen (1994) suggested that Hall's work, originally published as part of a series of Working Papers in Cultural Studies by the Centre for Contemporary Cultural Studies at the University of Birmingham, and later as an edited volume, *Culture, Media, Language* (Hall, Hobson, Lowe and Willis 1980), contributed to a paradigm shift in communication studies. Hall (1980) replaced the traditional model of mass communication involving a linear circuit or loop—sender–message–receiver—with a more complex framework which understood the media to be the result of a negotiation between institutional producers of meaning and audiences as producers of meaning. The media production process is discursive in that the television programme or newspaper or magazine that it produces is framed with meanings and ideas resulting from historically defined production processes, assumptions about the audience and personal and institutional agendas and identities.

The British Broadcasting Corporation (BBC) televised the Oxford and Cambridge boat race between 1938 and 2004 ('BBC Says Farewell' 2004). This event—a rowing race between crews from the universities of Oxford and Cambridge along the river Thames in London—was part of the British social calendar historically associated with the introduction of debutantes to high society. The race carries meanings associated with aristocracy and national identity and historical ideologies of amateur sport (an ethos that was used to prevent working-class professionals from taking part in sport). It is possible to argue that it was these characteristics that made it appear appropriate for the BBC to televise the race in its remit as a public service broadcaster. It is also possible to see evidence of the claims of cultural elitism and paternalism that have been targeted at the BBC (O'Sullivan 2000) in this decision. The broadcasts then can be said to be encoded with these values by the producers. However, the organisers of the race agreed to a five-year deal for the rival independent terrestrial television channel, ITV, to broadcast the race from 2005. The BBC (2004: para. 3) claimed that this decision was motivated by the organisers' 'desire to pursue a highly commercial agenda', something that would change the presentation of the race. Whannel (1992) documented the way that the commercial agenda of ITV historically shaped the production techniques used in the encoding of sport broadcasts. The reverential approach of the BBC to broadcasting major occasions drew 'upon the authority derived from its tradition of association with major national events' (Whannel 1992: 19), whereas ITV built large audiences by using techniques, such as the close-up, that dramatised the action (Whannel 1992).

The encoding process produces media texts as meaningful discourse, but this discourse requires decoding by the audience. This becomes more complicated as the producers and the audience of the media may not be the same. They need not share the same agenda, education, political position, gender, race, sexuality, age, ability or social class. The codes that exist within the media product may be understood by the audience differently from the way the producers understand them. There is no stable, unitary meaning that can be identified in television programming, but instead a range of potential ways it might be understood. Media texts are, therefore, always *polysemic* (carrying many meanings), and the task of media analysis is to consider not what a television programme or a newspaper article means so much as the ways in which it might be understood. One of the ways in which meaning is produced and imposed is through the use of combinations of texts. This can have the effect of limiting the potential range of meanings which might have been available. For example, images on their own can be very ambiguous, but in newspapers, the words that accompany photographs guide the reader in deciphering the picture.

During the Sydney 2000 Olympics, a photograph appeared in the British newspaper *The Independent* depicting two black women, one sitting cross-legged looking like she was about to cry, the other crouching next to her with a comforting arm around her shoulder. In itself, the photograph could have multiple meanings, but there are clues within the photograph that limit those meanings: both women were wearing uniforms, indicating they were athletes, one Australian and the other British, and the reader might have recognised the seated athlete as the Australian runner Cathy Freeman. Given this interpretation, a reader might have read the image as being a scene at the end of a race, but the outcome of the race is not immediately clear, given Freeman's disconsolate appearance. The written text above the image, however, directed the reader to make sense of the potential meanings of the photograph along specific lines. The words 'Olympic Games' appeared as a header to the page, asking us to understand the image as related to this international event. The headline over the image read 'Freeman Heals Pains of a Fractured Nation'. The athlete was confirmed as Cathy Freeman, and despite the ambiguous signs in the image, the word *heals* indicated that the result of the race was positive for her. The reader was asked to interpret the look of distress on Freeman's face in the context of the ethnic tensions in Australia—because of her identity as an aboriginal Australian, her victory was seen as symbolically bringing together aboriginal and white Australian communities.

Making sense of the words required the body of Cathy Freeman to be decoded in a particular way. The audience was provided with a preferred meaning and asked to adopt a specific position in relation to the text. The construction of meaning became a dynamic process where the audience was addressed by the newspaper's words and pictures, and in response, they adopted a specific reading position to understand what was being portrayed. As a result, it is important to consider not only what is being represented in the sport media, but also the way the audience is positioned by those representations. In this way, we can think of the audience as becoming part of the discourse of the sport media—subject to its meanings and definitions.

Analysing the Spectacle of Sport II:
the Discourse of Stargazing

> Racing hearts were the order of the day in Madrid on Tuesday as David Beckham had his Real Madrid medical examination under the intense gaze of excited nurses and anxious club dignitaries ... As if the moving hands of time wanted to signal a prodigiously fit sportsman' ability to last the span of a soccer contest, Beckham's medical test ran to fully 90 minutes.

... He was immediately surrounded by nurses, X-ray technicians and stethoscope-wielding doctor ... Beckham was quickly ushered into a room labelled 'Ecografica 2' for a blood test from which he emerged with shirt open, gold chain gleaming and smile flickering across his face ...

... Then came the X-ray of the metatarsal damage in his foot that almost ruined his World Cup, a break for orange juice and his first taste of Spanish ham, before he was whisked down another logo-splattered corridor for further heart and lung tests ...

... Beckham's medical test was relayed to Real fans on the club's in-house television station, the bulletin preceded by countless clips of other members of the Bernabeu ball-lover's union parading their own gifts ...

—Winter (2003: paras 1–10)

Winter's (2003) newspaper report of British football player David Beckham's medical examination following his move from Manchester United to Real Madrid illustrates strategies used by the media for the depiction of male sport celebrities. Male sport celebrities are regularly subjected to an invasive media gaze that moves beyond the surface of the body to probe beneath the skin. In this example, Beckham was probed inside and out in the full gaze of Real Madrid TV. Other football players have been subject to similar treatment. Before his death in 2005 at the age of 59, the Northern Irish soccer star George Best, known for his unparalleled football talent and partying lifestyle, regularly featured in the British media. On 25 June 2001, Channel 4 broadcast a documentary about the ups and downs of Best's career. The documentary was called *George Best's Body (Football Stories)*, and throughout the programme, X-ray images appeared in a split screen format alongside shots of Best in action. On one occasion, whilst discussing Best's excessive drinking, the screen showed images of him in a bar alongside an X-ray image of an upper torso, inviting the viewer to speculate on his liver. Later, when Best's relationships with women were profiled, the X-ray image was of a pelvis, and when the documentary talked about Best developing deep vein thrombosis, the X-ray panned down to the lower leg.

This attempt to model the interior of the celebrity body can be observed in other media formats. Reporting on George Best's liver transplant on 31 July 2002, *The Mirror* newspaper edged a double-page spread with close-up photographs of Best, drink in hand, toasting the camera, one for each year between 1967 and 2000. At the centre of the spread, a diagrammatic representation of the mechanics of a liver transplant asked the reader to imagine what was going on inside Best's body.

Similarly, former Manchester United football player Roy Keane featured on the cover of *The Observer* newspaper's *Sport Monthly* supplement in September 2002. Keane had a reputation for passionate but aggressive playing. Staring straight ahead, he was posed holding a dead bird's head in front of his face, its beak framing his right eye. The skull of the bird had caved in to reveal decaying brain matter, making an evocative connection with the title of the magazine's feature story, 'Inside the Mind of Roy Keane' (2002). The text below the image suggested that Keane was 'A Man Possessed' and promised 'his most candid interview ever'.

The regularities which emerge in the style in which the sport celebrities are represented can be considered as a discursive formation. Analysis of this discursive formation raises questions about the position of these sport celebrities within discourses of gender, race and class—a position which, on the surface, appears to confound received notions of the hypermasculinity accorded to sport stars within contemporary culture. There is a link here with the observations made by Cook (2000) in an article exploring discourses of masculinity in new Australian men's magazines. Cook (2000: 171) pointed to the ambiguities within the press coverage of men's health issues, finding 'representation of even the archetypically tough and resistant body (manual workers, sportsmen) overshadowed by penetrative, diagnostic technologies (X-rays, cancer screening)'. For Cook (2000) there was a conflict in discourses of masculinity within 'reports of regimes such as diet control, regular prostate screening, or various invasive surgical techniques used for high-masculinity sports-related injuries such as knee reconstruction or tendon repair' (Cook 2000: 172). The conflict pertained to the cultural association of authoritative scientific discourse with masculinity and their seemingly 'unquestionable right to scope and scalpel penetration of the body's surface' (Cook 2000: 172). This invasive, regulatory gaze identified by Foucault has further intensified with the development of new visualising technologies. Yet, if the medical gaze has been associated with a 'powerful masculinity', then it has traditionally been the female body upon which it has exercised its rights 'to examine, define and surgically penetrate' (Cook 2000: 172). However, in the representations Cook analysed, it was the unwilling flesh of male bodies which was subject to inspection by this invasive, masculine, medical gaze.

Cook examined three sites of representation of the male body: bodybuilding magazines, men's skin-care commodity marketing, and the surfing magazine *Waves*. In each site, Cook found a range of compensatory textual strategies to deal with the conflicting gender codings of the representations. For example, the body was represented as a mechanistic cyborg in the bodybuilding press, partitioned into its constitutive muscle groups. As a strategy to resist the 'scopic medical penetration of the body's interior', the bodybuilding press exteriorized anatomical detail, inscribing ' "soft" tissues onto the body's "hard" surface' (Cook 2000: 174). In another example, the photographs in the 'Slash of the Month' feature in *Waves* magazine (where readers send in pictures of gruesome wounds sustained while surfing) were described as 'trophy images: accounts of pain as its own inverse', refocusing attention onto 'the ultimate invulnerability of those very individuals who have reported the wound' (Cook 2000: 182).

There is a correspondence between the representations Cook described and the invasive, medical imaging of the bodies of Best, Beckham and Keane. Cook pointed to a clash of competing forms of powerful masculinity within the representations in her analysis. Similarly, the powerful, active bodies of professional sportsmen—representing what may be, to many, the ultimate in masculinity—were subjected to the lens of another, contrasting version of masculine authority. Yet, while the seemingly vulnerable bodies of these sport stars are laid bare for the X-ray eyes of the media, there is no exteriorizing strategy to compensate: the injuries and illnesses of the players remain irresistibly interior, hidden. Accusations that players are faking injuries or conversely hiding their seriousness remain testimony to the invisibility of the complaints that mysteriously take the convalescing player away from the action. The media's almost obsessive focus on injury and 'unhealthy' lifestyle (e.g. http://www.physioroom.com produces a table of English Premier League injuries) testifies to an unrelenting desire to penetrate beneath the visible surface of the players' bodies. This resulting media framing of the sporting body might provoke a range of feelings in viewers. In the next section, we turn to the capacity of the media to produce visceral effects in the sports spectator.

Affect and Media Sport

The focus so far on the signs and discourses surrounding sport celebrities draws attention to the importance of sporting bodies in the sport media. Sport is a highly physical experience: playing sport is an embodied activity, and it arouses embodied responses in its spectators. To consider media sport to consist only of signs or discourses which are cognitively decoded by knowing subjects risks missing some of its power. Watching sport can entail total absorption in the competition, with the events on the screen having the capacity to move one physically—from the edge of one's seat, hands tensely clamped to one's mouth, to leaping in the air, shouting, punching the air and even crying. This is more than simply understanding the meaning of what is happening. This is a bodily response beyond meaning.

Clough (2007) suggested that there has been an 'affective turn' in a range of academic disciplines across the humanities and social sciences. Thinkers have begun to focus on the power of affect to move us in ways that combine body and mind. For example, Grossberg (1992) used the term *affect* to explain the success of the connections forged between popular conservative politics and postmodern culture in the United States post-1970. He understood affect as an embodied response to something. For Grossberg, affect was not simply an emotional response, but embraced the kind of relationship to the world conveyed by terms like *commitment, will* and *passion*. Affect describes our investment in something, a particular experience or practice, like a sport spectacle. According to Grossberg (1992), affect could be 'the missing term in an adequate account of ideology' because it captures a sense of an individual's embodied, passionate investment in ideas and events that may not be easily understood, articulated or even rationalised in a cognitive sense.

Affect is a term that has been used in different ways by psychologists and sociologists to refer generally to the emotions. However, we need to distinguish between affect and emotion. Drawing on the work of Tomkins, Wissinger (2007) proposed an understanding of affect as specific physiological responses to stimuli which may or may not translate into emotions. Wissinger (2007: 232) argued that 'affect precedes emotions; affect is not conscious.' The concept of affect understood in this way can help illuminate the forces that flow between bodies and between bodies and technologies in the case of media sport. Affect can also be thought of as social, a contagious energy that binds people together in intimate relationships or social groups. The classic sociologist Durkheim (1966: 4), for example, was interested in the movements of feeling in crowds that 'do not originate in any one of the particular individual consciousnesses'.

In this sense, an understanding of affect asks us, in Hardt's (2007: ix) terms, 'to enter the realm of causality' and think about our capacity to affect our environment and be affected by it. However, as Wissinger (2007) observed, the effects of affect are not predictable or reducible to a single stimulus. Wissinger (2007) gave the example of the power of music to affect the body in multiple ways—the same piece may make some people dance or sing, cause some to leave the dance floor and send others to sleep. Affect is always dynamic, and the concept requires a rethinking of the body's relationship to representation.

Mediated sport often involves a mix of sounds, text and images. Media theory suggests that these images, words, sounds and symbols are woven together into narratives for the audience to understand. Once the audience has understood the narrative, they can be said to have stepped into the subject position constructed by the narrative. Yet mediated sport involves an array of signification that can move too quickly to be grasped consciously all at once—imagine an opening sequence of a sports show with a montage of staged and live action, overlaid by graphics and accompanied by music, sound effects and voices. Yet, despite the speed of delivery, mediated sport can have an immediate impact on the audience, and any or all of the sounds and images may generate affects, whether the audience is consciously aware of them or not, 'leaving impulses, intensities, and perhaps actions in their wake' (Wissinger 2007: 258 n. 13). Analysis of the sport media often involves a slowing down of the flow of the various channels of communication to investigate what they contain.

Wissinger's (2007) focus was the work of fashion models, which, she argued, involves affective labour. Modelling work manipulates affect by capturing and channelling attention. A model's allure lies outside the realm of consciousness or rationality. What constitutes the right look at any moment cannot be articulated, so that successful models need to cultivate a chameleon-like appearance to change at the whim of the industry. Having the right look means generating an affective response. It is possible to overlay this response with a narrative meaning, for example, labelling a look 'girl next door'. However, having a look that catches the eye involves an immediate impact outside of meaning.

For Massumi (2002: 24), 'the primacy of the affective is marked by a gap between *content* and *effect*.' There is no logical connection between the intensity of an image's effect and the structural qualities of the image. Affect neither resides in images and words, nor is it something that an audience brings to them. According to Grossberg (1992: 82), it is the 'unrepresentable excess which can only be indicated'. To focus, therefore, on the level of meaning of images and words is to neglect the intensity of the *event* of their expression. We could think of affect as the 'gratuitous amplification' (Massumi 2002: 27) of the intensity of certain words, images or sounds for some people.

Analysing the Spectacle of Sport III: the Affective Power of Media Sport

To consider the affective aspect of media sport, it is necessary to move beyond semiotic or discourse analysis to take account of an embodied response to the mediated spectacle of sport. The approach taken by Kennedy, Pussard and Thornton (2006) in their study of London's campaign to host the 2012 Olympic games was to combine discourse analysis with autoethnography. Ellis and Bochner (2000: 739) define *autoethnography* as 'an autobiographical genre of writing and research that displays multiple layers of consciousness, connecting the personal to the cultural'. Kennedy et al. (2006) collected impressions, images and texts from the campaign, including a series of representations of athletes leaping over, on or off famous London landmarks, that can be viewed at http://www.london2012.org.

Kennedy et al. (2006: 8) were surprised by their responses to the spectacle of the London 2012 bid campaign: 'despite some of our own criticisms of the Olympic Games' overt corporate and elitist practices and values, we were inexorably drawn into heartfelt conversations regarding the bid.' By adopting an autoethnographic approach, the researchers were able to record their experiences of being 'sucked in' to the spectacle, a sensation that made it matter to them in spite of their intellectual reservations. They noted patterns and gaps in the discursive formations that were being constructed in the 'Leap for London' campaign, working in a cycle of observation, recording, theorisation and retheorisation that is the hallmark of critical (auto) ethnography (Ellis and Flaherty 1992; Thomas 1993; Van Maanen 1988).

Discourse analysis showed that the images were characterised by the absence of a fully articulated message. The images brought together incongruent elements—for example, the black wheelchair basketball player Ade Adepitan appeared to be taking a shot at an imaginary basket at the top of Nelson's column (the landmark nineteenth-century monument to the British naval hero Admiral Nelson in Trafalgar Square, London). Kennedy et al. (2006) observed that the image drew together discourses of cultural difference, technocapitalism and British heritage, making links between historic and contemporary victories of British people. The image itself, however, was simultaneously unbelievable and convincing. Kennedy et al. (2006) argued that the wheelchair was the most 'jarring' element of the image because 'we normally don't see athletes with disabilities presented in the sport media' (Kennedy et al. 2006: 10). Old and new technologies were also contrasted in the image. The specialised wheelchair signified that contemporary Britain was a technologically advanced society, set against connotations of the column's evocation of the British Empire. However, by representing a black athlete with a disability, both the Olympics and British culture were figured as inclusive and meritocratic, overriding any associations of the scene with the social inequality of Imperial Britain and elite sport. Kennedy et al. (2006: 10) argued that it was the instability of the meanings and the clashes and gaps between them that resulted in their affective force: 'this image organises an affectively "positive" set of connotations because Ade Adepitan is reasonably well known in Britain and Nelson's column is a heavy signifier of Britishness for large swathes of the British population.' The image's ambiguous stylisation enabled mass affective investment.

To understand the process of experiencing the sport spectacle in terms of affect helps explain the passion that events such as the Olympics arouse. Sport spectacles are sites of short-lived but intense affective investments, enabling spectators to swing constantly between emotional highs and lows. Grossberg (1992: 229) described this as an 'occasion of an overindulgence of affect'. Our emotions are experienced as more real because of their excessiveness. 'That the excess is constructed precisely through the unbelievability and unintelligibility of the message makes it all the more powerful. In such practices, people get to live out affective relations which exceed their lives and always will (perhaps because they will have already experienced them on television)' (Grossberg 1992: 229). Sport spectacles like the Olympics are constructed on an unintelligible, shaky foundation of contradictory values: competition opposed to global participation; hierarchy and elitism opposed to unity and inclusiveness; equality of opportunity and fair play opposed to blatant privilege and visible corruption; hegemonic masculine values opposed to feminist triumphs. It is possible to understand these complex characteristics not simply as problems that the sport spectacle needs to solve, but as the very essence of its affective appeal. The sport contest at the heart of the sport spectacle crystallises the panoply of uncertainties and ambiguities into an unpredictable affective event.

Conclusion

In this chapter, we have described three approaches to analysing media sport. Taken together, they form a step-by-step guide (see the chapter summary) and will help direct readers in their own analyses of the sport media. Each of the remaining chapters in the book builds on the approaches presented in this one. The following chapters explore the specific characteristics of mediated sport in its many forms: film, television, newspapers, magazines, advertisements, objects, spaces and new media. Case studies in each chapter demonstrate the analysis in action, and the reader is provided with practical information detailing how a case study has been researched. The step-by-step guide in this chapter should be supplemented with techniques specific to a chosen media form found in the subsequent chapters. In this way, the book supports readers in conducting independent, critical analyses of sport, media and society.

CHAPTER SUMMARY

- Media sport can be analysed as *signs, discourses* or *affects*
- Semiotic analysis decodes meaning in media sport by isolating aspects that signify and corresponding concepts that are signified
- Myth and ideology in media sport can be illuminated by mapping the cultural connotations evoked by the denotative, literal meanings of signs
- Discourse analysis explores how the media asks us to 'know' sport, viewing it from particular perspectives or 'subject positions'
- Autoethnography offers the potential of recording our affective responses or embodied reactions to media sport events

---

Step-by-Step Guide to Analysing Media Sport

Step 1: Select your case study

- Choose an example of mediated sport such as the opening sequence of a sport broadcast, half an hour of live televised sport action, a sport magazine cover, an article in the sport section of a newspaper, an advertisement featuring a sport celebrity, a scene in a film with a sport theme or an environment such as a sports bar or a sports museum.
- Define the limits of your case study: decide where it begins and ends, for example, you might want to include the advertisement break in your analysis of televised sport, or you might want to focus on the advertisements alone. Your analysis of a newspaper article might be limited to one story, or you might want to take account of an entire page to consider how the story is positioned in relation to other items.
- Locate the original form of mediation. When mediated sport is presented again in a different format, it may accumulate new sets of meanings and lose some of its

original associations. For example, if you analyse a newspaper article, find the actual newspaper in which the article appeared, rather than relying on a Web archive that may not present an article in the same format. Avoid focusing on photographs alone because other texts accompanying photographs—a headline, an article, a caption—will have an impact on their meaning.

Step 2: Describe what you see (and hear … and smell and feel)

- This is the first stage of your analysis in its own right. Describe your case study at the denotational level. Be as accurate as you can, taking note of everything that is there, but trying not to make links to cultural meanings and associations.

For two-dimensional still images, articles or advertisements,
- describe the objects/people depicted
- describe the sizes and shapes of words and images
- describe the colours
- describe the lighting
- describe the fonts
- describe the layout.

For film or television sequences,
- describe the image, including
  - people, objects, colours, shapes
  - camera angle/position/movement
  - editing
  - lighting
- describe graphics and written words
- note spoken words
- describe sound effects
- describe music.

For three-dimensional environments,
- describe the things you can see as you move through the space, including
  - spatial design features
  - entrances and exits
  - markers that direct navigation or control flow (e.g. turnstiles, directional arrows)
  - objects
  - posters
  - photographs
  - television screens
  - advertisements

- logos
- signs
- describe the people you see in the space, including
  - what they are doing
  - how they interact with objects, images and texts in the space
  - how they interact with other people
  - points of surveillance or control (e.g. security checks)
- describe what you can hear, smell and feel, including
  - ambient sounds
  - music
  - textures
  - scents specific to the site (e.g. food, grass, petrol).

Step 3: Make Links to Cultural Associations

- Complete the second stage of your analysis by describing the connotations of the signs identified at the denotational level.
- Trace all the intertextual associations of the images, words and objects you have described.
- Find evidence to support your interpretations by referencing previous research. For example, histories of sport or representation might support arguments for the association of class or gender with clothing, body type, muscularity, gesture or pose.

Step 4: Consider How a Subject Position Is Constructed for the User, Viewer, Reader or Listener

- Reflect on the ways the connotations and associations you have identified construct a way of knowing sport for the consumer of mediated sport. What assumptions about sport are implicit in the way it is presented to media audiences? Consider
  - truth claims (statements)
  - references to so-called common sense understandings (discourses)
  - patterns of representation (discursive formations).
- On the basis of the results of stages 2 and 3, think about the way mediated sport forms communicate with spectators and users. Ask questions such as
  - who is being addressed?
  - how is he or she being addressed?
  - what are the presumed characteristics of the addressee?
- Consider both indirect and direct forms of address and take account of the way that mediated sport might play on the anxieties and desires of its consumers.
- You may find it helpful to use the subsequent table to record the stages of your analysis.

Denotation	Connotation	Address

Further Reading

Barthes, R. (1993), *Mythologies,* London: Vintage.

Berger, A. A. (2004), *Media Analysis Techniques* (3rd rev. edn), London: Sage.

Bignell, J. (2002), *Media Semiotics* (2nd rev. edn), Manchester: Manchester University Press.

Hall, S., ed. (1997), *Representation: Cultural Representations and Signifying Practices,* London: Sage.

Kennedy, E., Pussard, H., and Thornton, A. (2006), ' "Leap for London"? Investigating the Affective Power of the Sport Spectacle', *World Leisure,* 48: 6–21.

Mills, S. (1997), *Discourse,* London: Routledge.

–2–

Sport on Film

KEY CONCEPTS	
Camera	Mise en scène
Lighting	Superfield
Editing	Narrative
Sound	Genre

Sport films have emerged as a recognisable category of film that focuses on events, athletes and themes relating to sport, drawing on the excitement, challenge, drama and tragedy of sporting experience. Rowe (1999: 15) differentiates between televised sport, which attempts to recreate a sense of 'reality' in its portrayal of events, and film, which moves from 'the "invention" of the fictional world to the "truth" of sport and human existence'. For a sport film to succeed, it must contain the elements that make other films successful, relating a story that can appeal to a broad audience. Sport films use sport as a way of exploring relationships, values, identities, social issues and life dilemmas. To convey the story, sport films draw on a set of recognisable techniques and codes. Analysing these filmic techniques can help to unpack the manifest and latent meanings of the narrative.

The first part of this chapter discusses the ways signifying systems operate in sport films. The importance of sound for rendering the power of sport through film is explored with reference to *Raging Bull* (1980), the first of two film case studies. The second part of the chapter addresses the importance of narrative and genre for making sense of sport films, and the second case study considers baseball movies as a possible film genre.

Signifying Sport in Film

Sport films use signifying systems that the audience is expected to understand from prior experience of cinema-going. Audience members recognise the conventions used by film and develop competence in 'reading' film, which enables them to follow the narrative. The codes are so well established and well understood that we expect film to convey reality in ways that conflict with our everyday experience of the world. For example, the entire sporting career of baseball player Roy Hobbs is delivered in 118 minutes in *The Natural* (1984). A whole lifetime is communicated through flashbacks, musical signifiers of changing eras and editing. Turner (1994) identified five signifying systems which construct meaning in film: the camera, lighting, sound, mise en scène and editing.

The Camera

Turner (1994) suggested that the manipulation of the camera provides a complex set of codes that convey meanings in film. Aspects of camera use that are exploited for their capacity to signify include the film stock, angle, position and movement, focus and framing. The choice between colour and black and white film stock immediately evokes a host of associations that frame the events. Colour can render drama, action, immediacy and realism and has become the expected format for contemporary film. *Any Given Sunday* (1999), a film set in the world of American football, uses stark primary colours in the final game scene. The blocks of bright red on clothing worn by spectators in the crowd and the striking yellow and red of the uniforms of the home team contrast with the green of the field and the black worn by the visiting team. The use of colour helps convey the excitement and occasion of the sport spectacle. The use of black and white (or sepia) film is significant because of its difference from colour stock. In contrast to the contemporariness and immediacy of colour, black and white's associations with older films enable it to evoke the past. For example, the inclusion of black and white sequences of baseball players at the beginning of *Field of Dreams* (1989) sets the mood of nostalgia which runs throughout the film.

The position of the camera is effective in constructing the audience's relationship with the sport action, the narrative and the characters. The contest narrative form of most sport films is often given dramatic power through techniques which portray the extremes of emotion experienced by an individual athlete, including close-ups at the beginning or end of a competition. The close-up shots of individual competitors in *Chariots of Fire* (1981) depict their concentration and determination prior to the Olympic 100-metre final, emphasising the importance of the upcoming event. Shots from above create a sense of power over a character, making him or her appear small and vulnerable. In contrast, shots from below signify increased size and stature, conveying power, strength and importance. In the movie *Coach Carter* (2005), the eponymous character of the coach, played by Samuel L. Jackson, is usually portrayed standing with the camera slightly below head height, looking up to demonstrate his physical and personal dominance, or straight on to portray him as a powerful, serious and influential leader. However, the camera position changes during a scene at a school board meeting, where Carter's future as a coach is in question, and his vulnerability is highlighted by a camera shot from above looking down on him sitting at a table.

Camera angles can offer the characters' points of view by showing an event from a perspective corresponding to what we imagine the character would see. This can increase the sense of being part of the action. For example, the camera may put us in the position of a batter viewing a pitch, a goalkeeper waiting for a penalty shot, or a basketball player viewing the basket. In the *Loneliness of the Long Distance Runner* (1962), we can see part of the race from the hero Colin Smith's point of view, as he watches the runner ahead and faces in the crowd as he approaches the finish. The effect of this audience identification with a character increases a sense of involvement in the competitive dimensions of the action—the audience cares about the character winning or losing. Sport films use point-of-view shots to encourage the audience to step into the position of characters and experience their vulnerability, anxiety, power or dynamism.

The shot/reverse-angle shot is typically used in dialogue when the camera moves back and forth between speakers. In *Remember the Titans* (2000), the shot/reverse-angle shot is used to highlight differences between listeners and speakers. The movie is based on a story about the integration of a high school American football team in Virginia during the 1960s. A central theme of the movie is the relationships formed between players and coaches from differing ethnic backgrounds. Within this film, shot/reverse-angle shot is used to accentuate the initial feelings of separation and conflict between black and white players, coaches and athletes and black and white members of the coaching staff. Placing individuals within the same shot later in the film illustrates a sense of community and bonding as the coach and players come to respect and appreciate each other.

There are a number of other techniques that may be used as well. For example, camera movement can often be used to give the impression of rapid or violent action within sport events, and camera roll makes the world experienced by a character appear out of control, muddled, confused or disoriented. A tracking shot involves the camera moving with the action. A slow tracking shot can make the scene appear dream-like, and a fast tracking shot may carry connotations of being out of control or frenetic. Changes of focus have significance because most films aim to have everything in a shot in crisp, clear focus. Departures from this have an effect—for example, soft focus can be associated with romance or sentimentality. Techniques which appear to create a halo around a character's head can have a range of associations such as glamour, dreaminess, divinity or magic.

The movie *The Loneliness of the Long Distance Runner* has been noted for employing film techniques associated with the poetic social realism of the free cinema movement, including changing the sequencing of events, speeding up the film and the use of jazz music (Hughson 2005: 43). In particular, Hughson suggested that the camerawork in the movie was central to the success of these techniques. In the film, Colin Smith, a rebellious, working-class youth, is sent to a borstal (a British young offenders institution). While there, his running ability becomes apparent and he begins to train for an upcoming competition against a 'public school' (a private school for the privileged classes). The governor decides to let Smith train outside the gates of the borstal. In the scene where he leaves for the first time, Smith is shown outside the gate as it closes, separating him from the rows of other youths still inside. Camera shots from far away create distance from Smith and reinforce his characterisation as isolated and alienated. As he begins to run, it is clear he is enjoying his freedom, and the camera movement is slightly out of control, suggesting a buoyant air. On occasions, the camera points towards the sky and is quickly rotated again, providing a sense of almost giddiness as Smith runs through a path in the woods. Smith's freedom and high spirits on his run are contrasted with the grim, static reality of borstal life.

Lighting

The choice of lighting in a film is related to its thematic content or mood. High key lighting aims to reduce shadows and create bright, even illumination. For example, light-hearted comedies or musicals tend to be lit in this way. By contrast, low key lighting deliberately exploits shadows to create atmosphere, ambiguity or a sense of unease. Crime thrillers often make use of expressive lighting to create a mysterious or threatening mood. Documentary-style films, such as *The Loneliness of the Long Distance Runner* or *Friday Night Lights* (2004), often rely on natural lighting and shooting on location to communicate a sense of realism. Spot lighting can be used to direct the viewer's gaze to particular objects or characters with significance for the story, while floodlighting creates a diffuse effect.

Movies often draw on different styles of lighting in accordance with the development of the character and narrative. The opening scene of *The Natural* (1984) depicts the central character, Roy Hobbs, waiting, half in shadow, at a train station. The partial illumination establishes a sense of uncertainty about him, who he is and where is he going. The screen fills with the image of a train arriving and departing, with fleeting glimpses of Hobbs through the gaps between the cars. As the train pulls off, an empty platform is revealed. The next scene shows Hobbs on the train, a pattern of light and dark playing on his face, cast by the slats of the window blind. The striped effect of the lighting accentuates the mystery and ambiguity surrounding the character. This lack of clarity around the adult Hobbs contrasts with the next scenes, which show him as a child playing baseball with his father in a wheat field. The bright lighting creates clear, sharp definitions of the images, conveying a sense of certainty. Backlighting intensifies the glow of sunshine on Hobbs's blonde hair, creating a halo effect which adds to the mood of innocence. The difference in lighting suggests to the audience that something tragic or mysterious has happened to change Hobbs from a carefree child to a troubled adult.

Editing

Relationships between camera shots are created through editing and montage. Editing is a central way that the narrative progresses throughout the film, as shots are juxtaposed with other shots and structured into sequences. The demands of realism mean that editing remains largely invisible or seamless in most films, giving the impression of a natural transition between shots. For example, documentaries tend to use fewer edits than fictional stories. *Hoop Dreams* (1994), a documentary about two young, black basketball players from Chicago, has long sequences of interviews with the boys, the coach and their families.

Film-makers employ multiple editing techniques. The simplest methods involve straightforward cuts between one scene and the next or the use of techniques such as a fade or dissolve, where one image gradually disappears and is replaced, or a wipe, where one image is pushed aside to reveal another. The fade or dissolve may be used in flashbacks to denote a change in time while maintaining a sense of continuity or to indicate the passage of time, as the hero, as a child, transforms to his adult image. There are also a range of transition devices that are used to move between scenes such as overlapping sound, sudden cuts and action that begins in one scene and ends in the next. The editing technique can help to create an emotional context, establish a new setting or develop the action. Sudden cuts produce surprise, horror and disruption. The use of short establishing shots above a new location can help to place the narrative within a physical context. The timing of cuts between shots can intensify energy or slow it down. In *Any Given Sunday,* cuts during games are quick and explosive, highlighting the fast-paced, dynamic action of the game. Cuts in a scene of relative stasis can slow it down and instil significance in the moment.

Montage editing involves a quickly changing set of different shots whose meaning emerges within the combination of shots (Hayward 2006). The spectator supplies the third meaning that connects the shots that are positioned together. Montage often disrupts a film's sense of realism by drawing attention to the editing process. It can effectively speed through time. In *Raging Bull* (1980), a home movie sequence, which combines title cards documenting fights, stills from the fights and home movies depicting scenes of marital harmony, condenses more than three years of the boxer's personal and professional life into two minutes thirty-five seconds (Phillips 2002). Phillips (2002) suggested that the montage of shots at the end of *Breaking Away* (1979) has the effect of altering the metanarrative of the film. The film depicts four working-class young men taking on university students in an annual team bicycle race. The last few scenes of the film indicate that the characters have changed personal direction by depicting them pursuing different life choices such as going to university or getting married. Despite the film's engagement with the politics of class and sport, Phillips (2002: 133) argued that the scenes 'quickly shift emphasis from social class to individual psychology' in keeping with 'so many American movies'.

Sound

Film is not just a visual phenomenon. A film's soundtrack can bring a scene to life, a capacity further enhanced by developments in sound technology. Chion (1994) drew attention to the importance of Dolby stereo for increases in clarity and detail in sounds and noises used in contemporary films. He explained that 'Dolby offers a gain in resources on the level of sound space and sound dynamics' (Chion 1994: 153). Dolby stereo and multitrack recording gave directors and sound designers the ability to broaden the way that scenes are constructed. Chion called this the 'superfield': 'the space created, in multitrack films, by ambient natural sounds, city noises, music, and all sorts of rustlings that surround the visual space' (Chion 1994: 150). This technology enables individual sounds to be heard and placed with much more definition, so that contemporary soundscapes are less dominated by what is seen on the screen. Increased definition of sounds has also provided sound designers with the means to extract greater depth to the portrayal of feelings and emotions that are not only in the present, but also the past and the future. Chion called this 'rendering': 'the use of sounds to convey the feelings and effects associated with the situation on screen—often in opposition to faithful reproduction of the sounds that might be heard in the situation in reality' (Chion 1994: 224).

Sound also has a narrative function. It can move the plot forward, help define characters, indicate mood, locate the film historically and highlight particular actors, objects and actions. Soundtracks may be used to situate movies in particular historical times, such as the 1960s soundtrack that plays throughout *Remember the Titans.*

Chariots of Fire uses sound and editing to develop the drama surrounding the men's 100-metre Olympic final. Rowe (1999: 160) has described *Chariots of Fire* as the 'definitive sports film of the 1980s' and highlighted the importance of the evocative electric soundtrack by Vangelis. The film deals with issues around the exclusivity of the British middle and upper classes, nationalism, ethnic prejudices and the amateur ethos. In the scene before the race begins, the hero, Harry Abrahams, is shown in the changing room, where he finds a letter from his coach, Sam Mussolini. Mussolini's voice reading the letter is heard, creating the effect of listening to Harry's personal thoughts. In the letter are final instructions for the race and a good luck charm that was given to the coach by his father. While the letter is read, the camera focuses on each of the main competitors as they sit quietly, seriously thinking about the upcoming event. There is very slow music playing, along with soft lighting to indicate the quiet, individual and methodical preparations for the event. Suddenly, there is an abrupt edit, accentuated by loud band music, and we see and hear the cheering crowd, as the athletes walk onto the track in a blaze of sunlight. In this sequence, sound is employed as a transitional device, and the solitary, quiet scenes of the changing room are contrasted with the very public nature of an Olympic event. The sound changes again as the runners get into position on the track. The camera moves in slow motion, and the only sounds are music, which is slow and almost eerie. The absence of crowd noise, dialogue and band music is noticeable. We hear the sound of the trowel as the runners dig into the cinder track to create their starting places and there is a sequence of close-ups highlighting parts of the body in preparation such as shoes, hands digging, faces and runners' legs. A close-up of the charm demonstrates its emotive and narrative significance. The slowness builds tension as the runners prepare. The camera cuts to the coach pacing and looking at his watch, again creating a sense of tension. As the runners get into place, there is a camera shot from Abrahams's perspective, and we see ourselves looking down the empty track. This image is accompanied by the sound of beating hearts. The quiet tension is broken by the crack of the starting gun, and the noise of the crowd rushes back in as the race begins. At the end of the race, the camera returns to slow motion, as a replay of the race is interspersed with shots of Abrahams being congratulated, and there are close-ups of the key runners' straining faces. The band plays 'God Save the Queen' as the British flag is raised. Within this sequence sound is used as a way of developing the emotional, sensory and dramatic elements of the story, creating tension, emphasising the importance of the moment and further developing the narrative.

Mise en Scène

Mise en scène is a term used to describe all the visual elements in the frame of a shot: the set design, the costumes, the placing and movement of objects and characters. The frame encloses certain objects and characters and leaves others out, lending significance to both. The position of materials within the frame carries connotations of power and importance. Giannetti (2005) describes the mise en scène of a scene in *Bend It Like Beckham* (2002). The scene takes place in the bedroom of the central character, Nagra, a British Asian young woman passionate about playing soccer. Nagra is positioned on the floor at the end of her bed. The sloping ceiling, walls and door of the room are covered with David Beckham paraphernalia, including a replica Manchester United football shirt, posters and cut-out images. Nagra is looking up at a large, black and white poster of David Beckham's face. The position of the poster at the top of the frame evokes power befitting Beckham's hero status within global soccer culture. The slant of the wall brings the image into an intimate relationship with the character of Nagra. She is depicted as a supplicant at a shrine to football.

Costume invariably plays a role within sport movies since sporting action requires particular types of clothing. Costumes can evoke a range of associations such as historical era, professionalism, class, gender and membership in subcultures. In *Field of Dreams,* the costume of Shoeless Joe Jackson immediately locates him as a historical figure transplanted into the present. The uniforms of the female players in *A League of Their Own* (1992) are part of the league's attempt to ensure that they display appropriate femininity by wearing skirts instead of more traditional baseball uniforms. The boxer Rocky Balboa's appearance in an oversized maroon robe with gold edging and an advertisement for a meat-packing company helps construct him as a sympathetic figure in *Rocky* (1976). Rocky's poor clothes contrast sharply with the flamboyant, tailored costume of his competitor, Apollo Creed. The use of the Stars and Stripes motif in Creed's attire, in its signification of old-fashioned American values, builds tension as his character sacrifices sporting ideals in favour of entertainment and an easy victory.

Case Study: *Raging Bull*—Feeling the Fight

Raging Bull is a powerful film of the life of the boxer Jake La Motta. La Motta's self-destructive career is narrated through fight scenes interwoven with scenes from his domestic life, often providing striking contrasts. During the film the image and sound of the fight scenes convey La Motta's state of mind and show how the various signifying systems can work together in the film to render the experience of the fighter. If we consider the three scenes featuring fights between Jake La Motta and Sugar Ray Robinson at different points during La Motta's career, we can see how different codes of camera, lighting, sound, mise en scène and editing can combine to create different impressions from superficially similar events. In particular, the use of sound during these scenes is central to marking changes in La Motta's mindset and fortunes, while also creating a sense of continuity throughout the film. Yet, while sound is important, no music is used in the fight scenes. Instead, the sounds of the ring are given preeminence. A boxer in the midst of action will experience sound all around. In *Raging Bull,* all the crowd sounds from the boxer's perspective are recorded in stereo. This helps to place the cinema audience in the ring and, in Chion's (1994: 151) terms, exploits the superfield to provide 'a continuous and constant consciousness of all the space surrounding the dramatic action'.

The use of heavy filtering and the slowing down of crowd sounds give the impression of silence in *Raging Bull,* but low modulation fluctuations are always present. The filtering of the crowd sound is often used to clear an acoustic space for the dramatic intervention of a new sound. Films before the 1970s suffered from a continuous noise accompaniment and a poor sound quality in the higher frequencies. The standardisation of Dolby changed this. Unwanted tape hiss could be removed, leaving room for crisp, clear audio. As Chion (1994: 149) observed, Dolby sound 'vibrates, gushes, trembles, and cracks (think of the crackling of flashbulbs in *Raging Bull)*'. The sounds of flashbulbs in *Raging Bull* are always dramatic. They have a chilling, mechanical quality and appear especially brutal when placed in a negative situation such as a boxer taking a count. Occasionally they are heard when La Motta is prowling around the ring after a successful attack on his opponent. Flashbulbs and cameras are also synonymous with the intrusion of the media gaze into the life of a sporting celebrity. The camera flashes are used to link public and private in the film. After his final defeat by Robinson, La Motta is shown being interviewed at home with his wife and children as he announces his retirement. La Motta asks the photographer to take some pictures of his wife, children and himself. The resulting flashes remind us of the brutal fights. Evoking the sound of metal on metal, they give the impression of clashing swords, which brutally render the feeling of gloved punches landing on bare skin.

In the scene depicting La Motta's first fight against Sugar Ray Robinson, the ring is brightly lit and the space created by the camera angle is open and wide. The camera shots are in sharp focus and the commentator's voice is crisp and loud. La Motta's career is on the way up. The combination of signifying elements in the scene renders La Motta's experience as he emerges as a potential champion with a long career in front of him. The sound of whistling, a signifier of crowd excitement, heard by the boxer in the ring is slowed down, mirroring the use of slow motion in the visuals. At one point it evokes the sound of a factory hooter or a steam whistle, as if the boxing match is like a day in the factory. Thom (1999: para. 4) discussed the use of slow motion in film, noting that '*Raging Bull* and *Taxi Driver* contain some obvious, and some very subtle uses of slow motion. Some of it is barely perceptible. But it always seems to put us into a dream-space, and tells us that something odd, and not very wholesome, is happening.' In this case, the unwholesome happening is signified by La Motta circling around the ring waiting for the moment to charge in for the kill. We are also aware of the voyeuristic, almost vulture-like qualities of the reporters all around the ring, with their abrasive-sounding cameras and the clear sounds of the punches and the grunts from La Motta as he lays into Robinson. Here, these sounds reflect his boxing success. We hear them again in the last fight with Robinson.

ANALYSING *RAGING BULL*

Raging Bull (1980), directed by Martin Scorsese, was selected by the American Film Institute as the best ever sport film in its '10 Top 10' greatest films list. At the 1980 Academy Awards, *Raging Bull* was nominated for eight awards, winning Best Actor for the lead, Robert De Niro, and Best Editing for Thelma Schoonmaker. In our analysis, we wanted to focus on the skilful use of sound and image in the film's construction of the narrative of the life of the boxer Jake La Motta. We selected three fight scenes from the movie, at different points during La Motta's career, to show how signifying systems were used to render the different experiences of the boxer. For each of the scenes we noted the camera angles and position, lighting, editing, everything in the soundtrack and the mise en scène. This process required us to replay the scenes many times, focusing on each of these dimensions individually, and then in conjunction with each other. For example, we listened again and again to the soundtrack—including sound effects, music and dialogue—to identify precisely the character of the sounds. Then we noted the ways the sound interacted with the images. We then noted the ways the varying use of audio and visual communication changed across the three scenes. Finally, we considered the way that the viewer was positioned to make sense of the narrative constructed within and between the shots.

Low sounds have become associated through convention with a sense of un-ease. For Chion (1994: 108), 'the impression of realism is often tied to a feeling of discomfort, of an uneven signal, of interference and microphone noise'. In between rounds seven and eight, a low-frequency rumble is heard. Although hard to distinguish, it has an animalistic quality that reflects La Motta's nickname, the 'Bronx Bull'. Similar sounds become much more common in subsequent fight scenes.

In the second fight scene with Robinson, La Motta is beaten following a controversial decision by the judges. In this scene, both audio and visual fields are altered in various ways. A dense, smoke-filled atmosphere indicates La Motta's blurred vision. The crowd sounds have increased bass frequencies, rising and falling in pitch, creating a sense of disquiet. Low howls and animal screeching and roaring sounds exacerbate the fearful mood and accentuate the brutality of boxing. In this fight La Motta takes punishment throughout the fight but mounts one last desperate attack, which is preceded by a sound like a skidding car. A high-frequency modulated sound is used to accompany the announcement of La Motta's defeat. The crowd sound is distant and muted, rendering La Motta's dislocation from the reality in the ring.

The final fight scene with Robinson, when La Motta loses his world title, is shot from two perspectives: 'live' and on television. Barred from the ringside, La Motta's brother watches at home with his wife on a small television set. The monophonic, tinny quality of the television sound is contrasted and mixed with the rich stereo sound from the ring. The sound of the crowd on the television is heard as indistinguishable white noise. A beer advertisement is superimposed on the image of the fight, indicating the objectification of the boxer by the media spectacle. In the ring, the same sound is in stereo but has a fluctuating presence, as though his fans are leaving him for the soon-to-be-crowned new champion. The suppressed coverage of the violence in the match on television (e.g. the Pabst Blue Ribbon sponsor's logo announcing 'Round 13' obscures the image of La Motta recovering from one of the beatings) contrasts dramatically with the brutalism of the reality as experienced by La Motta in the ring. Yet the monophonic, televisual mediation effectively renders the impotent displacement experienced by La Motta's brother.

The sequence featuring Jake and his wife's home movies is the only part of the film in colour—the rest of *Raging Bull* is shot in black and white. Yet there is an inversion of the usual codes of colour within the film. Romantic nostalgia often signified by black and white film stock gives way in *Raging Bull* to a gritty evocation of the past. The lack of colour in the film delivers a sense of the reality of the times experienced by La Motta. The camera dwelling on blood soaking the ropes after La Motta's defeat to Robinson is even more redolent as we are asked to imagine its colour in the absence of red.

Raging Bull positions the audience in the ring, experiencing with the boxer a heightened sensitivity to sound and image. The accumulated sound of Robinson's punches have the 'duty of "rendering" weight, violence, and pain' (Chion 1994: 112). The editing creates a barrage of sounds and images as La Motta's head is punched repeatedly: camera flashes, animal noises, blood splatters, saliva and sweat. Scenes of reporters in the crowd beyond the ring baying for blood contrast with the bowed head of Jake's wife. Robinson is seen from La Motta's perspective. The slow motion image dwells on his raised fist, the light shining through the smoky ring creating a halo effect, giving him the appearance of an avenging angel. The sound fades out almost to silence and comes crashing in, accentuating the weight and violence of the punch as it lands. The shots of Jake's wife's head fearfully looking up and dropping down at the moment of impact mirror La Motta's physical defeat.

Narrative and Genre in Sport Films

The signifying systems of film create meanings within and between shots, constructing a narrative or a way of knowing the events they depict. Narrative can be thought of as 'the recounting of two or more events (or a situation and an event) that are logically connected, occur over time, and are linked by a consistent subject into a whole' (Stam, Burgoyne and Flitterman-Lewis 1992: 62). However, narrative does not simply recount what happens, but in so doing actively constructs meaning. The audience is thus engaged in a dynamic process of figuring out and interpreting the unfolding events. The organisation of events in a film provides its narrative structure. The choice of where and when to begin and end the film and what is presented in between has consequences for the way we understand a film. Sport films typically employ a classical narrative structure that moves predictably towards a climactic big game or contest. Deviations from this pattern require the audience to reconsider conventional ways of knowing and making sense of sport. For example, *Rocky* employs a classical narrative structure, as the film follows Balboa's preparation for the big fight that concludes the film. By contrast, *Bull Durham* (1988) does not feature a 'big game', and when the hero, Crash, breaks the minor league home run record, it is an anticlimactic moment that does not even appear on the screen.

When films display shared elements—recurring plots, conventions, themes and values—it is possible to group them into separate genres or types. Both the producers and consumers of film use their knowledge of the conventions of different genres in making meaningful sense of events on screen. For example, some recognisable film genres might include the western, the musical, the 'coming of age' film, the war movie, the science fiction film, the romance, the horror film or the comedy. Sometimes actors and directors are associated with particular genres. For example, John Wayne, Glenn Ford and Clint Eastwood are associated with westerns. Sport movies are less likely to be associated with particular actors or directors as they rarely specialise in this type of movie. Sylvester Stallone has starred in the series of Rocky movies and Kevin Costner has starred in three movies featuring baseball: *Bull Durham, Field of Dreams,* and *For the Love of the Game* (1999), as well as a golf movie, *Tin Cup* (1996), and a cycling movie, *American Flyers* (1985). However, neither actor can be identified primarily as a sport film hero.

Movie-goers are so familiar with generic characteristics of film that film-makers are able to condense plots or sequences by relying on the audience to fill in the gaps. For example, in sport films, we rarely see a competition in its entirety; instead the event is signified by highlights that convey in shorthand the drama of the contest. This might include shots of the scoreboard to locate changes in time, a quick half-time talk or an emphasis on particular key moments in the game.

O'Sullivan, Dutton and Rayner (2003) highlighted two consequences of the reliance on genre as a convention: the marginalisation of media that challenge traditional genres and the potential limitations of formulaic narrative conventions. In westerns, it is expected that the hero will defeat the bad guys and restore law and order to the community. In sport movies, it is typically expected that the hero will win the big game and demonstrate qualities of hard work, effort, skill and determination. Originality in genre films is a result of the combination of this formula with elements of unpredictability. The pleasure for the audience may be 'as much in the conventional base as in the surprise twist' (Phillips 2000: 23).

While genre films may vary the details, they use the same underlying pattern repeatedly, so that the 'same fundamental conflicts are resolved over and over again in similar fashion' (Altman 1999: 25). Berger (1992) delineated aspects of films that can be considered formulaic, thereby forming the basis for a particular generic category: time, location, heroes and heroines, villains, secondary characters, plots, themes, costume, locomotion and weaponry. Using the western as an illustration, he showed how these elements remain stable across the film genre. For example, Berger (1992) observed that

- westerns take place at the turn of the 20th century
- they are located on the edge of the frontier
- they have certain kinds of heroes (cowboys) and heroines (schoolmarms)
- the villains can be the corrupt sheriff, the psychotic killer, the criminal banker; secondary characters tend to have certain needs—the townsfolk may be too weak to resist the criminal element that may be attacking them
- plots usually involve actions that restore law and order—gunfights, chases
- themes involve justice
- costumes worn by characters include cowboy hats and boots
- the dominant forms of locomotion in the western are the horse and the stage-coach
- the weaponry of westerns is the six-gun.

Berger's (1992) criteria may be useful in considering whether an identifiable genre exists that unites all sport films, or whether there are separate genres or subgenres for films featuring different sports. Genres overlap with each other, so it is also possible to consider whether sport is merely incidental to the narrative of films of another genre: action movies, comedies, romances. There is considerable debate as to whether sport films do constitute a particular genre (Jones 2005). There have, however, been attempts to identify their shared qualities. For example, Jones (2008) argued that sport films do have regular conventions such as the story of the underdog competing against the favourite in *Rocky, The Bad News Bears* (1976; remade in 2005) and *Hoosiers* (1986). Similarly, Cashmore (2008) suggested that sport films have shared plot elements relating to the potential triumph or disaster associated with the film's climax. Rowe (1998: 352) also suggested that the genre of sport films includes a preoccupation with 'the extent to which (idealized) sports can transcend or are bound by existing (and corrupting) social relations'. If we apply Berger's (1992) criteria to a number of sport films featuring the same sport—baseball—we can begin to consider whether certain features form a pattern within these films.

Case Study: the Baseball Movie—a Genre of Nostalgia?

Many movies have been based around baseball and baseball players. The Web site http://www.baseballmovie.com lists seventy-eight baseball films that have been made since 1942. Twenty-six of the movies on the list have been released since 2000 alone. Just as the popular genre of the western says something about American culture, baseball also reinforces particular stories of social life. Ogden (2007) drew on Barthes's discussion of mythology to demonstrate how baseball has been constructed throughout history as a sacred American national pastime that embodies its moral character and core values. From its beginning, baseball was conceived as a uniquely

American game representing democracy, competition, skill, honesty and courage. The myths surrounding baseball may in part be sustained through the use of familiar, repeated elements, suggesting ongoing, 'natural', even inevitable social meanings. This case study explores the ways that reoccurring narrative conventions are used to tell and arguably reinscribe the story of baseball.

Time

Baseball movies are situated in different historical periods, from *Eight Men Out* (1988), based on the White Sox scandal of 1919, to *Fever Pitch* (2005; also known as *A Perfect Catch*), which depicts the Red Sox winning the 2004 World Series and breaking the curse of Babe Ruth. Many baseball films, however, are located in the past such as *The Natural, A League of Their Own, The Babe* (1992), *Eight Men Out* and *The Rookie* (2002). Others that were made a long time ago, such *as The Jackie Robinson Story* (1950), *Angels in the Outfield* (1951) and *The Pride of the Yankees* (1942), were contemporary at the time but now look dated and are evocative of baseball's history. Others are set in the recent past or present such as *Bull Durham, Bad News Bears* (2005) and *Major League* (1989). There are also films that combine past and present, such as *Field of Dreams,* which is situated in the 1980s (when it was released) but contains characters and scenes from the early part of the twentieth century, and *The Winning Season* (2004), which includes a return to the 1909 World Series. So, while baseball films do vary in relation to the specific era in which they are set, there is a continuing intertextual association with baseball's history, roots and traditions. This nostalgic turn can be understood as an attempt to reaffirm America's inherent character and core values through the representation of its national pastime. For example, in *Field of Dreams* and *The Winning Season,* individuals from contemporary times are transported back to the past to learn lessons about the importance of family, self-belief and honesty.

Place

The key events in baseball films occur in and around the ballpark. The ballpark, with its expansive, green fields, evokes the countryside. In addition, movies are also situated in small towns with ballparks located in open spaces and rural environments. For example, the opening scenes of *The Natural, Field of Dreams* and *A League of Their Own* occur on farms. The father and son playing catch in the field in *The Natural* are visually associated with the growing plants in the field, locating the game as a 'natural', pastoral part of life. Hunter (2005: 72) critiqued this image, arguing that it is 'of course, anything but [natural], giving white middle class masculinity a privileged sense of national belonging and entitlement by making it the primary occupant of the building and reiteration of a baseball mythology'. This predominately suburban or rural middle-class representation of the baseball player reinscribes the past and its association with heartland values and contrasts with the contemporary demographics of baseball. In 2006, a total of 40.5 per cent of Major League Baseball (MLB) players were Latino (29.4 per cent), African American (8.4 per cent), Asian (2.4 per cent) or 'other' (0.3 per cent), and 30 per cent of the coaches in MLB were either African American (16 per cent), Latino (13 per cent) or Asian (1 per cent; Lapchick 2006). In addition, 31 per cent of the players are international.

Heroes

There are recurring qualities associated with main characters that make them heroic. Roy Hobbs, in *The Natural,* plays for a team called the Knights, emphasising the sense that baseball players are heroes, protecting their country's way of life. This heroic motif is reinforced through references to Homeric heroes and Sir Lancelot (Hunter 2005). The central characters of films such as *The Jackie Robinson Story, The Pride of the Yankees, The Stratton Story* (1949) and *The Natural,* are baseball players who have persevered through adversity. Their heroism resides in their purity of focus as well as their determination to succeed in sport. Often films portray players as naive, inexperienced, talented and enthusiastic rookies who encounter temptations or problems when they reach the big leagues. The capacity for heroes to persevere, retain their integrity and maintain or reacquire an innocent love for, and commitment to, the game is a central motif in many films. In *The Stratton Story,* Jimmie Stratton, a promising baseball player, loses part of his leg but continues to fight to return to the sport he loves. *Bull Durham* presents a more complex hero in Crash, a world-weary veteran who very briefly made it to 'the Show' (the major leagues). Despite the disappointment of a career spent in the minor leagues, Crash maintains his love of baseball, his commitment to sport and his desire for success.

Villains

The typical villains in baseball movies are mercenary, cut-throat capitalists and sportsmen who exploit or corrupt the innocent hero. These cut-throat capitalists are motivated by profit, rather than love for the game. In *A League of Their Own,* the villains are the capitalist organisers who 'feminise' the game to sell it and, at the end of the war, shut down the entire women's league. *Eight Men Out* relates the story of the 1919 Black Sox scandal and portrays young, financially poor ballplayers being duped by more wily, sophisticated organisers. The multiple villains in *The Natural* include an agent and a reporter who hound the hero, Hobbs, and other players to get a story; a sophisticated femme fatale, who stalks him and damages his career; and a corrupt owner, who attempts to bribe him.

Secondary Characters

Baseball in rural areas can be portrayed as a transformational space through the celebration of small town values. The local community, represented by parents, fans and, particularly, young people serve as secondary characters who reinforce the redemptive features of sport. These community ballparks offer young people a chance to develop and world-weary ex-players the opportunity to gain a new lease on life by coaching them. The misfit group of young people and the alcohol-loving coach in *Bad News Bears* transform themselves into a successful, integrated team. The alcoholic is saved by the innocence of the children on the team, and the children develop skills and confidence by being part of a winning baseball team.

The family also serve as secondary characters, particularly in the form of the supportive wife or girlfriend. In *Field of Dreams,* the wife supports her husband in what appears to be a foolish endeavour, and the high school sweetheart in *The Natural* maintains her loyalty to Hobbs even though they do not see each other for twelve years. The supporting wife also appears in *The Stratton Story* and *The Pride of the Yankees.* The character of Annie in *Bull Durham* may be more of a heroine, but her role is portrayed as helping her chosen young players to develop the skills and knowledge that will enable them to succeed in the major leagues. The hero is supported as he follows his dreams or perseveres through adversity. The supporting role of women in the movies reinscribes baseball as a masculine space and asserts the importance of traditional gender roles.

Plot

The central character in many baseball films can be viewed as a hero on a quest for success. This success must be achieved while maintaining or acquiring particular values perceived as central to idealised American culture such as honesty, hard work, kindness and integrity. In *The Pride of the Yankees* and *Bang the Drum Slowly* (1973), the superstar heroes are faced with debilitating and ultimately fatal illnesses, yet they maintain their love of the game, their desire to play and their integrity until the end. Success in baseball films results from sustained effort and desire. The climax of baseball films can often be a game, with the outcome left until the end of the movie. The game is the ultimate test of the hero, and success may represent the reward of hard work and perseverance as well as the fulfilment of the hero's dreams.

Themes

Rowe (1998) highlighted the tendency for baseball films to explore the sport's potential for helping the nation regain values that have eroded in the face of an increasingly capitalistic and competitive society. Baseball is often portrayed as an authentic, communal and wholesome experience that can lead people back to important things in life, the antithesis of an individualistic and commercialised rat race that is out of control and dehumanising. Other recurring themes include nostalgia, the value of family, the pure love of the game and the importance of community.

Locomotion

Baseball players travel on the team bus or, in some cases, on a train. These scenes focus on the dynamics between players or players, coaches and management as well as outsiders such as journalists and fans. Key scenes, such as the seduction of Roy Hobbs in *The Natural,* initial arguments and the eventual bonding of coach and players in *A League of Their Own,* and Crash's training of young superstar Nuke in the ways of baseball in *Bull Durham,* are all located in the context of travelling to the next game. The contained space of the team bus, car or train positions players in close proximity to each other, and here they may bond, work through conflicts and learn about the self and others. As the film progresses, changes in interactions between players may indicate maturation, integration and friendship. For example, in *Bull Durham,* the relationship between Nuke and Crash changes from antagonism to trust as Nuke begins to take his mentor Crash's advice and develops from an arrogant rookie to a more mature player.

Costume

Baseball uniforms are distinctive and locate characters as players for particular teams as well as situating them in a specific historical period. The uniforms in *A League of Their Own* also signify the players' gender. Donning a uniform can communicate that a player has made it to the top and achieved at least one part of his or her quest. In *Bad News Bears,* the uniforms bearing the logo of the sponsor 'Bo-Peep's Gentleman's Club'—a silhouette of a female in a suggestive pose—connote the dissolution of the coach and the positioning of the team as outsiders.

Weaponry

The baseball bat serves as a player's way of expressing dominance, skill and success. Scoring the winning run represents the epitome of the hero's quest. The bat is most clearly marked as significant in *The Natural,* constructed by the youthful hero Hobbs from a tree struck by lightning. Hobbs emblazoned it with the name 'Wonder Bat' and an image of the lightning bolt. The childlike bat recalls his past innocence and lost dreams and ultimately serves as his signature weapon as he leads his team to victory after victory.

Applying Berger's (1992) categories illustrates that baseball films seem to share a number of themes and conventions. It might be argued on this basis that the baseball movie is a genre in its own right. However, some of these elements are generalised among sport films—for example, the 'against all odds' plot line. The baseball movie might be considered only a subgenre of a wider sport movie genre. Considering components of genre, however, can help to reveal the strategies that film-makers use to (re)create the mythic qualities associated with baseball. Narrative conventions and systems of signification work together in sport movies to construct a particular vision of sport and society. The analysis of narrative and formula can help illuminate the assumptions on which they rest.

CHAPTER SUMMARY

- Sport films use signifying systems that the audience is expected to understand; it is useful to think about the ways meaning is constructed by the camera, lighting, editing, sound and mise en scène
- The creative use of audio and visual communication in film can render a powerful experience of sport for the audience
- The signifying systems of film create meanings within and between the shots, helping the audience to construct a narrative by interpreting and connecting events portrayed
- When films display shared elements, such as recurring plots, conventions, themes and values, it may be possible to group films into a genre
- We can consider whether sport films constitute a specific genre by analysing the extent to which certain features, such as time, place, heroes, villains, secondary characters, plots, themes and costumes, occur with regularity across a number of individual films

---

Suggestions for Analysis

There is an ongoing debate about whether sport films constitute a genre in their own right. Select a range of films with sport-related content and apply the parameters suggested by Berger (1992), to consider commonalities across time, place, heroes, villains, secondary characters, plot, themes, locomotion, costume and weaponry. Are there sufficient similarities to identify a sport genre or sport-specific subgenres (e.g. a soccer film genre)? Are other aspects of recognisable cultural narratives present in the films (e.g. fairy tales, Christian parables)? How are themes central to sport treated in different sport films? For example, how is damage to the body discursively constructed in boxing films and baseball films?

Further Reading

Chion, M. (1994), *Audio-Vision,* New York: Columbia University Press.

'The Greatest Sports Films of All Time', <http://www.filmsite.org/sportsfilms.html> accessed 26 March 2008. [rankings of the greatest sport films by different media sources]

Hughson, J. (2005), 'The Loneliness of the Angry Young Sportsman', *Muse,* 35: 41–8.

Jones, G. (2008), 'In Praise of an "Invisible Genre"? An Ambivalent Look at the Fictional Sports Feature Film', *Sport in Society,* 11: 117–29.

Metz, C. (1974), *Film Language,* Chicago: University of Chicago Press.

Nine: A Journal of Baseball History and Culture, <http://muse.jhu.edu/journals/nine/index.html> accessed 29 November 2007.

Poulton, E., and Roderick, M., eds (2008), 'Introducing Sport in Films', *Sport in Society,* 11/2–3 [special issue].

Rowe, D. (1998), 'If You Film It, Will They Come?' *Journal of Sport and Social Issues,* 22: 350–9.

'SI.Com Goes to the Movies', <http://sportsillustrated.cnn.com/features/2003/movies/> accessed 26 March 2008. [rates top sports movies overall and by sport]

Televised Sport

KEY CONCEPTS

Five channels of communication	Gendered genre
Simultaneity	Clarity
Flow	Banter
Televisual convention	Megaevents

This chapter builds on the identification of the importance of signifying systems, narrative and genre in making sport meaningful in film by extending these concepts to the analysis of sport on television. Televised sport can be understood as comprising five channels of communication, graphics, image, voice, sound effects and music, operating at the same time to create a narrative or way of knowing sport. Approaches to the analysis of the five channels of communication are demonstrated and linked to the construction of sport programmes. Sport is the only type of television programme that globally attracts more male than female viewers (Cooper-Chen 1994). This chapter considers sport as a gendered genre, which contains features designed to attract a male audience, while also employing techniques associated with other types of programming. The case studies for this chapter are the use of narrative in the televising of the Salt Lake City Winter Olympic spectacle and the televising of men's and women's football in the United Kingdom.

Televised Sport and Communicative Excess

The experience of televised sport is one of communicative excess: constantly changing sounds and images confront the senses; moving bodies are laden with logos; graphics surround the screen showing player statistics, keeping time and updating the score. Around the pitch, field or court, the colours and shapes of advertisements vie with images of the crowd draped in fan paraphernalia. Music is played or sung to the spectators, who also sing their own songs, and yell and cheer or whistle and boo, while the voices of commentators overlay a constant narrative on the action. The sounds of the sport are also present such as players crashing into each other, shouting above the din or running down a court. At the start or end of play, intro and outro sequences present a collage of images and sounds, and the entire coverage may be punctuated with advertisements, commercials and station identification breaks.

To analyse television sport, therefore, we need a model of communication that takes account of all of this activity. In an article on semiotics and television, Seiter (1992) adapted the work of Christian Metz, originally developed in response to film, to consider the ways television creates meanings. Seiter (1992) observed that while semiotic approaches to analysis emphasise the smallest unit of meaning (e.g. the phoneme in linguistics), television makes it difficult to identify discrete building blocks of meaning. To 'freeze' an image would be to lose the voices, sound effects and music which may well be occurring simultaneously. Metz (1974) identified five channels of communication for cinema: image, written language, voice, music and sound effects. Seiter (1992) suggested that television could also be understood in these terms, but she substituted graphics for written materials, to include logos, borders, frames, diagrams and computer-animated images, which, she said, were far more prevalent on television than in cinema.

Seiter's approach to characterising communication in television has echoes of Williams's (1974) insistence on the importance of 'flow' for understanding the complex operations of meaning in television. Williams (1974) argued that watching television diverged from more traditional cultural forms because the typical experience was one of flow. Williams (1974) criticised television reviewers for focusing on individual programme items, as if they could be separated from the experience of an evening's viewing:

> It is not only that many particular items—given our ordinary organisation of response, memory and persistence of attitude and mood—are affected by those preceding and those following them ... it is also that though useful things may be said about all the separable items ... hardly anything is ever said about the characteristic experience of the flow itself. (p. 96)

Live sport broadcasts are preceded, followed and interspersed with an array of short items—prerecorded sequences detailing a team's campaign, live pundits' speculations, competitions, advertisement breaks—all of which help frame the event for the viewer. This flow of multiple, simultaneously occurring channels of communication creates a complex structure of intertextuality, accumulating a web of associations. The full significance of images, words, music, sounds and narratives in televised sport can only be understood in relation to other, previous instances that they evoke. The analysis of televised sport involves consideration of how meanings occur within and across the five channels of communication and in relation to a host of intertextual references. Following Seiter, then, it is possible to think about how each channel of communication might figure in the signifying process, and how each contributes to the experience of televised sport.

Image

Metz (1974) argued that it was not possible to discern the smallest unit of meaning in cinema, suggesting that film should instead be analysed at the level of shot, its largest minimum segment. Television can also be considered in this way. However, while the concept of the shot may take account of the interrelationship of sound and image, it is still very reliant on its visual dimension. Berger (1992: 27) developed a 'grammar of television' to cover the ways camera shots and editing techniques operate (see Figure 3.1).

Berger's (1992) suggestions for ways of decoding the connotations of shots can be thought of as a starting point for analysing aspects of image construction in televised sport. Nevertheless, the television image is complex, with potentially limitless combinations of signs that are not reducible to the predictability of a 'grammar'. Shot type, camerawork and editing techniques are all part of the make-up of the image of television sport. So, too, are lighting, colour, clothing, composition and replays (show motion or otherwise). All these factors need to be considered as imagery in sport television.

Signifier	Definition	Signified (Meaning)
Close-up	face only	intimacy
Medium shot	most of the body	personal relationship
Long shot	setting and characters	context, scope, public distance
Full shot	full body of person	social relationship
Pan down	camera looks down	power, authority
Pan up	camera looks up	Smallness, weakness
Zoom in	camera moves in	Observation, focus
Fade in	image appears on blank screen	beginning
Fade out	screen goes blank	ending
Cut	switch from one image to another simultaneously	excitement
Wipe	image wiped off screen	imposed conclusion

Figure 3.1   Berger's (1992: 26–7) 'grammar of television'.

Characteristics of the imagined spectator of televised sport can also be detected in a programme's choice of shot type. Whannel (1992) found that in the 1950s, British sport producers were concerned about broadening TV sports' appeal beyond the expert to the less committed majority. Conventions adopted during this period, which have remained with televised sport—the magazine format, long shot–close-up patterns, commentary styles—were intended to liven up a broadcast to appeal to a floating audience of novices or occasional viewers. Whannel (1992: 30–1) concluded that one distinctive feature of the assumed audience model during the 1950s was that 'two oppositions—expert/novice and male/female became condensed together' so that the 'implicit assumption becomes one of male expertise and female ignorance'. The features used to attract novices, therefore, could also be seen as an attempted address to a female viewer. For example, the *Guidelines for Cricket Production, 1952* state, 'During the day, particularly on a weekday, our audience must, generally speaking, be of the female sex, and I feel they would prefer more commentary than the average male viewer' (cited in Whannel 1992: 31).

The use of close-ups was very much part of the attempt to add colour to sport broadcasts. For example, Whannel (1992) traced a 1956 memo from the then controller of British Broadcasting Corporation (BBC) Television, who, having compared BBC and ITV's coverage of Wimbledon on two sets placed side by side, commented that he felt ITV's coverage was better because they gave many more close-ups and showed the face more often. Interestingly, Modleski (1984: 99) suggested that the close-up is characteristic of 'popular feminine visual art' like the soap opera. It is easy to forget, she said, that in soap opera, 'characters even have bodies, so insistently are close-ups of faces employed' (Modleski 1984: 99). The omnipresence of close-ups in this programme type activates the 'gaze of the mother', according to Modleski, providing viewers with training in reading other people's emotions. Of course, it is not possible to ignore the importance of the body in sport, but the prevalence of the close-up in some televised sport forms (tennis, snooker) might be viewed as a strategy to attract a wider audience.

Written Language and Graphics

The use of graphics is prevalent in television. Seiter (1992) observed,

> Diagrams are superimposed over news or sports images to invite a quasi-scientific scrutiny of the image. Borders and frames mask out the background of already pared-down images. Words constantly appear on the screen to identify the program, sponsoring corporation, the network or cable station, the product name, the person portrayed. (p. 44)

Statistics, diagrams, logos and computer-animated images are inseparable from sport broadcasts and are often a constant feature. Graphics provide an eye-catching visual marker of a range of events within a broadcast, including scores, time, players and logos. Graphics may be in motion, superimposed on the playing field, flashing or accompanied by sound. Graphics may also refer to events occurring beyond the immediate broadcast such as a scoreline running underneath the match that refers to other results. Words and graphics play an important role in creating the televised sport experience by marking, labelling and highlighting particular features of the broadcast.

Voice

It has been argued that the medium of television is dominated by its soundtrack: 'the sound track serves as a value-laden editing function, identifying better than the image itself, the parts of the image that are sufficiently spectacular to merit closer attention on the part of the intermittent viewer' (Altman 1986: 47). The voice of the commentator in sports television has this effect—if your attention wanders, a yell from the commentator immediately refocuses your gaze. Altman referred to this as 'italicizing'.

It is interesting to consider the way that the voice in sport television differs from other television genres. Unlike dramas, for example, sport broadcasts can be watched without the sound with relatively little loss of comprehension. Yet, in studies of televised sport, the words of the commentators are often given most attention (Duncan and Hasbrook 1988). The voices of the commentators and presenters could be thought of as not so much adding to the meanings of the event, but limiting their polysemy. The comments they make often close down the number of possible meanings the images may have. For example, the sight of a player leaving the field of play may be interpreted by the viewer as an instance of injury, poor play or coaching strategy. Commentators may supply the explanation with inside knowledge or their own speculations. Voices of players, spectators in the crowd or referees (e.g. in rugby) occasionally insinuate themselves into the soundtrack, altering the television audience's sense of distance from what is happening and providing further information about how to interpret the events on screen, and even those out of shot. The sound of booing from a crowd may indicate an off-screen scuffle, a perceived poor refereeing decision or a response to a player's unsportsmanlike behaviour.

Music

Music is a central feature of sport programming. Music heralds the start of shows or events (national anthems), creates atmosphere and indicates a programme's content. The recurrent association of a particular sport with a theme tune allows it to evoke all of the associations of that sport in a few bars. The BBC's soca theme tune that is regularly used for cricket programming evokes Caribbean sunshine, relaxation and joie de vivre, drawing on historical associations with the Test Match series between England and the West Indies in the 1970s and 1980s, which drew capacity crowds.

Sound Effects

There are plenty of sources of sound in televised sport in addition to voices and music. We could call these 'sound effects' or, perhaps more accurately, simply 'sounds'. The ambient sound of a stadium, bats hitting balls, shoes squeaking on a court surface, starting pistols, car engines roaring and players grunting all make up the soundscape of sport. The sound of commentators speaking adds to this soundscape, but the content of what they say is not the only aspect worth noticing. Much of the atmosphere of televised sport, and a lot of its affective appeal, is conveyed through sound. It is illuminating to compare televised sport broadcasts from the 1970s to current programmes. One of the greatest differences is the quality of sound. A video clip of Brazil versus England from the Federation Internationale de Football Association (FIFA) World Cup held in Mexico in 1970 is available on the BBC Web site at http://news.bbc. co.uk/sport1/hi/football/world_cup_2006/4850280.stm. The soundtrack is muddy and indistinct. The tinny sound of the commentator appears distant from the action, and while there is constant crowd noise, it merges with ambient sound, including wind noise over the microphones, so that the overall effect is an indistinguishable low hum. Sounds emerging from the players or play itself or crowd songs or chants are not heard within the soundtrack. Listening to this old footage indicates the important role that sound has come to play in the broadcast of sport. Contemporarily, microphones placed along the touchline or even closer to the action, for example, on the middle stump in cricket broadcasts, help render the 'liveness' of sport through sound. Increased sound clarity made possible through developments in digital technology heighten the effect of being close to, or even part of, the on-screen action.

Made for TV: the Construction of Sport for the Camera

In the mid 1970s, Buscombe (1975a) wrote about the televising of football in Britain. An important part of his analysis was the identification of three types of 'pro-filmic event':

- events which exist independently outside the control of television (e.g. football)
- events produced expressly for inclusion in a television broadcast (e.g. studio shots)
- graphics (including lettering, abstract designs and cartoons).

However, Buscombe reflected that the distinction between the first two types of events would be at best difficult to make since television has been known to affect many kinds of independent events, blurring the difference between what is real and what has been created for television. Developments in the staging of megasport events such as the Olympics make Buscombe's observation ever more salient—sports that make it onto prime time television do not occur independently of television; rather, the interests of television are taken fully into account in constructing the event. For example, Rowe (2004a: 183) discussed the way one-day cricket has been adapted to the demands of television: 'unlike viewers of Test cricket, impatient audiences with busy lives will not be required to watch at least thirty hours of live action over five days only for the event to end inconclusively as a draw.' Moreover, the staging of sport events specifically for television is only one way that the televising of sport confounds a simple distinction between actuality and fiction. The wealth of intertextual evocations that accumulate across the five channels of communication allow for generation of meaning to take place without either the participation or intention of the producers of televised sport. In no way can television be said to relay neutrally a 'pro-filmic' objective world.

Televised Sport: a Gendered Genre?

Reflecting on the observations made previously, certain features of the televising of football construct a particular kind of viewing position for audience members to step into. Although sport is typically thought to address a male viewer, it may also be deliberately packaged to address or include other groups such as females or young people. In 1996, the National Broadcasting Corporation's (NBC) coverage of the Olympics was specifically designed, produced and packaged to attract 'stereotypical' female viewers: 'NBC sought to hail, or interpellate, female members of the television audience by proffering essentialized feminine subject positions within its prime time Olympic discourse' (Andrews 1998: 12). They employed strategies such as creating personal, emotional dramas about particular athletes and reconstructing sporting events for prime time viewing. In addition, the coverage of female athletes was provided with intertextual references within other media forms which also celebrated the prowess of the United States' female Olympians. A critical review of NBC's production techniques in *The Humanist* highlighted the substitution of sport and expert commentary with sentimental dramas or 'soaps', and the pretence of live sport, which was actually taped and represented in a narrative format. Mayberry, Proctor and Srb (1996: 2) argued that the excessive use of close-ups to highlight the emotions and reactions of US competitors was the most controlling of 'NBC's arsenal of tricks'. As stated earlier, close-ups have been understood as having characteristics that make them particularly popular with a female audience (Fiske 1987; Modleski 1984).

There are other aspects of the televising of football, however, that deemphasise qualities of drama, obeying conventions of realist cinema to convey a sense of unadulterated reality, despite the necessary mediation of reality that television involves. Techniques of realism within the televising of football and other sports could be understood as the 'style of truth' that Easthope (1990) identified as one of three elements of masculine address in popular cultural forms. Easthope argued that it was possible to explain how certain features of popular cultural texts effectively appealed to men. These aspects of 'masculine style' included clarity and banter, both of which are discernible in televised sport forms.

Clarity in Televised Sport

For Easthope (1990), when information is presented as an apparently plain statement of truth without obvious personal bias, it can be understood as a masculine style. This is because it 'goes along with the masculine ego and its desire for mastery. Truth in this style is presented as something to be fully known, seen in complete detail ... Vision is supposedly "clear" as water, as "transparent" as glass' (Easthope 1990: 81). The transparent style treats itself as invisible, not really a style at all. In this way, meaning can be presented as 'fixed, free-standing, closed round on itself' and truth as 'objective and impersonal, something revealed once and for all and so there to be mastered and known' (Easthope 1990: 82).

Techniques that give the effect of realism in televising football were identified by Buscombe in 1975 and remain contemporary characteristics of both football and other televised sports today. The naturalistic colours and the simple editing techniques, along with on-screen graphics displaying group and team statistics, team lists, diagrams, players' details, scores and ticking clocks are all associated with the knowledge claims of scientific discourse. These features of televised sport, along with other technological innovations, such as the Hawk-Eye electronic line-calling system used to track the ball in tennis and cricket, and the subsequent replays that indicate a ball's trajectory and bounce, can be considered an important aspect of sport's appeal to clarity.

Commentary and half-time studio discussions during the play inevitably touch on rules and rule infringement. As a rule-bound activity, sport can itself be understood as appealing to clarity. Nevertheless, commentators often question the calls of officials and appear to have limited faith that the rules are being enforced without bias or errors in judgement. Once again, vision, often in the form of the action replay, is invoked to reinforce the possibility of certainty, which seems constantly to shift and slide away. The question of just deserts is a repeated theme, asserting the fairness of sport despite the inconsistencies of the match. The move to digital, high-definition television may increase the clarity of the action, but it may not silence the debates.

The content of football talk, however, is not its only significant aspect. It is possible to discern another aspect of masculine style in the form that football talk takes. Easthope's second dimension of masculine style, banter, is also a part of televised sport.

Banter in Sport Talk

The regular use of nationalistic cliché and ironic humour in televised football opening sequences (Kennedy 2000) can be thought of as a further aspect of masculine style. During the build-up to the match between England and Holland in the European Football Championship in 1996, ITV showed a sequence with the title 'The Story So Far' imposed on a fluttering English flag. England team members were then shown lined up, mouthing the words to the national anthem, but with the soundtrack replaced by one featuring a deep operatic voice singing the song 'He Is an Englishman', from the comic opera *H.M.S. Pinafore* by Gilbert and Sullivan. The sequence used all available channels of communication to present an intertextual, humorous report on the uneven media coverage of the England football team, referencing their drunken behaviour during a flight, their unexpected draw with Switzerland and their improved performance against Scotland. Comic newspaper headlines passed across the screen, over a series of images. The sense in which the visual montage should be read was conveyed by a selection of pop songs. The lyrics to rock tunes accompanying the images implied that the footballers were 'crazy horses' who would do well to listen to the 'message in the air', but were occasionally dynamic and 'fire like this'. An abrupt change to yodelling music accompanying a film of Switzerland scoring a goal presented a hackneyed reference point with clear humorous connotations. There was humour, too, in the use of rock music and bright orange dancing graphics of the sequence that followed—a summary of the qualities of the Dutch side—which made links with the letters *D-U-T-C-H* with phrases like 'U is for Usually beat England.'

While the use of banter may not be confined to men, Easthope (1990) argued that it is used so often as a form of male exchange that it can be seen as a second feature of masculine style. The defining aspects of banter relate to both its form and content:

> As humour or comedy, banter makes use of every kind of irony, sarcasm, pun, clichéd reply, and so is an example of the joke ... The content of banter has a double function. Outwardly banter is aggressive, a form in which the masculine ego asserts itself. Inwardly, however, banter depends on a close, intimate and personal understanding of the person who is the butt of the attack. It thus works as a way of affirming the bond of love between men while appearing to deny it. (pp. 87–8)

Finlay and Johnson (1997) considered football talk programmes as instances of banter. They analysed the ITV Saturday lunchtime show from the early 1990s, *Saint and Greavsie,* pointing to 'the playful antagonism between St John (the Scotsman) and Greaves (the Englishman), which is employed to legitimise racist and/or chauvinistic remarks' (Finlay and Johnson 1997: 137). The authors argued that the ostensibly aggressive sparring was offset by unspoken understanding between the two presenters, indicated, in part, by the proximity to each other in their seating arrangements.

Finlay and Johnson (1997) suggested that televised football talk operates in a similar way to women's gossip, which has been understood as having social function. The programmes establish a discursive space 'in which men can interact without women and begin to perform masculinity' (Finlay and Johnson 1997: 140–1). However, they concluded that, unlike women's gossip, football talk stops short of genuine intimacy and the sharing of personal experience, instead focusing on the game and the professional lives of the players.

To understand televised sport as a gendered genre is to acknowledge that what may appear to be gender-neutral is, in fact, culturally coded as masculine. Nevertheless, other elements of televised sport are more associated with programme types attracting female viewers such as close-ups and never-ending narrative structures. Sports competitions go on and on, after all, much like soap opera. Gender is not fixed, and nor are the ways in which males and females view televised sport. Gendered styles are often based on stereotypical views of masculinity and femininity that mask the blurring of boundaries and the presence of shared identities and interests. The following case study explores characteristics of the televised coverage of women's and men's football.

The Changing Face of Football on Television

A precedent in the media analysis of sport was set by Buscombe's (1975a) British Film Institute television monograph, which focused on the televising of football on

British television. Buscombe (1975b), Ryall (1975), Barr (1975), MacArthur (1975) and Tudor (1975) each took aspects of the televising of the 1974 FIFA World Cup, from scene-setting in listings magazines to analysis of cultural and televisual codes in the title sequences, the make-up of the expert panels and an international comparison of televisual styles. This analysis is useful both as a point of reference to inform the contemporary analysis of televised football and to compare how the televising of football has changed over time. In 1975, women's football was not shown on British television. Despite its long-standing popularity in other countries (e.g. the United States), the ingrained associations of football with masculinity in the United Kingdom have resulted in low visibility for the women's game. More recently, however, television coverage has increased, and during the 2007 FIFA Women's World Cup, women's football matches were regularly shown on BBC TV (albeit mostly on its second, specialist-interest terrestrial channel, BBC 2). This case study will consider the televising of international men's and women's football matches on British television to highlight the similarities and differences in the conventions of televising football from the 1970s to the present day.

Case Study: Men's and Women's Football on British Television

Following the approach taken by Buscombe and his colleagues in 1975, this case study focuses on unpacking the techniques used in title sequences, live action and half-time studio discussions of two games, England versus Russia (men) and England versus Japan (women). Attention was paid to the full extent of the simultaneous signification within the five channels of communication identified previously by recording activity relating to graphics, image, voice, sound effects and music.

Title Sequences

Buscombe (1975b) observed an abundance of colour and graphics in title sequences, including the plentiful use of national signifiers such as a tartan motif for Scotland. For Buscombe, the use of nonnaturalistic colour in the titles drew attention to the overwhelming naturalistic conventions of colour use in the broadcast of live action, where the sky is shown to be blue and the grass is shown to be green. The title sequence for England versus Russia played on this contrast. The programme was announced as 'a game we can't afford to lose' and a 'crucial *Match of the Day Live*', indicating that partisan support on the part of the BBC has now become acceptable, a change from the corporation's early years (Whannel 1992). Following this dramatic build-up, the titles opened with shots of a gleaming Wembley Arch (the architectural signifier of the new Wembley Stadium in West London) to an almost silent soundtrack. Aerial shots of Wembley accompanied quiet crowd noise, which became louder as football fans were shown milling outside the stadium, and a muffled 'England' chant could be discerned.

The bold, brass notes of the *Match of the Day* theme tune started as a sequence of live action highlights were shown. The theme tune has been associated with football on the BBC since the 1970s and evokes nostalgia and tradition (BBC theme tunes can be heard at http://www.bbc.co.uk/fivelive/programmes/holmes_vote/). Close-up shots of England players were shown, altered by an effect that made it appear as if the spectator was looking through red-and-blue-tinted glass shapes. The sequence of players in moments of triumph (including clearly identifiable shots of Steven Gerrard, Joe Cole, Paul Robinson, Ashley Cole, Peter Crouch, Wayne Rooney, Sol Campbell, Owen Hargreaves and John Terry, followed by the manager, Steve McLaren) ended as the camera zoomed out to reveal that the images were being shown through the

---

ANALYSING MEN'S AND WOMEN'S FOOTBALL

The two matches analysed for this case study were both shown as editions of *Match of the Day,* a long-running football highlights programme on the BBC, which occasionally broadcasts live events. The first match was a qualifying men's football match for UEFA Euro2008 played at Wembley Stadium, London, England, and broadcast on BBC 1 on 12 September 2007. The second was a group stage match of the FIFA Women's World Cup 2007, played at Shanghai Hongkou Stadium, China, and broadcast on BBC 2 on 11 September 2007. In our analysis, we wanted to focus on the simultaneity of the five channels of communication in televised sport: graphics, image, voice, sound effects and music. Televised sport is packed full of signification moving at pace, and to capture the overall effect, we needed to record the two matches, then replay short segments of one or two minutes, noting activity in all five channels, including, for example, the words of the commentators, the camera shots and the noise of the crowd. Repeated rewinding and replaying was necessary to make sure all of the signification had been accurately identified. This process constituted the first stage of the analysis: denotation, or the laying out of the interplay of sound and image in the flow of televised sport. Re-presenting this complex information in a table like the following graphically demonstrates the simultaneity of the communication channels and provides a basis for the second stage of analysis: connotation.

Graphics	Image	Voice	Sound effects	Music
	Shots of Wembley Arch Aerial shots of Wembley Football fans milling outside stadium			
			Quiet crowd noise Crowd noise becoming louder	
	Live action highlights		Muffled 'England' chant	
				Match of the Day theme tune

England three lions logo, positioned at the centre of the red and white St George's cross, the English flag. The three lions were replaced by the championship trophy, with the BBC Sport logo superimposed, changing into the words 'Match of the Day Live'. Within this title sequence, the colours of the pitch and the crowd in the stadium were distorted as they passed beneath the shapes of the three lions but otherwise appeared bright and naturalistic. The sequence, with its deliberate image manipulation, emphasised the realist conventions of live football television.

The FIFA Women's World Cup match between England and Japan was introduced in similar terms to the men's match—'a win is a must'—but the title sequence was very different. Opening with a grey landscape evoking Chinese brush paintings, with accompanying sounds of crickets and the wind rustling through foliage, the camera panned across pink flowers and a turquoise butterfly, as Chinese calligraphy slowly appeared, only to suddenly transform into a female footballer taking an athletic overhead shot at a ball. On contact with the player's foot, the ball transformed into the head of a Chinese dragon with a multicoloured tail, and the soundtrack changed to the *Match of the Day* theme tune. As the tail of the dragon swooped across a grey cityscape, it curled around more Chinese letters that scattered and reassembled in the form of female footballers. All the players were shown in long shot, making them difficult to identify. Finally, the dragon's tail wound around the World Cup trophy, before trailing off screen. The sequence ended with a shot of the trophy in an empty stadium and the intermingled titles for *Match of the Day*/BBC Sport/FIFA Women's World Cup 2007 appearing on top of the image. The colours and images appeared nonnaturalistic and stylised throughout the introduction.

Live Sport Action

Ryall's (1975) analysis of the visual style of the televising of the 1974 World Cup led him to distinguish four main shot types used during a match:

1. primary image or normal shot: shots from a camera in the grandstand, halfway up, in line with the halfway line, constituting the normal view of the game, 'sufficiently close to the play to enable a comprehensible image to be formed … and far enough away from the immediate action to give some sense of its content' (Ryall 1975: 38)
2. secondary image A or close shot: shots from a camera in the same position, offering a closer view of the action
3. secondary image B or goal shot: shots from cameras positioned behind each goal, for goal mouth action and 'action replays'
4. secondary image C or bench shot: shots from cameras on the touchline near the halfway line for images on the trainer's bench, the substitutes, and so on.

It is interesting to observe the continuing prevalence of these shot types over thirty years later. During the England versus Japan match, the primary image, or normal shot, was a shot of the pitch from the halfway line, supplemented by shots of players, shots of the bench and a shot of the whole pitch from above the goal. The men's match, England versus Russia, used similar shot types but included an aerial shot capable of looking down on players from above the stadium. The men's match was shown in widescreen, whereas the women's match was not, probably dictated by the origin of the World Cup images in China.

Buscombe (1975b: 30) noted, in the men's game, the lack of the kind of close-up shot that he considered to be characteristic of drama, observing that most shots were 'either of about one-eighth of the pitch or of one or two players, their bodies more or less filling the frame from top to bottom. Anything closer than the latter or further away than the former is very rare.' By contrast, in the England versus Japan match, there were a great many close-up shots as well as long shots. Inevitably, this greater frequency of close-ups has an effect on the framing of sport. Modleski (1984: 99) argued that the effect of the close up in soap opera is to enable the audience to 'witness the characters' expressions, which are complex and intimately coded, signifying triumph, bitterness, despair, confusion—the entire emotional register, in fact'. In doing so, Modleski maintained that the close-up activated not only a feminine gaze, but a maternal one, provoking anxiety about the welfare of others. Since televised sport has long been considered a masculine media genre, the increasing prevalence of close-ups has the capacity to alter the way the viewer is positioned. Close-ups of players anxious before a penalty kick, jubilant after a goal or in pain from an injury could be said to have a similar effect of constructing an intimate viewing position for the spectator.

Live action from both matches was broadcast with colours at all times approximating the natural. Buscombe (1975b) saw naturalistic colour as part of a general neglect of the technical possibilities of television in its broadcast of football, leading to an effect of realism. Buscombe noted that the camera positions—on one side of the pitch, approximately on the halfway line—were in accord with the 180 degree rule of classic realist cinema (dictating that if two people are placed opposite each other and the camera is showing them from one side, the director may not cut to a shot showing the characters from the opposite side). Such a position, Buscombe suggested, was the simulated viewpoint of an older, richer and more neutral football spectator seated in the stands at the halfway line. This was because in 1975, football stadiums in Britain had limited seating, with cheaper spots available for standing spectators on the terraces behind the goals. Simple edits between camera shots during the match added to an overall effect of realism in the televising of football.

Various graphics of the same type were overlaid on the image during both matches. The BBC logo, the digital clock showing time elapsed, abbreviations for the national teams and the score all remained constant during the play. Before the match, graphics showing team formations were shown and, occasionally, punctuating the play, identifiers of players and coaches appeared at the foot of the screen accompanying close-ups.

What is remarkable in considering the early analysis provided by Buscombe and Ryall is the minimal difference in the codes used to televise football in 1975 and now. Since 1975, television technology has advanced rapidly; nevertheless, the conventions of televised football in Britain have remained largely constant. Despite a greater number of cameras available, the normal shot type remains, with the supplementary shots also fulfilling similar roles. The 180 degree rule is also largely still in operation. On the rare occasion that it is flouted, a reverse angle indicator appears in the corner of the screen to avoid confusing the viewer.

The sounds of the crowd were identifiable beneath the commentary in both matches, but certain ambient sounds were clearer during the men's match. For example, during England versus Russia, it was possible to hear the names of the teams being introduced to the crowd. Each match featured a commentary team, with one commentator focussing on play-by-play action and the other supplying colour. However, this division of labour was more sharply made during the women's match, where Guy Mowbray followed the action and his partner, Lucy Ward, provided a personalised perspective on the match. Using comments such as 'you can see the nerves of the girls', Ward was able to demonstrate her empathy with the players.

Studio Discussion

During half-time in the men's match, three pundits, Alan Shearer, Ian Wright and Alan Hanson, all dressed in sharp suits and ties, joined the anchor, Gary Lineker, to discuss the action. Against a plain red background, with the England logo and the stadium visible through a large picture window, Lineker introduced the section direct to the camera, using ironic understatement—'That was really rather good'—to set the light-hearted tone of the discussion. One of the England players in the match, Shaun Wright Phillips, is the adopted son of Ian Wright and the subject of much banter among the pundits, indicating that this was knowledge assumed to be shared by the TV audience. For example, Alan Shearer, placing a hand on Ian Wright's shoulder, joked, 'We would have been 3 nil up if Shaun Wright Phillips could head the ball.' While this relationship created an unusual intimacy among the presenters, the discussion maintained a focus on the match. The pundits were animated and relaxed in their roles. Each presenter had his own chair, and they were positioned comfortably around a low table littered with paper. Despite the laughter and jokes, they appeared well organised, speaking at the appropriate cue and talking in turns.

The relaxed tone was also evident in the half-time discussion of the England versus Japan women's FIFA World Cup match. The anchor, Gabby Logan, addressed her opening remarks not to the camera, but turned towards the pundits, as if the viewer had come upon a conversation in flow. Nevertheless, the three pundits (Karen

Walker, Jo Potter and Gavin Peacock) looked ill at ease, with all three crammed onto one sofa, unable to look at each other comfortably when speaking. Logan occupied a matching sofa facing the others. All were casually dressed. There was no England logo visible in the background, which was dominated by pink, picking up themes from the title sequences. Unlike the pundits of the men's match, who were assumed to be familiar to the audience, each of the women's match pundits—all former players—were identified by graphics giving details of numbers of games played. The graphic identifying Potter, for example, read 'made England debut in 2004, 13 appearances, 1 goal'. The most experienced pundit, Peacock, was the most animated, and he provided the analysis of the action. Despite some humour, there was less banter than during the men's match discussion and more use of camera angles to heighten interest.

Since 1975, the conventions for televising football appear to have only been refined rather than altered substantially. Numbers of cameras may have increased, but largely, the angle of shots they provide remains constant. Close-ups are more frequent, and title sequences feature sophisticated graphics. Women's football is shown with more regularity, and the style of production approximates men's football. Nevertheless, the relatively short history of women's football on British television resulted in uneasy, inexperienced pundits during the half-time discussion. It appears that women's football is not yet given the same polished production quality that the BBC affords the men's games. Despite technological innovations, conventions in the televising of sport appear resistant to change, indicating that these conventions carry high connotative value.

Case Study: Narrating the Nation through Olympic Spectacle

Television is inseparable from the staging of sports megaevents such as the Olympic Games. Hogan (2003) reported that the sale of Olympic broadcast rights was the biggest source of revenue for the International Olympic Committee (IOC) and local organising committees. Jobling (2005) recorded that 300 channels broadcast the 2004 Olympics to 220 countries and territories, providing 2,000 hours of coverage a day to 3.9 billion people. The huge international audience enables the host nation to construct an image of itself through the opening ceremony which acts as 'an extended advertisement ... to promote tourism, international corporate investment, trade and political ideologies' (Hogan 2003: 102). Hogan (2003: 102) observed that Olympic opening ceremonies 'are elaborately staged and commercialized narratives of nation' that take place amidst the cultural and political dynamics of globalization which appear simultaneously to threaten the nation and rekindle nationalist assertions of identity. The discursive constructions of the nation that result are, therefore, threaded through with gaps and fissures in meanings, as various material and ideological tensions compete with each other. Arguably, this is the source of the affective power of the opening ceremony, which Tomlinson (2000: 168) described (in relation to Muhammad Ali's lighting of the Olympic flame in the Atlanta ceremony) as reaching 'unknown heights of collective catharsis. It brought a lump to the throat.'

One of the most controversial opening ceremonies was the 2002 Winter Olympics in Salt Lake City, Utah, in the United States, which occurred months after the 11 September 2001 aircraft hijacking and terrorist attacks in New York and Washington, D.C. The setting for the event was the frozen arena of the Rice-Eccles Stadium of the University of Utah. The ceremony commenced with a series of individual skaters dressed in historical costumes crossing the ice carrying a flag for each of the host cities of the previous Winter Games. The connotative impact of the sequence combined continuity with difference. The current Games were positioned within a tradition evoked by the nostalgic memorialisation of past events. The variations in the costumes and sport disciplines of the skating athletes conveyed the distinction of each Olympics, culminating in the present. Following the sequence of skaters, the 'difference' provided by the Salt Lake City Games was underscored by the unprecedented exhibition of patriotic symbolism encoded into the display of the American flag that flew at the World Trade Center on 11 September. The torn and battered flag was carried into the stadium by noted American athletes, members of the New York City police and fire departments and the New York City Port Authority. The soundscape that surrounded the events went from solemn silence to the Utah Symphony and Mormon Tabernacle Choir's traditional, controlled, classical orchestration of the American national anthem. Images of President Bush, hand on heart, flanked by Jacques Rogge (President of the IOC) and Mitt Romney (President and Chief Executive Officer of the Salt Lake organising committee) were interspersed with shots of tears in the flag, views of the stadium and close-ups of saluting uniformed personnel. Hogan (2003) produced a critical reading of the visual and sonic signifiers in these scenes:

> The segment was richly layered, evoking the divine through the use of the choir; evoking the nation through its most potent symbol of nationhood, the flag; evoking the power of the state through the presence of the enforcers of law and order; and serving as homage to the victims of the September attacks. (p. 107)

In addition, Olympic sport became the vessel used to carry the accumulated signifiers of power and nation. Sport framed the event.

The interpretative programme that followed the national anthem can also be read as an ideological narrative of nation. The nation was figured as the 'child of light' skating through an icy storm, assisted by 'the fire within' to triumph over adversity. Commentary accompanying the sequence emphasised that the young white boy in this role was an ice hockey player, not a figure skater, who 'has had to learn', thereby confirming his gender-appropriate sporting heritage. Hogan (2003: 116) pointed to the gender and racial signification in this sequence: 'White males personified both humanity/America (the child) and its will and drive (the fire within) [which] reveals the extent to which White male perspectives and experiences are still dominant in discourses of American identity.'

Following this episode, the hugely semiotic parade of nations took place, with the disparity of team sizes redolent of the significance of the nation itself. The second interpretative sequence engaged differently with issues of race and nation. Representatives from the five Native American nations (Ute, Goshute, Shoshone, Paiute and Navajo) emerged onto the ice in traditional costume performing tribal dances. Spiritual leaders of the five tribes then welcomed the athletes from the five continents in indigenous language. This section was highly affective in its performance of communication across the division of culture and language. Hogan (2003) saw similarities in this sequence with the Sydney Olympics opening ceremony's incorporation of indigenous peoples. She suggested that it was unclear whether 'the indigenous performers are guiding and teaching their young White observers or performing for them' (Hogan 2003: 116). Hogan (2003: 116) argued that this 'useful ambiguity' allowed the spectators to interpret for themselves the relationship between colonizer and colonised in the performance. There was similarly useful affective ambiguity in the synthesis of funk, rock and Native American music in the performance by Robbie Robertson and the Red Road Ensemble, which helped construct a fragile, momentary feeling of multicultural unity.

In the 'Pioneers' sequence, the child of light and a solitary Native American led varied groups of settlers to Salt Lake City. Hogan (2003) pointed to the absence of historical tensions or lethal conflict represented in this segment, as people of all backgrounds marched together and joined in a hoedown. The triumph of technology was figured in the joyful coming of the railroad, as the contemporary country group the Dixie Chicks provided a musical bridge from past to present. As a link back to the seriousness of the sporting event, the composer John Williams conducted the Utah Symphony and the Mormon Tabernacle Choir in 'Call of the Champions', which included firework accompaniments to the Olympic motto '*citius, altius, fortius*' (faster, higher, stronger). Sounds and images were used throughout the ceremony to weave together a narrative of nationhood around diverse and contradictory elements. Kellner (2003: 25) discussed the ways that the array of signifiers within the opening ceremony of the Salt Lake City Winter Olympics combined to construct an 'orgy of patriotism' that benefited President George W. Bush. The nationalism of Bush's opening speech—'On behalf of a proud, determined and grateful nation, I declare open the Games of Salt Lake City'—was interwoven with signifiers of the 9/11 flag and the sounds and images of a momentarily unified, multicultural nation. While Mike Eruzione and the 1980 US ice hockey team that defeated the Soviet Union in Lake Placid lit the Olympic flame, the crowd chanted 'USA, USA'. Kellner (2003: 25) argued that Bush's decision to surround himself with the team made for 'a spectacular photo opportunity that combined patriotism, power and US victory in the cold war'. Television provides a global audience of viewers ready to consume the image of the nation constructed during this and other Olympic opening ceremonies. Spectacle is central to contemporary production of televised sport.

CHAPTER SUMMARY

- Television uses five channels of communication simultaneously to render the experience of sport: graphics, image, voice, sound effects and music
- Clarity and banter are elements of 'masculine style' in televised sport, but other elements, such as the use of close-ups, are associated with programme types traditionally associated with female viewers
- Despite technological innovations, conventions in the televising of sport appear resistant to change, indicating their connotative value in constructing the way sport is viewed
- Sport megaevents are staged specifically for television, and sport spectacle is a central way for nations to present historical, political and economic narratives of themselves for consumption by a global audience

---

Suggestions for Analysis

Some sports, particularly those where action is fast and space confined, like American football or the Olympic 100-metre final, seem to translate better to television than others. Sports that take place over a large area, such as cross-country, cricket, surfing or the Tour de France, arguably create more of a challenge for television. Select an international event and consider the ways that television's five channels of communication (graphics, image, voice, sound effects and music) are used to construct the spectacle of sport. How are other aspects of the sport media, such as newspapers and the Internet, intertextually referenced in the televising of the event?

Further Reading

Bignell, J., and Orlebar, J. (2005), *The Television Handbook (Media Practice)*, London: Routledge.

Buscombe, E., ed. (1975), *Football on Television*, London: BFI.

Criswell, A. (2006), *A Study of Modern Television: Thinking inside the Box*, Basingstoke: Palgrave Macmillan.

Duncan, M., and Hasbrook, C. (1988), 'Denial of Power in Televised Women's Sports', *Sociology of Sport Journal*, 15: 1–21.

Hills, L., and Kennedy, E. (2006), 'Space Invaders at Wimbledon: Televised Sport and Deterritorialization', *Sociology of Sport Journal*, 23: 419–37.

Hogan, J. (2003), 'Staging the Nation: Gendered and Ethnicized Discourses of National Identity in Olympic Opening Ceremonies', *Journal of Sport and Social Issues*, 27: 100–23.

Kennedy, E. (2000), 'Bad Boys and Gentlemen: Gendered Narrative in Televised Sport', *International Review for the Sociology of Sport*, 35: 59–73.

Kennedy, E. (2000), '"You Talk a Good Game": Football and Masculine Style on British Television', *Men and Masculinities,* 3: 56–84.

Seiter, E. (1992), 'Semiotics, Structuralism and Television', in R. Allen, ed., *Channels of Discourse Reassembled,* London: Routledge.

Stempel, C. (2006), 'Televised Sports, Masculinist Moral Capital, and Support for the U.S. Invasion of Iraq', *Journal of Sport and Social Issues,* 30: 79–106.

Whannel, G. (2005), 'Pregnant with Anticipation: The Pre-history of Television Sport and the Politics of Recycling and Preservation', *International Journal of Cultural Studies,* 8: 405–26.

Williams, R. (1974), *Television: Technology and Cultural Form,* London: Fontana.

–4–

Sport and the Press

KEY CONCEPTS

Newspaper narratives   Photographic codes

Journalistic practices   Community of readers

Headlines   Discourses of doping

Language codes   Intersections of race, class and gender

This chapter unravels the ways that newspapers use words and images to construct discourses of sport. The particular combinations of codes that are specific to newspapers are explored, and the meanings of sport news stories are considered as effects of connotation and intertextuality. The chapter highlights the narrative and linguistic strategies that journalists employ to tell stories about sport. The chapter demonstrates ways that theses techniques serve to construct points of identification with readers on the basis of class, nation, ethnicity and gender. Newspapers are thus shown to use sport to engage in a dialogue with readers, constructing mythic communities based on assumptions of shared values. The two case studies in this chapter involve stories from the Olympics. The first case study analyses the media's coverage of Ben Johnson's positive drug test at the 1988 Olympics, and the second explores discourses of nation, gender and ethnicity in British newspaper reports and photographs of Kelly Holmes's double Olympic victory in 2004.

Making Sport News

Newspapers do more than report the news; they determine what news is and present it in accordance with particular values and organisational needs. Van Dijk (1983: 28) advised against understanding news as 'simply an (incomplete) description of the facts' since it is a 'specific kind of (re)construction of reality according to the norms and values of some society'. The media chooses from a large pool of events and issues what they wish to include and how they wish to tell about them. Journalists select those stories deemed newsworthy with reference to their own definitions of news and with the broader constraints of organisations that are structured to deliver news to the public. As Graber (1979: 9) observed, the mass media 'not only survey the events of the day and make them the focus of public and private attention, they also interpret their meanings, put them into context, and speculate about their consequences'. What results from this process is an unusual presentation of information known as the news story. Reah (1998: 5) pointed out that 'other texts that deliver information are not referred to as "stories". We don't talk about "report stories" or "lecture stories" or "textbook stories"'. News stories occupy a strange middle ground between factual reporting of past events and fictional accounts. It is necessary, therefore, to consider the importance of the sports writer in constructing the news.

All journalists work within the constraints of publication deadlines and news space limitations, but sports writers may have additional pressures such as game deadlines and their relationships with sport organisations. Sports writers have to depend upon athletes, coaches and teams for information day after day; because of this, their stories may reflect a need to maintain amicable relations. As Trujillo and Ekdom (1985: 265) noted, 'sportswriters rarely make overt and/or critical value judgments that might endanger circulation and profit.'

Rowe (2004a: 38) suggested that by paying attention to the practices of sport journalism, 'it is possible to "de-naturalize" media sport texts and so to understand that they are particular creations and constructions arising from the complex, contradictory forces that make culture.' Rowe (2004a: 39) argued that the process of producing media sport involves 'many decisions, calculations, dilemmas and disputes'. Whannel's (2002) examination of the repeating characteristics of sport biographies indicates that sports writers draw on preexisting formulaic narratives to mould the raw material of the sport world into stories designed to appeal to their readers. The 'punishing, stressful deadlines' (Rowe 2004a: 43) of the sport press are likely to exacerbate journalists' reliance on culturally prescribed framing techniques to produce dramatic stories at a moment's notice. Games that finish late, upsets, scandals, unexpected heroes and other challenges mean that journalists must often work quickly to transform a surprise event or unanticipated outcome into a fully formed narrative.

As Whannel (1992: 121) observed, 'star performers are characters within a set of narratives.' The media reconstructs the sporting contest as a story, identifying heroes and villains, developing a plot and creating drama and interest. Narrative is, therefore, a way of making sense of events. Narrative does not simply reflect what happens; rather, it constructs possibilities for what can happen, generating and interpreting sporting moments as significant elements within a meaningful whole. Considered in this way, analysis of narratives in cultural texts can contribute to illuminating values and discourses within specific cultures.

The media presents the news within a framework of certain values, usually associated with the dominant industries in society. News has a tendency to legitimate existing social norms (Fishman 1980; Gans 1979; McKay and Rowe 1987; Tuchman 1978). Trujillo and Ekdom (1985: 264) argued that sports writing is ideological as sports writers 'continuously present and affirm social consensus on a broad set of cultural values'. However, techniques used by journalists tend to obscure this process. For example, Richardson (2007) considered that objectivity could be understood as a journalistic practice to enable a reporter to distance himself or herself from the truth claims of the journalist's report and avoid criticism.

Journalists use 'practices of objectivity' (Richardson 2007: 87) to produce a report that appears unbiased. These practices include removing the authorial voice so that the reporter's opinion is hidden, presenting sources that contradict each other to achieve the effect of balance, providing supporting evidence in the form of background information and using so-called scare quotes to indicate a contentious truth claim. What appears to be an objective report is, therefore, far from being a neutral report. As Gans (1979: 39) commented, 'values in the news are rarely explicit and must be found between the lines—in what actors and activities are reported or ignored, and how they are described. If a news story deals with the activities which are generally considered undesirable and whose descriptions contain negative connotations, then the story implicitly expresses a value about what is desirable.'

Narrative in News Stories

A first step in unpacking the way the sport news story is constructed is to distinguish between the content of the report and the way the story is presented. Events in a news story are rarely introduced in the chronological order in which they happened. As a result, we need to isolate the form of the narrative from its content. Richardson (2007) argued that the news is generally structured around a three-part plot: the setting, the event and the outcome. News stories presented as unfolding events often ask readers to make links between people and situations, relating current happenings to their wider knowledge of the world. As a result, the presentation of current news as an ongoing narrative requires much meaning work on the part of the news consumer.

Sport narratives are often organised around a central question: who will win? Prematch stories generate interest in upcoming events, while postmatch stories recount explanations for the outcome and implications for the future. Harris and Hills (1993: 108) suggested that sports have an 'inherent storylike structure. Whether the story involves a single game, a tournament, a season, or a series of seasons, initial tensions or uncertainties—usually connected with winning—are at least partially resolved as the actions unfold.' Sporting narratives must also keep readers interested in the next 'instalment' and provide an ongoing sense of the importance and uncertainty of upcoming events. Why/when/how suppositions speculating on the reasons for winning and losing, the contribution of various characters (athletes, coaches, crowds, owners, etc.) and the possible repercussions of a particular outcome create a sense of drama, generate interest and sustain tension.

Richardson (2007) pointed to the prevalence of the inverted pyramid format for the presentation of hard news narratives. This organisation of news differs from many fictional narratives by presenting the climax first, with all the who, what, where and when information in the opening paragraphs. As Bell (1991: 149) explained, the 'lead as summary or abstract is obligatory in hard news ... [it] is the device by which copy editor or audience can get the main point of the story from reading a single opening sentence, and on that basis decide whether to continue.'

In sport stories, often the who, what and where information is contained in the scoreline preceding the actual story, reinforcing the emphasis on victory and success in sport (Carrard 1988). For example, a story in *The Observer* about a fifth-round Football Association Cup match between the two English soccer teams Liverpool and Barnsley (Jackson 2008: 2) presented the following information about the final score, players who scored and times of the goals, as a lead:

Liverpool 1
Kuyt 32
Barnsley 2
Foster 57 Howard 90

In smaller text below, details about the location and attendance of the match, the roster for both teams, match statistics, game rating and referee were all included prior to the written report. The presentation of the key information in this way enabled the report to concentrate on the drama of the event: the much lower ranked Barnsley beating Liverpool, a team placed near the top of the Premier League. The story began,

> A FAMOUS afternoon for Barnsley ended deliriously with ladles of the stuff dreams are made of.

The ready availability of up-to-the-minute information about the progress of sport contests on radio, television and the Internet has arguably emphasised narrative flourish in sport news stories over simple descriptive, play-by-play reporting. For example, the Liverpool–Barnsley match report included detailed play descriptions in half of the story and framed the rest around the Barnsley goalkeeper Luke Steele's 'stand out moments'.

The inverted pyramid style of narration, however, is not the only way a story can be presented. A more literary approach can be achieved by leading with a seemingly unconnected statement that cannot be understood without reading further. Richardson (2007) suggested that this kind of narrative tends to start with a pronoun—*he, she, it*—creating a sense of anticipation for the reader who does not immediately know to whom (or what) the pronoun refers. The more typical newspaper report, by contrast, provides all the information the reader needs the first time a person is mentioned. For example, following a controversy around the eligibility of sprinter Dwain Chambers to run for England, *The Sun*'s front page report started, 'Doping scandal sprinter Dwain Chambers begged for forgiveness last night' (Orvice 2008: 1). The story then used the pronoun *he* to refer back to this information (an anaphoric reference): 'He WILL run for the UK.' By contrast, the use of a pronoun can be more dramatic as information is withheld until later in the narrative (a cataphoric reference). This style is discernible in a story (Malloy 2007) about Daisuke Matsuzaka, a pitcher for the Red Sox baseball team, which began,

> It wasn't a fair fight.
> The Red Sox paid $103 million for Daisuke Matsuzaka, who stood on the mound last night facing the perpetually awful Tampa Bay Devil Rays, who boast a team payroll of $24 million. (p. D5)

The identification of different narrative forms in sport news stories gives an indication of the ways that newspapers use language to construct the events they report. The next section focuses on the 'unique type of text' known as the headline (Reah 1998: 13).

Newspaper Headlines

Richardson (2007: 64) proposed that journalism is best approached as 'an argumentative discourse genre' dependent on various rhetorical figures of speech. Examples of these include hyperbole (excessive exaggeration), metaphor (perceiving one thing in terms of another), metonym (when something associated with a thing is substituted for it), neologism (recently created words), puns and wordplay. Richardson (2007: 69) suggested that one of the most common neologisms in journalism is the use of the suffix *-gate*. The *USA Today* headline 'Flap about Pats' "Spygate" Cools Off' (Weisman 2008: 4E) combined a neologism with alliteration and a familiar nickname to reference the New England Patriots' illegal taping of the Jets' defensive signals early in the 2007–2008 National Football League (NFL) season. Words used in these ways carry associated ideological meanings. In this case, the reference to the Watergate political scandal, which ultimately led to the resignation of former president Richard Nixon, contributes connotations of dishonesty, intrigue and corruption.

Much use is made of rhetorical devices by headline writers to draw the readers' attention to a story. Reah (1998) observed that words selected for headlines often enable writers to play on the ambiguities between words and meanings, using homophones (words identical in sound but not spelling), polysemes (words with several closely related meanings) or homonyms (words with more than one meaning which are not obviously related). Headlines often use readers' awareness of the sound of the word to make meaning through alliteration or rhyme. Loaded words that generate affective responses are used to make an impact and commonly appear in headlines.

Words may be omitted to deliver as much information as possible within a limited space. The result of leaving out grammatical words is often to increase ambiguity since many lexical words (nouns, main verbs, adjectives, adverbs) rely on grammatical words (auxiliary verbs and determiners) to indicate what kind of word they are (e.g. a noun or a verb). On 22 February 2008, the British press reported that the left-wing Mayor of London, Ken Livingstone, had invited the former athlete Linford Christie (who is banned for life from competing in the Olympics as a result of a doping test) to carry the Olympic torch through London. The *Guardian* (Phillips 2008: S9) used a long noun phrase (combinations of nouns with other words) to form the headline 'Christie Torch Role Sparks Uproar in Olympic Circles'. The wordplay on *torch* and *sparks,* and the use of 'circles' to invoke the Olympic rings, is aided by the removal of grammatical determiners so that sparks can be understood as either a noun or a verb. Intertextual references to words and phrases from a range of cultural sources extend the meaning of headlines. The graphological features of headlines (font size and style) operate in conjunction with other visual aspects of the page, such as layout and photographs, to construct the overall meaning. Font size may indicate the importance of an event, which may be reinforced by the presence of a photograph. The next section looks more closely at the linguistic devices used in newspapers to frame sport stories, focusing on word choice and sentence construction.

Newspaper Language

The choice of words (lexis) in newspapers requires careful consideration since the connotative power of words enables them to 'convey the imprint of society and of value judgements in particular' (Richardson 2007: 47). For example, there is a clear difference between describing a player's movement towards a goal as 'going forward' or 'attacking'. The way people are named in newspapers, and the way that attributes are assigned to them, can affect how they are perceived. Similarly, by changing the construction of a sentence, a writer can profoundly alter the sense in which an event is communicated. Richardson (2007: 55) argued that newspaper sentences often transform transitive actions (where someone does something to someone or thing) into passive constructions by deemphasising or deleting the agent. For example, 'Sarah kicked the ball' can be rearranged as 'the ball was kicked by Sarah', which retains both subject and object but puts more emphasis on the ball. More passive still, the agent, Sarah, can be removed altogether, as in 'the ball was kicked.'

The connotative value of these constructions can be enormous since they communicate to the reader who or what is important in the action. *The Times* reporting of the Linford Christie incident selectively removed and replaced the agent of the contentious decision. The headline on the back page of *The Times* (O'Connor 2008: 96) read, 'Games Torch Invitation for Christie Sparks Anger', with a subheading, 'Livingstone Attacked for "Perverse" Decision'. While the use of the passive voice in the headline leaves Christie as the only person named in the action, the remainder of the story focuses the issue firmly around Livingstone: 'Ken Livingstone, the Mayor of London, came under intense pressure last night to withdraw his invitation to Linford Christie, a convicted drugs cheat, to be part of the Olympic torch relay in the build up to the Beijing Games.' The invocation of authority in the quotation from the International Olympic Committee (IOC) and the use of the phrase 'official sources' enabled the paper to maintain the appearance of objectivity while simultaneously personating a negative reaction to the decision to involve Christie in the relay.

The connection between newspapers and their assumed audiences can be illustrated by comparing differing ways of reporting the same story. On 1 February 2008, the British press widely reported the controversial decision of Fabio Capello, the recently appointed England soccer manager, not to select David Beckham to play for the national team. Players who represent their country in international matches are awarded a cap for each appearance, and Beckham had previously accumulated ninety-nine caps. Capello's team selection meant that Beckham would not get his 100th cap in the upcoming friendly match. Beckham's celebrity status meant that the story was not just confined to the sport news section of the British papers. The front page of *The Times* had an image of Beckham in tears next to '99 and out Capello drops Beckham'. The front page of the *Daily Mirror* used a picture of Beckham looking composed next to the word 'AXED,' followed by 'and Becks flees home after England snub'. The familiarity of using a nickname is a common technique in tabloid reporting of sport celebrities, which are thereby coded as part of an extended national family. The hyperbolic use of 'AXED' by the *Daily Mirror* implied reader outrage at Capello's 'snub' to the former England captain.

A different lexis was noticeable in *The Times*' headline, however. *The Times* used a cricket expression 'not out' for its wordplay, indicating distance from the events on behalf of its readership. The ironic slant was underscored by the image of Beckham crying and throwing his arms up in an infantile gesture. Beckham's black armband made him look all the more ridiculous because of its signification of his captaincy.

Inside *The Sun*, a double-page spread (Irwin 2008: 74–5) carried the headline, 'Is It Any Wonder? Since England's Last Match Becks Has Played 2 Games … Gerrard Has Played 15'. The intertextual reference to David Bowie's song 'Fame' introduced the ensuing critical slant on Beckham's lack of match fitness. The article began with a list of attributes that made connections between his lifestyle and his nonselection: 'International Celebrity, Male Model, Trophy Husband, Shirt Salesman … and Occasional Footballer' (Irwin 2008: 75). The implied contrast between the appropriate masculinity of football and the inappropriate masculinity of celebrity was inscribed into the resulting image of Beckham. The article invoked the persuasive power of scientific discourse to lend truth to the account by including a graph of Beckham's club and international appearances each season between 2003 and 2008.

The different perspectives found in the reporting of the Beckham–Capello story demonstrate how the newspapers constructed their relationships with their imagined readerships. Both tabloid papers, the *Daily Mirror* and *The Sun*, assumed interest and knowledge about soccer amongst their working-class readership, but the *Daily Mirror* anticipated reader sympathy with Beckham, while *The Sun* expected its readers to share its critical perspective on Beckham's celebrity lifestyle. *The Times*, addressing a more ambivalent middle-class readership, adopted an ironic distance from the events by using cricket terminology. As Reah (1998) observed, consistency within a newspaper's choice of words and grammatical structure construct the text as a coherent unit of meaning conveying the cultural politics of the paper. This works to 'establish a relationship with the audience; and establish the nature of that audience, in the sense that newspapers often address an implied audience rather than an actual one' (Reah 1998: 109). The next section further explores newspapers' address to their readers.

The Imaginary Community of Newspaper Readers

Bignell (1997) argued that newspapers use combinations of linguistic signs to represent the readers' own discursive idiom. This results in the language of the newspaper acting as a reflection of the readers' speech codes. The reader identifies with the style of language used and takes his or her place within the mythic community constructed by the newspaper. In Reah's (1998: 109) terms, it is possible to consider the newspaper text as 'a conversation between individuals who have a shared—and therefore unchallenged—value system'.

The use of modal verbs (*may, could, should, will, must*) enables a writer to express attitudes towards what is being reported. The use of modality can create a sense of community between the newspaper and its audience since there is an assumption that the opinion conveyed by the article is shared by the reader. For example, *The Sun* headline 'This Will Hurt Becks Like Hell No Matter How Much He Has in the Bank' (Dillon 2008: 72) assumes agreement from the paper's readership. Reah (1998) and Richardson (2007) identify other textual features that assume shared knowledge on the part of the newspaper and its readers. The use of change-of-state verbs or implicative verbs (*stop, begin* or *manage, forget*) presupposes shared meanings. For example, if an athlete is said to 'have forgotten his duty to his fans', there is an implication that an athlete's duty to fans is well understood by everyone. Similarly, the use of the definite article *the* presupposes that something exists. For example, an article about the NFL team the New England Patriots in *The Observer* referred to 'The Patriot Way' (Wetherell 2008: 19). Presupposition is also contained in journalists' use of *wh-* questions—for example, 'when did it all start to go wrong?' implies that it has indeed gone wrong. These presuppositions direct the reader towards a particular interpretation of the events reported (Reah 1998).

Bignell (1997) suggested that two sets of language codes are observable in the British tabloid and so-called quality press. For Bignell (1997: 93), '"popular tabloids" use an orally based, restricted set of vocabulary and sentence structures, while "quality" newspapers use a more elaborated and complex set of codes which have more in common with written communication than spoken communication.' These codes map onto a class division in the respective readerships. Readership of the quality press in Britain (*Financial Times, The Times, Telegraph, Independent* and *Guardian*) is dominated by those employed in top managerial and professional occupations, while the tabloids are predominantly read by unskilled manual workers or the unemployed (Richardson 2007). Orality in the tabloids is signified by various rhetorical features such as deliberate misspellings, slang words, first names and nicknames, puns, modality and short, incomplete sentences. Typography is also used to convey speech, either by underlining or capitalisation or using dots and dashes for hesitation. For example, a headline in *The Sun* (Knox 2008: 53) referenced the striker Darius Henderson's goal for Watford as 'A Happy Hending'. The *Daily Mirror* (1 February 2008) described the England manager Fabio Capello's team selection as 'It's Fab New Look' (Lipton 2008a: 71), and the rivalry between the two London soccer teams Chelsea and Tottenham in the Carling Cup Final was described as 'Snarling Cup Final' (Lipton 2008b: 75).

The style of the quality press, by contrast, uses fewer of these features and so appears formal. Bignell (1997) argued that the authority associated with the quality press is as much a mythic code as the familiarity of the tabloids, both being founded on specific language styles. The quality press uses longer sentences and the codes of written, rather than spoken, discourse. For example, the headline in *The Times,* 'Beckham Pledge: I'll Be Back' (Dickinson 2008: 104), uses punctuation marks associated with formal grammatical language style.

Words and Images: Newspaper Photographs

Bignell (1997) draws on Barthes's (1977) analysis of the photographic message to point to some of the ways words and image combine to create meanings in newspapers. Despite being presented as transparent documents of an event, news photographs are painstakingly selected and modified to construct the right image for the story. Images may be cropped to emphasise an aspect or digitally altered to render an effect. Trick effects are common, for example, after the British tennis player Tim Henman was knocked out of Wimbledon in 2004, *The Sun* created a photographic montage on its back page, under the headline HENMAN CAPS MONTHS OF AGONY. Faces of the stars of English sport (Tim Henman, David Beckham, Michael Vaughan and Lawrence Dallaglio) were superimposed against a backdrop, evoking the police identity parade in the film *The Usual Suspects,* under the word GUILTY in enormous red letters, with smaller red text beneath reading,'... of Crimes against English Sports Fans'. Beneath each face were details of recent English defeats in the sports of tennis, football, cricket and rugby. The words, colours and images worked together to construct a range of meanings around sporting success, nationhood and masculinity.

Newsworthy individuals are commonly the subject matter of newspaper photographs. The camera angle adopted for depicting individuals, their facial expressions or the ways they are posed helps to discursively construct a viewing position for the reader to adopt in relation to the person portrayed. Other people or material objects featured in the photographs can ask the reader to make connections from one thing to another. A story from the *Daily Mirror* (Sloan 2008) about the success of a female jockey was accompanied by a main image of the jockey, Kirsty Milczarek, in a glamour pose, wearing a shoulderless evening dress and jewellery and gazing into the camera, smiling with her lips slightly apart. A small circular inset below depicted a young woman with a child (Milczarek as a toddler). To the right of the main photograph was an image of Milczarek on horseback during a race, above another of her as a young showjumper. Underneath the main headline there was a further image of Milczarek in her racing silks shot from below, posed with her hands on her hips, looking into the distance. The poses and content of the photographs conveyed divergent significations of femininity in relation to sport. The glamour pose emphasised the jockey's femininity, coding her as conventionally heterosexually attractive. The images of her as a child and as young showjumper both infantalised her and contextualised her sport in more 'feminine appropriate' terms (Hargreaves 1994). In contrast, the action photograph of Milczarek on horseback during a race minimised the impact of her gender, and the profile of her dressed as a jockey connoted strength and heroism. The images as a group portray a somewhat ambiguous array of traditional codes of femininity and sporting prowess that allows readers to construct their own narratives around their understandings of women in sport.

Photographs presented in sequences require the reader to fill in the gaps between the images by constructing a narrative. As Bignell (1997: 102) suggested, 'the repetition and variation of the signs in the pictures "add up" to produce particular connotations for the sequence as a whole, which become the signifiers of the mythic meaning of the event, like "tragedy" or "triumph" for instance.' For example, *The Sun*'s story about Beckham's lack of fitness (discussed previously) was accompanied by a sequence of images of him in various locations around the world between 22 November 2007 and 22 January 2008. In the series of shots, Beckham is depicted engaging in celebrity diplomacy, publicity and socialising, alongside one image of him playing soccer in New Zealand and another training in London, England. The image sequence was laid on top of a shot of Beckham playing football barefoot and bare-chested on a beach in Brazil. Together the images told a story of constant international travel and celebrity engagements, with little time devoted to serious sport. The headline IS IT ANY WONDER? overlaid on the spread carried a presupposed shared knowledge of the story ("is it any wonder that Beckham was not picked for the England team?"), and the images together provided the answer.

Newspapers use specific language codes in combination with layout and pictures to produce rich meanings. Using multiple layers of visual and textual signification, newspapers frame sport and sportspeople within broader social ideologies. While appearing to celebrate achievements, the press can use subtle forms of implication to contradict its explicit message. The two case studies that follow show how images and text construct particular viewpoints from which readers are invited to view Olympic athletes. The first case study discusses the way newspapers in the United States reported Ben Johnson's positive drug test in 1988. The second discusses the way Kelly Holmes's double gold medal success in the 2004 Olympics was narrated by the British press.

Case Study: Ben Johnson and the Spectacle of Drug Use in Sport

Since the 1980s, drug use has remained a recurring theme in a newspaper's sport pages. The initial proliferation of stories about drug use in the 1980s has been attributed to a range of factors, including an increase in the number of athletes using drugs, the ongoing acceptance of athlete transgressions as a topic in sport sections and, in particular, high-profile reports, arrests, suspensions, bans and even deaths

(Donohew, Helms and Haas 1989; Jensen, Gurber and Babcock 1987; Padwe 1989). Arguably, however, it is the story of Ben Johnson's positive drug test in the 100-metre at the 1988 Olympics that most effectively encapsulated the media's coverage of performance-enhancing drug use, and Jackson (1998: 23) referred to the story as 'the genesis of the modern sport-steroid controversy'.

This case study draws on data from *The New York Times* to explore the characteristics of the media's coverage of the Ben Johnson story during 1988 and 1989. One method of examining media stories is to analyse 'events which are matters of controversy or events which could attract a range of competing interpretations and then to examine whether a variety of viewpoints is present in the reporting of such events' (Davies and Walton 1983: 8). Exploring the reporting of controversial issues such as steroid use can help to provide insights into the ways that media coverage adheres to and diverges from normative values and narratives. The Ben Johnson story framed the issues around drug use in sport in relation to the vilification of athlete users, the role of governing bodies and the increasing threat of drugs to the world of sport.

Cheating, the Nation and Sport

Stories on Ben Johnson highlighted the significance of the event in dramatic, even hyperbolic terms for the runner, the nation and sport itself. Worrall (a Canadian IOC member) was quoted as saying, 'Ben Johnson has just been killed as an athlete, and probably his complete life has been ruined.' Coverage featured his transformation from a hero to a villain, a man whose 'Stellar Career' was 'Abruptly Clouded' (Goldaper 1988). Other signifiers of the ruined life of the athlete included speculations about his potential financial losses: '[the positive test] will probably mean a loss of several millions. It will definitely hurt his name, his image, his credibility, and his future marketability' (Caulkins, as cited in Burns 1988: D31).

The event was framed as having ramifications for his nation: a Canadian news anchorman was reported to have said, 'It is indeed a tragedy, not only for Ben Johnson, but for Canada' (Burns 1988: D31). Olympic spectators were also portrayed as distraught and betrayed. One technique that sports writers used for emphasis was ironic juxtapositioning, which places together two extremes: 'In one day, the watching world had been carried from shocking fraud [Ben Johnson] to genuine excellence [Greg Louganis's performance] and genuine tears' ('One Day' 1988). Johnson's positive test was portrayed as the opposite of 'genuine' sport. Similarly, Charles Dubin, associate Chief Justice of Ontario, stated that 'cheating is the antithesis of sports competition, and it encourages a lack of moral values' (Burns 1989: A29). Each of these ways of describing the significance of the event distances Johnson, 'the stained symbol of steroid use', from the world of sport and his country, differentiating between the villain and his victims (Anderson 1988: para. 20).

Discourses of Performance Enhancement

The event instigated speculation by the media on the pervasiveness of drug use within Olympic sport and the effectiveness of steroids in enhancing performance. Because the issue is typically kept quiet due to its illegality, it is difficult to gain reliable figures. Media estimates ranged from 'ten percent' to 'at least half of the 9,000 athletes who competed at the Olympics in Seoul used performance-enhancing drugs in training' (Janofsky and Alfano 1988: D31). The uncertainty surrounding steroid use was also present in speculations about their efficacy. The discourse from laboratory officials or testing agencies was relatively cautious, due in part to the ethical restrictions on conducting scientific tests with the levels of steroids athletes are thought to take. Dr. Donald Catlin, head of the laboratory that oversaw drug testing for the United States Olympic Committee (USOC) and the National Collegiate Athletic Association, said that 'the sense I get is that more people in the scientific world feel that they [steroids] do have some perceived beneficial effect on athletes' (Altman 1988: A34). The media coverage overall, however, reified the power of steroids. Emphasis was placed on Johnson's transformation from a skinny kid to an Olympic-calibre athlete. In contrast to the more reticent scientific discourse, athletes and coaches were confident that steroids worked. The decision to use drugs was portrayed as a strategy for levelling the playing field and attaining 'competitive fairness' (Kidd, Edelman and Brownell 2001: 156). Coach Charlie Francis described Ben Johnson's decision to use steroids: 'either he wanted to participate at the highest level or he didn't. He could decide he wanted to set his starting blocks in the same place as the others or one meter behind. It was pretty clear that steroids were worth about one meter at the highest level' (Janofsky 1989: D27).

One of the side effects of the coverage was that for the first time, the public were provided with a portrayal of the performance-enhancing capabilities of steroid use. Dr. James Garrick, a San Francisco sports medicine specialist, lamented that the notoriety given to the Johnson case might increase the use of steroids by athletes at all levels. 'I can't think of a better advertisement for anabolic steroids than the Ben Johnson thing,' he said (Kaufman 1988). *New York Times* columnist George Vecsey (1989: A29) provided a simple but striking equation: 'people around the world know that steroids = medals = money, unless you happen to get caught.' The media coverage consistently reinforced the power of steroids to facilitate performance and led to the rewards of success in elite sport creating a dramatic, sweeping narrative of sport and scandal.

This discourse was mixed in with speculations about the effectiveness of testing and the way to proceed. The media coverage discussed the belief that athletes can beat drug tests: 'the cheaters are winning. They know how to beat the tests, and what I'm hearing from a lot of people is that they have a fantastic new blocking agent that our labs cannot pick up ... Until we begin some kind of unannounced testing essentially surprising the athletes, what we are doing is a waste' (Dr Robert Voy, Chief

Medical Officer for the USOC, as quoted in Janofsky 1988a: D29). At this point in time, the way forward was perceived to be random, out-of-competition testing: 'more regular and sensitive tests would surely eliminate drugs from most athletes' training program' ('Winking at Steroids' 1988: A26). One of the key issues at this time was whether or not random testing would be an infringement on athletes' civil rights: 'athletes should agree to not only train, but also agree to year-round random testing which is done in a way that preserves their dignity and their civil rights' (Helmick, President of the USOC, as cited in Wallace 1988: B16). Perhaps the only discourse that was critical of governing bodies addressed the need for independent testing agencies to eliminate the possibility of organisations concealing positive tests to protect their athletes and themselves. A simile (a strategy for comparing unlike things that have one type of resemblance, typically using *like* or *as*) was used to reinforce the point: 'you can't have a sport test itself and be trustworthy. It's like the fox guarding the henhouse' (Janofsky and Alfano 1988: D31). Johnson's positive test, therefore, was viewed as proof of the IOC's seriousness about stopping drug use: 'no matter who is offsides, we are prepared to act' (Pound, Vice President of the IOC, as cited in Janofsky 1988b: D32). Overall, the tone of coverage portrayed governing bodies as reformers who must 'clean up' sport by controlling deviant athletes and, to a lesser extent, their coaches and doctors. The definition of the issues was primarily reliant on official discourses and views that prevailed in setting out and framing the issues and solutions (Gans 1979).

The vilification and distancing of drug-using athletes, the creation of a sense of their threat to sport and society and the emphasis on surveillance and punishment contributed to the ongoing themes of stories of drug use that have continued for the past twenty years. The issue of performance-enhancing drug use seems to have evolved into a subgenre of sport reporting, a regular feature that is addressed as a part of a newspaper's overall coverage of sport alongside injury, violence, racism, gamesmanship and other sporting 'problems'. A search of *New York Times* articles on the term *steroids* shows that 4,733 articles have been published since 1981 and that 2,688 of these are in the sport pages. In the year from 14 February 2007 to 15 February 2008 alone, there have been 496 articles on steroids in the sport pages of *The New York Times*. One-hundred-metre sprint stars have continued to make the headlines for their associations with drug use, and a number of high-profile and even world record–holding 100-metre runners have been suspended for steroid use, including Justin Gatlin, Marion Jones, Linford Christie, Dwain Chambers and Tim Montgomery. Many of the stories that have been sensationalised have featured African American or African Caribbean athletes infusing intertextual, racialised discourses into the ongoing narrative (Jackson 1998). Stories of performance-enhancing drug use appear to have become intertwined with sport and sport reporting as a sensationalised, controversial topic that contributes to the spectacle of sport.

Reports of spectacular victories also require journalists to draw on a range of social meanings to dramatise an event. Hills and Kennedy (2009) discussed the intersecting themes of race, class, nation, gender and sexuality in the press coverage of Kelly Holmes's double gold medal–winning performance at the Athens Olympics. The next section explores the way this event was mediated in the British press.

Case Study: All Gold—Kelly Holmes's Double Olympic Victory

The British athlete Kelly Holmes was an unexpected hero of the 2004 Olympics. Hills and Kennedy (2009) argued that this was evident in the repeated theme of surprise in newspaper reports. *The News of the World* (29 August 2004) followed their back page headline of 'Kelly's All Goold', substituting Olympic medals for the *O*s, with 'Double Has Her Gobsmacked', drawing on her own words 'I'm gobsmacked' after the race. Page 3 of the *Sunday Mirror* presented a photograph of Holmes holding 'her head in her hands, unable to take it all in', with the headline, 'I Can't Believe It … '. *The Sunday Times* sport section ran a headline across pages 14 and 15 that

---

ANALYSING THE PRESS COVERAGE OF KELLY HOLMES'S VICTORIES

Kelly Holmes was an established British athlete who had been beset by repeated injury during her career. She was thirty-four years old when she won gold medals in the 800-metre and the 1,500-metre at the Athens Olympics in 2004. This was an historic accomplishment for British athletics. Holmes's medals were the first British double gold for both events since Albert Hill had achieved the same in the 1920 Olympics. These factors combined to make her victory both unexpected and unprecedented in recent years. The day after Holmes's second medal, her victories were reported in the British Sunday newspapers.

We were struck by this coverage and wanted to compare the different reports. We decided to collect newspapers that represented both populist tabloids and quality press, and occupied both right and left of centre political positions. Our sample included, therefore, *The News of the World*, the *Sunday Mirror*, *The Observer* and *The Sunday Times*. It was important to use the paper edition of the newspaper to be able to analyse the placing of the story on the page and the way the event was accompanied by photographs and other reports. We considered that the online editions of the newspapers would not present the story in the same way since meaning accrues from the accumulated intertextual associations of words and images both within the report and surrounding it. Online newspapers give only the words of the story and sometimes an image, but they are removed from their original context and fonts, and formatting and placement are altered.

Once we had decided on the newspapers, we located all references to Holmes throughout paper, looking in all the various sections. We identified repeated themes in the written reports, paying attention to linguistic devices that were used to construct the story. We analysed the images using techniques from semiotics, drawing out the connotations of the varying depictions of Holmes, her family and other athletes. We then considered the way that the words and images interacted with each other to tie down the range of possible meanings. Finally, we analysed the narratives that were constructed through the combination of these linguistic and photographic codes and identified the way that the Kelly Holmes story was made known to the reader in each of the newspapers.

read WAKE ME UP, IT'S A DREAM SAYS KELLY, with an image of a surprised Holmes as well as other assorted images. Steve Ovett's (2004: 27) column in *The Observer* alluded to a wider feeling of astonishment at her achievement: 'to me, Kelly's double gold medal in the 800m and 1500m is a classic case of what the Olympics are really about: unpredictability, not world records.' The press responded to this unpredicted and significant event by narrating Holmes as an instant national heroine. However, Hills and Kennedy (2009) argued that the multiple and changeable storylines that appeared in the press were a result of the challenge Holmes presented to the established image of national sporting hero.

Uneven Narratives for an Unusual Champion

Hills and Kennedy (2009) identified inconsistencies in the narratives of two articles in *The Sunday Times*. A profile of Holmes was included in the paper's 'Comment' section. The profile was accompanied by a cartoon head-and-shoulders image of Kelly Holmes grinning broadly, with arched eyebrows and staring eyes, which Hills and Kennedy (2009: 15) suggested gave her a slightly crazed look. The headline 'Bad Luck Finally Runs Out for Our Golden Girl' departed from both 'golden success' and 'ups and downs' narratives by constructing a different kind of story. The headline began with a negative and ended by embracing Holmes as 'our golden girl'; the story was framed not as a rise to victory, but as the end of a long, drawn-out fall. Hills and Kennedy argued that the mood of the headline continued into the first paragraph of the profile:

> Kelly was a broken figure. Defeated, humiliated and hobbling on crutches outside Atlanta's Olympic stadium in 1996, she concluded that if athletics could be so cruel she didn't need it. In an act of renunciation, she threw her spikes into a dustbin. (Bad Luck, 2004: 15)

Hills and Kennedy argued that it was unusual to begin a piece celebrating a momentous event involving one of Britain's greatest Olympic athletes with an almost sadistic interest in the low points of her career. There was a marked change to the narrative in the second paragraph with an allusion to a better-known tale—that of Cinderella:

> That was the poisoned apple moment in the fairy tale. The happy ending seemed chalked in for last Monday night, when Holmes surfaced from years as the forlorn 'bridesmaid' of British athletics to find Lord Coe, her childhood hero, gently removing her spikes in an act of homage to her stunning victory in the women's 800m at the Athens Games. (Bad Luck, 2004: 15)

The quotation marks surrounding *bridesmaid* referenced the use of the word by Holmes herself in an interview. However, Hills and Kennedy suggested that by marking out the word in this way, the romantic storyline was lent an air of incredulousness.

The following paragraph reinforced this with another change of narrative direction: 'the former army sergeant was not simply going to the ball: the golden coach was heading for her coronation' ('Bad Luck' 2004: 15). As an army sergeant, Holmes was not straightforward as a bridesmaid or fairy tale princess.

A few lines into the article, the profile reported that Holmes's Olympic achievements had actually surpassed those of Coe, who had been constructed as her Prince Charming. In so doing, the article punctured any cohesion that the Cinderella narrative might have had. The profile went on to characterise her as a 'geriatic' (she was thirty-four) and suggest her injuries were so numerous they would 'condemn a horse to the knackers' yard' (for the slaughtering of worn out livestock). This rather less romantic storyline gave way to another: 'she could destroy the world's fastest runners with searing bursts of speed' (Hills and Kennedy 2009: 121). Hills and Kennedy argued that this narrative unevenness typified the press coverage of Holmes's victories. Multiple storylines were arranged around her, without any appearing to be a good fit. Holmes was not easily incorporated into any of the existing narratives of athleticism, heroism or female stardom.

At the time of her gold medal–winning performance, Holmes was an unprecedented heroic figure in terms of the enormity of her achievement. The British medal haul was substantially greater in the subsequent Beijing Olympics, but in 2004, Holmes's victory had not been paralleled for eighty-four years. Holmes was also unusual in the particular intersection of race, class and gender that made up her social identity.

The photograph of Holmes on the cover of *The Sunday Times* depicted her smiling, giving a thumbs up sign while holding a Union Jack flag around her shoulders. The caption underneath praised her as 'the most successful British middle-distance runner of modern times'. The accompanying article, however, qualified this by pointing to her gender—'the most successful female runner this country has ever produced'—reinforcing perhaps the inability of a woman to embody the national heroic without question ('Golden Joy' 2004: 1).

Hills and Kennedy (2009) observed that this uneven marking of gender characterised much of Holmes's coverage in the press—*The Sunday Times* cover story described her (perhaps tellingly) as the 'nearly-woman of British athletics', while on page 3, inside the paper, Sebastian Coe was quoted as saying, 'She ran with great confidence and massive authority ... when it came to flat-out speed she could beat anybody'. Rather than trivialise her sporting achievement, the language used to describe her performance emphasised qualities that have previously been associated with masculinity: skill, strength, speed, power, tactics. *The News of the World* used both '*Focus*' (Harrison 2004: 104) and '*Strength*' (Sabey and Bhatia 2004: 6) as headers, and quoted her saying, 'I used all my guts and strength' (Sabey and Bhatia 2004: 6). Clavane (2004: 84), in the *Sunday Mirror,* described her characteristics as 'keep on going. Guts. Tunnel vision' and said she 'powered over the line'.

There were suggestions that Holmes's qualities of strength and determination also affected her personal life. *The Sunday Times* profile discussed her relationship with the runner Mutola as formerly 'one of the closest' in athletics, but now in a 'glacial phase' ('Bad Luck' 2004: 15). Hughes described her attitude as one of 'cold, calcu-lated determination' and suggested that 'when she cruised round the finalists yester-day, there was an eerie lack of camaraderie, an initial lack of human response to her' (Hughes 2004: 14). *The Observer* quoted her former coach Arnold, who said, 'She can be very aggressive, and very, very determined' (Smith 2004: 3), and described her 'ascetic lifestyle', which meant 'no drinking and few nights out' (Smith 2004: 3). *The News of the World* revealed 'the secret that drove Kelly to win a second gold medal—Alicia Keys' song *If I Ain't Got You* playing over and over in her mind'. This love song was interpreted by Holmes as being 'about my gold medal' (Sabey and Bhatia 2004: 6), giving an indication of Holmes's personal priorities. The same qualities that were viewed positively in relation to Holmes's sporting success were treated more ambivalently with respect to her personal life, questioning her ability to perform successful femininity and achieve at sport simultaneously.

Kelly's Secret Dad: Class and Gender in the Press Narratives

Hills and Kennedy (2009) pointed to the ways that the press portrayal of Holmes's naked ambition conflicted with the upper-middle-class, amateur gentleman legacy of British sport culture, which devalues trying too hard. Simultaneously, however, the reports of her discipline and self-control departed from typical media portrayals of the British working class as excessive and unrestrained (Skeggs 2004). Nevertheless, the press coverage continued to draw on traditional framing devices for representing sportswomen and working-class Britons, combining infantalisation with a focus on an ill-disciplined and turbulent home life.

The front page of the *Sunday Mirror* previewed a story inside the paper with 'Golden Kelly's Secret Dad' against an image of Holmes at the moment of victory and a smaller photograph of a smiling black man with greying hair. The story was given a double-page spread inside the paper, with the headline running across both pages: KELLY'S REAL DAD TALKS FOR THE FIRST TIME (Stretch 2004: 4–5). Another headline taking up a third of the first page of the article was a quote from Derrick Holmes: 'I Wish I Could Hug My Little Girl Again ... but She Doesn't Want to Know Me' (Stretch 2004: 4). The photograph of Derrick Holmes on the next page presented him in a light-hearted pose and was captioned: 'LADIES' MAN But Derrick Is Desperate for a Reconciliation'. The article's reference to Derrick Holmes as an 'emotional', 'happy-go-lucky' 'ladies man', inhabiting a 'down-at-heel' area, some-one who 'struggles financially' 'touting for work door-to-door' or 'in some pub with a pint in one hand and a young lady in the other' (Stretch 2004: 5) evoked the media stereotype of dissolute working-class behaviour patterns that could not be used to frame Holmes herself.

Hills and Kennedy (2009) pointed out that the tabloids were not alone in focusing on Holmes's childhood and family background. *The Observer* presented a rags-to-riches storyline to emphasise disturbance in her upbringing: 'like some of our other Olympic winners, Holmes is a success story from a broken home' (Smith 2004: 3). The article combined reports of a happy home life with references to 'domestic flux' and lack of contact with 'her biological father'. The article reported that her mother did not possess a passport (and could not therefore be present at her daughter's victory in Athens), thereby subtly conjuring an image parochialism for Holmes, in contrast to the international travellers to be found amongst *The Observer* readership. As Skeggs (2004: 112) observed, a 'way of signifying unmodernity is through spatial fixity, through not being mobile'.

Yet Hills and Kennedy (2009) observed that Holmes herself had none of the characteristics that the newspapers associated with her parents. This narrative of uncontrolled and turbulent working-class origins contrasted with other reports of her self-discipline and work ethic. Holmes had lived with Mutola in South Africa, a long way from her mother's house in the village of Hildenborough, England, and competed all over the world. The attempt to construct her as somebody's daughter is contradicted by her reported lack of interest in her 'biological father' and her mother's statement that 'I was never out for saying you have to do this or that; Kelly's done it for herself' (as cited in Smith 2004: 3). Similarly, there was a striking contradiction between the descriptions of Holmes as both a 'geriatric' and a 'little girl'.

Both Smith in *The Observer* and Hughes in *The Sunday Times* discussed 'speculation' (Smith 2004: 3; Hughes 2004: 15) about her relationship with Mutola. Both papers carefully avoided an outright suggestion of the existence of anything more than a training partnership or friendship between them, but talked about 'gossip' (Hughes 2004: 15; Smith 2004: 3). Hills and Kennedy (2009) argued that the rumours of a lesbian relationship made it difficult for the papers to fit her into a narrative of heterosexual femininity. Interestingly, the tabloids made no attempt to do so, but *The Observer* tracked down 'Holmes' childhood sweetheart, Simon Wixen, now a 34-year old computer analyst' (Smith 2004: 3), who appeared unwilling to discuss the question of Holmes's sexual orientation.

The Long Road to Glory: Heroism, Race and Nation

The Observer headline accompanying its feature article read, 'Victory for a Very Modern Heroine' (Smith 2004: 3). There was a series of images accompanying the article with the caption 'The long road to glory', which required the reader to construct a narrative to fill the gaps. The main image was of Holmes immediately after her success, raising the British Union Jack flag above her head. Three smaller photographs showed Holmes in different scenes: Holmes as a child in the back garden of a typical, working-class house with a white boy and a dog (the boy was her 'childhood sweetheart'); Holmes as a young woman smiling in her army uniform; and Holmes with her mother, posing with an honour she received from the Queen for her service to the armed forces. Hills and Kennedy (2009) argued that the selection of photographs depicted Holmes disrupting many categories: nation (a black woman against the British flag); sexuality (the absence of a current romantic partner); gender (the army career); ethnicity (the picture of a white mother with a black daughter); class (the ordinary garden, the ordinary clothes, the extraordinary feat). The newspaper presented Holmes's relationship with Britishness as complicated—the text described her as achieving her dreams 'despite—or thanks to—the state of modern Britain' (Smith 2004: 3). This confusing sentiment was echoed in *The Sunday Times,* which constructed a similarly incoherent narrative:

> Her story is not one of being a minority, the only child in a family of five who is black, the recipient of genes from a Jamaican father and an English mother. Nor is it specifically about being one of the few mixed-race children growing up on a council estate in Kent. But it is a fusion of those things, and a response in life to being a more driven individual than her siblings, and a remarkable obsession to push herself towards that podium. (Hughes 2004: 14)

Hills and Kennedy (2009) observed that the portrayal of Kelly Holmes, therefore, demonstrated attempts by the media to relate her story using traditional narratives of sporting success, femininity, class, ethnicity, sexuality and nation. Holmes's qualities and background, however, did not fit easily into these disrupting prevailing discourses surrounding Olympic heroism within the British press. While elements of traditional narrative frameworks were apparent in the press coverage of Holmes's victory, the instabilities and discontinuities within them indicated that Holmes's story could not be easily contained within dominant cultural constructions of sport and heroism.

CHAPTER SUMMARY

- Sport journalists do more than report the news; they decide what counts as news
- Different narrative forms are used to construct sport news, requiring us to distinguish between sporting events and the way that the sport news story is presented
- Rich meanings are produced in the sport press by the use of rhetorical devices, multiple visual and linguistic signs and the construction of an imaginary community of readers
- The connotations of the words and images used in newspapers combine to frame the way that sportspeople and sport events can be understood

Suggestions for Analysis

Newspapers address their imagined community of readers by framing sport in ways designed to accord with their interests and values. Issues of rule infringement in sport illuminate newspapers' different social and political perspectives well. Trace the reporting of an incident or scandal, such as a sport star involved in recreational drug use, in different national or local newspapers. How is the player's behaviour celebrated, disciplined or monitored? What assumptions do the papers make about how players ought to behave, and how do they use language to indicate the assumptions they expect readers to share? What combinations of linguistic and visual signs are used to emphasise particular perspectives? Consider how this framing of players' behaviour relates to the media construction of the sport star as 'role model'.

Further Reading

Jackson, S. (1998), 'A Twist of Race: Ben Johnson and the Canadian Crisis of Racial and National Identity', *Sociology of Sport Journal,* 15: 21–40.

Kian, E., Vincent, J., and Mondello, M. (2008), 'Masculine Hegemonic Hoops: An Analysis of Media Coverage of March Madness', *Sociology of Sport Journal,* 25: 223–42.

Markula, P., ed. (2009), *Olympic Women and the Media: International Perspectives,* Basingstoke: Palgrave Macmillan.

Richardson, J. (2007), *Analysing Newspapers: An Approach from Critical Discourse Analysis,* Houndsmill: Palgrave Macmillan.

Rowe, D. (2004), *Sport, Culture and the Media: The Unholy Trinity* (2nd edn), Maidenhead: Open University Press.

Whannel, G. (2002), *Media Sport Stars: Masculinities and Moralities,* London: Routledge.

Sport and Magazines

KEY CONCEPTS

Producers and consumers	Mirror stage
Ideal reader	Cover and editorial
Textual address	Health and fitness
Subject position	Specialist sport magazines

The sport media is as diverse as its audience. This chapter explores some of the techniques that the sport media uses to engage the different segments of its audiences, focusing on sport and fitness magazines. Sport-related magazines use both direct and indirect modes of address to interpellate their prospective readers. The chapter provides a close analysis of magazine covers, editorials and contents to show how the text, image, layout, typeface and cover lines all combine to hail readers to buy the magazine. As readers make the decision to purchase their sport magazine, they actively step into the address of that magazine. In this way, the identities of readers are shown to be constructed in interaction with the sport media. The two case studies for this chapter demonstrate the ways that social identities are implicit within the subject positions presented to the reader by two specialist sport magazines, *Climber* and *Crush.*

The Characteristics of Magazines

Magazines represent a large and diverse section of the media industry. Around 9,000 different titles exist in the United Kingdom and 19,000 in the United States (Holmes 2007). Sport-, exercise- and fitness-orientated magazines form an important sector of the market. *Sports Illustrated,* for example, has circulation figures of over 3,000,000 (Audit Bureau of Circulations 2007). Yet, despite their popularity, magazines are considered lowbrow media forms (McLoughlin 2000). In part, this reputation is a result of the way magazines are structured. The magazine is designed for readers to browse, dipping into and out of stories, flicking through the pages and admiring the images. Magazines vary greatly and incorporate a range of formats from slickly fashioned glossy publications to home-produced, stapled pages. Typically, magazines are issued in regular intervals and include a number of articles on a range of topics (Holmes 2007). Historically, there have been connections made between this format and the popularity of magazines, with women needing short breaks from domestic chores. However, as gendered working patterns have changed, so has the range of magazines targeted at men, for example, Beynon (2002: 125) called *Men's Health* 'one of the publishing successes of recent years'.

Abrahamson (2007) argued that magazines are different from other forms of media in their 'exceptional' capacity to shape social life. Magazines typically focus on some aspect of contemporary culture and help to define its characteristics, norms and values. One unusual feature of magazines is the way that they can allow for a unique connection between media producers and consumers. This is particularly the case with specialist magazines, such as *Climber,* where the editors, writers and readers may identify themselves as part of the same community with a shared interest in a particular activity. The term *journalistic distance* refers to the ideological and material differences between those who create and consume media products. Unlike other media formats, there may be little journalistic distance between the producers and the consumers of a magazine in terms of their approach to the activity and interest in their topic. In addition, specialist sport magazines are often attempting to provide their readers with information that will lead to action and enhance their enjoyment of participating in an activity. 'This connection between the reader's appetite for information and interest in some resulting action may lie at the center of the impulse which brings many readers to magazines in the first place' (Abrahamson 2007: 670).

The magazine is a material object—it is not only the look, but the size and feel of a magazine that is important. Magazines can be deliberately produced to be small enough to carry around, or use glossy paper to add a sense of luxury to the reading experience. Magazines seek to mobilise consumers' desire—to sell themselves to the readers along with a host of associated products. According to Holmes (2007: 514), major magazine publishers engage in a process of 'finding and fostering' a community of readers and base content on 'the needs, desires, hopes and fears of that defined group, thus creating a bond of trust with their readerships'. This establishes a relationship that encourages interaction between the magazine and the readers and allows the magazine to respond to readers' potentially changing needs and interests. The magazine may also sell this created community of readers to advertisers.

McCracken (1993) found that over 95 per cent of American women's magazines were made up of either explicit advertising or editorial comment recommending items to buy. By taking account of the kinds of products and services advertised in a magazine, as well its format, content, images and look, it is possible to build a picture of the magazine's ideal reader. The magazine uses the prospect of contact with this ideal reader to persuade advertisers to pay for space in its publication, and advertising revenue can account for half of the cost of some magazines (Bignell 1997).

Addressing the Ideal Reader

The racks of magazines at the book store, newsagent or supermarket compete for the attention of both the casual and committed shopper. Casting an eye over the array of titles and images and cover lines, consumers decide which magazine is for them. This decision may be made in a fleeting moment despite the myriad of signs that require evaluation. Magazines call out to their imagined readers, talking to us in ways that share our concerns, politics and values. The consumer is drawn to the magazine's content by the indications given on the cover. When we recognise ourselves and our interests in the visual codes of the magazines, we step into their address. We become their idealised reader and make our purchase. Althusser (1970) suggested that this is how ideology confers identity on individuals. On hearing a figure of authority, such as a policeman, shouting, 'Hey you!' in the street, and turning round in response to that hail, the individual recognises himself or herself as a potential suspect the policeman might want to question. In this process, the individual becomes subject to the meanings that the policeman bestows upon him or her. This is similar to the way magazines call out to us and ask us to consider ourselves within their terms. When we do, we become subject to their meanings, our identities being formed as part of this interaction with the text of the magazine.

Mills (1992) drew on an analysis of pop songs and the way radio DJs talk to their listeners to construct a model of direct and indirect address that is useful for making sense of the way the reader is positioned by a magazine. When a love song is played on the radio, the listener can adopt a range of different positions in response. If the song is sung by a man invoking the name of a woman as his love object, a heterosexual man might identify with the speaker in the interaction. A heterosexual woman listening might identify with the supposed addressee of the song. Alternatively, the listener might think he or she is overhearing an interaction between two people, of which the listener has no part (in this case, gender, sexuality or a recent bad experience in love might have an impact on the position adopted). Mills (1992) argued that this positioning is not stable and can shift. Mills demonstrated this by referring to the way radio DJs address their audience. The listener is not implicated in the address the same way all of the time: sometimes the DJ can use 'you' to mean the entire audience, sometimes an individual listener. In the meantime, the talk remains available to the rest of the audience. This model of speaker–addressee–overhearer can be used to analyse what makes a potential purchaser step out of the position of overhearer into that of addressee.

Positioning the Subject in Sport and Fitness Magazines

The magazine offers us a subject position to occupy. Since identity is not fixed, or unitary (Hall 1992), individuals are engaged in a quest for completion. Magazines offer us a way of understanding ourselves that appears to offer this more finished sense of self. Our choice of magazine, therefore, reflects our sense of who we are and who we might like to be. A golf magazine may use codes to speak to potential readers in ways that say 'you are a white middle aged man who works hard during the week, but that is not all you are and it is not as important as your real passion—golf.' It is possible that a potential purchaser is looking for a magazine as a distraction from work, as he imagines his golfing holiday that is still a long way off. The information contained within also encourages us to learn more about the area of interest and take action towards moving towards a future self. The way the magazine addresses us makes us feel part of a larger community of individuals with shared interests. The magazine presents a version of identity that the potential purchaser would prefer to have. In this sense, the magazine cover is presenting the reader with an idealised self (McCracken 1993).

The work of the psychoanalyst Jacques Lacan can help explain this process of identity formation. Jacques Lacan (1901–1981) was a French psychoanalyst whose work has been used to explain the complex relationship we have with images. Lacan's understanding of the unconscious reveals identity to be forever fluid and unstable. An important phase in the development of identity for Lacan was the mirror stage. Lacan described this stage of child development as one where the child begins to understand itself as a social being, separate from its mother. Lacan observed that a six-month-old baby may be unable to walk or even stand up, but will become fascinated with its reflection in a mirror. Even though the child experiences its body as out of control and disconnected, in the mirror, it appears as a whole, fully formed person. The child learns, therefore, to identify with an idealised image of itself. The child sees itself in the mirror as both itself (its reflection) and not itself (only its reflection). As Sarup (1996: 36) suggested, we need not take the mirror in this account literally; rather, we can see it as 'a point outside the self through which the self is recognised'. This process enables the child to understand itself as a subject, to enter into language—as a speaker (I), addressee (you), and someone mentioned in others' speech (he or she). However, the mirror only gives the child an imaginary experience of what it is like to be whole. Since this identification is based on an illusion or misrecognition, at the heart of identity is a sense of lack. For Lacan, the aim of psychoanalysis was to enable 'human subjects to recognise and name their desire—the relation of being to a lack' (Sarup 1996: 38). Lacan's account of identity and lack is useful for making sense of the feelings associated with the consumption of magazines and other media and the fantasy of wholeness and fulfilment they induce.

According to Lacan (1977), therefore, an inescapable sense of lack exists at the core of our identity, which we spend our lives attempting to overcome. Magazines offer something to us that might compensate for our feeling of lack. They present us with idealised images of ourselves to identify with, but to sell us the magazine, they encourage us to feel insecure or empty without it. Imagine the process of going to the store to purchase the latest edition of your favourite magazine. Scanning the titles, you may experience disappointment that the magazine you are looking for is not there. Finally, you recognise it, and you feel a sense of relief that you have found it. This pleasure is heightened by the expectation of satisfaction from reading the articles, looking at the images and exploring the contents. In this way, the magazine presents the promise of creating a more fulfilled and complete self.

This chapter will, therefore, examine in detail the ways that magazines address their readers. The following sections will refer to a number of health and fitness magazines to show how they construct both a direct address and more subtle indirect address to a potential purchaser. Different aspects of the magazine will be considered for the way they contribute to the overall address, creating differences within the market for health and fitness publications. The magazines discussed are British editions of *Runners World, Zest, Health & Fitness, Ultra Fit* and *Men's Health* (September 2007) and US editions of *Women's Health* and *Men's Health* (March 2006). The cover of the magazine acts as a kind of advertisement for the magazine as a whole and so will be given attention in its own right. In particular, the cover image, cover lines and layout will be considered for their contribution to the address to the reader.

Then, specific aspects of the content will be considered: the editorial, the contents and the composition of pages.

The Magazine Cover

The cover of the magazine is its first point of contact with a potential consumer and functions both to identify itself and the target reader for that magazine. Features of the cover, such as the title, the images, the layout, the graphology, the texture of the paper and the cover lines, operate as explicit and implicit markers of the identity of the ideal reader. Text and image work together, asking the reader to interpret them in a particular way.

The Title

The title of the magazine crystallises the expectations of the readers, summing up in one or two words the meaning of the magazine. Health and fitness magazines tend to provide exercise and nutrition advice, so the straightforward information-giving nature of some of the titles, like *Health & Fitness,* connote seriousness and trustworthiness. Some titles explicitly narrow down the potential pool of consumers by gender: *Men's Health, Women's Health.* Others do the same thing more subtly by implying a gendered reader through a combination of fonts, colours, words and images. *Zest,* for example, implies a bubbly personality type likely to be associated with femininity. The title is written in a block white typeface with the letters placed unevenly on the page, so that they appear to bounce. This gives the impression of light-heartedness. Alongside the title is the slogan: 'Health, diet, fitness, looks: feel 100% confident'. This emphasis on looks and feelings helps construct an indirect address to a heterosexual, female consumer, which is underscored by other signifiers on the cover of the magazine like the image of a smiling woman, lettering in shocking pink and indications of content like 'Diet Success Couple' and 'Blast Fat Sculpt Curves'. The titles of *Ultra Fit* and *Runner's World* do not contain a direct address to a gendered reader, and the slogans that accompany them ('Diet and fitness plans that work'; 'World's best-selling running magazine') are factual and informative. Nevertheless, both magazines have an image of a woman running on the cover, which has the effect of feminising the broader address of the title.

While some of the slogans are very clear, others are more playful. The ambiguity of the seemingly flippant, but simultaneously no-nonsense, slogan on one copy of *Men's Health,* 'Tons of useful stuff', uses banter both as an indirect address to its masculine readership and as a guide to the contents. Easthope (1990) suggested that banter was one marker of masculine style, and this is similar to the humour that Benwell (2004) called ironic discourse in men's magazines. Similarly, *Women's Health* consciously plays on the well-worn advertising cliché 'New and Improved' to create the slogan 'You and Improved', thereby using intertextuality to construct the consumer as the commodity herself.

The Cover Image

As indicated earlier, the image that takes up much of the space on the cover of the magazine is crucial in identifying the magazine's ideal reader. While it can be argued that cover models are chosen to reflect the kind of reader the magazine is targeting, the way the codes work may be more complex than this. Critics such as Fuss (1992) have pointed to the importance of desire as a reader's gaze is directed at magazine cover models. Similarly, White and Gillett (1994: 26) discussed the way the images of muscular bodies in bodybuilding magazines are presented as desirable but not necessarily reflective of the body of the typical reader. Instead, they argued, photographs of muscular bodies framed in a self-evidently positive light affirm 'the insecurity of the reader who does not measure up to the envied image on the page'. Other commentators have suggested that the formats used by magazines like *Men's Health* have adopted conventions associated with women's magazines, and in playing with reader's desire to be the ideal body on the cover, risk creating tensions by simultaneously mobilising a potentially homosexual desire for that body (Beynon 2002). To avoid this, Beynon (2002: 126) suggested that *Men's Health* must chart 'a careful course ... to steer clear of the homosexual and promote the desirability of heterosexuality'.

In contrast to women's lifestyle magazines, which tend to feature close-ups of women's faces on their covers, *Ultra Fit* and *Runner's World* both have a full-length image of a running female on their covers. The woman on the cover of *Runner's World* is set against a background of blue sky and a strip of sandy ground, providing a minimalist context for her activity. There is no contextual information on the cover of *Ultra Fit,* which has a stark white background for the runner. These images of active women could be considered to mark a positive difference from the sexualised, passive images of female athletes that many studies have suggested characterise the sport media (Kane and Greendorfer 1994). Information inside the magazine indicates the cover photograph is of a real athletic female ('Personal Trainer Jenny Pacey') rather than a model chosen for her looks. Nevertheless, neither woman appears to have discernible muscle development (except for Pacey's upper arms). Instead, the photographs seem manipulated to give the bodies a smooth, glowing appearance.

These images of active women belong to the magazines with a less obviously gendered address. The images on the cover of *Health & Fitness, Zest* and *Women's Health* are all of women shown from head to upper thigh. The model on the cover of *Zest* is shown with the greatest amount of contextual information. She is depicted in a tropical beach scene, wearing a shocking pink bikini, arms raised, head tilted, mouth open and back arched in a pose associated with sexual ecstasy. The model on the cover of

Health & Fitness is similarly shown wearing a bikini, but this time it is orange, and while her arms are also raised above her head, her back is straight and she is looking directly at the reader. The resulting connotations are more wholesome than sexual. The model on the cover of *Women's Health* has more clothes on than the others, but Hargreaves (1994) has argued that certain items of clothing can exaggerate the areas they conceal, making bodies look more sexualised than if they were naked. The model is leaning against a rock, wearing a dark sweater. However, the sweater extends no farther than her waist, and her bottom half is clothed only in white bikini briefs.

The image on the cover of *Women's Health* is in black and white. This is in the conventionalised style of *Men's Health* cover models. Masculinity theorists such as Beynon (2002) have pointed to some of the strategies used by *Men's Health* to make the cover images of seminaked male bodies less challenging to heterosexual, male consumers. Beynon (2002: 126) suggested that 'masculine-on-masculine looking is permitted' by the emphasis in these images on musculature (particularly the biceps and abdominals) and the outdoor setting that connotes wholesome ruggedness and provides a justification for the lack of clothing. The black and white coding is also interesting in this regard. While black and white may connote a classic, iconic image (and therefore one that deserves to be admired), the black and white is equally effective in detracting from the fleshiness of the body on show. In this way, the colour scheme intersects with the hard outlines provided by the muscle tone and the confident gaze of the model (looking, it seems, straight into the eyes of the magazine reader) to present an image of invulnerability that negates the connotations of femininity associated with the display of the body.

Cover Lines and Layout

The magazines' cover lines give a preview of the contents, so they need to make prospective readers want what is inside the magazine. One way for health and fitness magazines to do this is to play upon the insecurities or weak points of their consumers. They create a need, then, offer a solution. Following the Western cultural convention for reading left to right, the most important cover lines are positioned in the top left-hand corner (McLoughlin 2000). In this spot, all of the magazines except *Runner's World* placed text referencing ways of losing excess body fat in bold, capital letters:

Ultra Fit: TOP 3 FAT FIGHTING WORKOUTS
Zest: BLAST FAT SCULPT CURVES
Men's Health (UK): GET BACK IN SHAPE!
Men's Health (US): LOSE YOUR GUT
Health & Fitness: SLIM WITHOUT THE GYM
Women's Health: FLAT ABS NO CRUNCHES!

While there appears to be a consistent emphasis on fat reduction, variations in fonts, colours and punctuation communicate this message differently to the magazines' specific readership. The wordy cover lines of *Ultra Fit* use a literate and scientific discourse to address a knowledgeable and serious consumer. THE BEST DRUG-FREE WAYS TO PACK ON MUSCLE AND SIZE suggests that readers are so committed to building muscle that they may have considered (and rejected) performance-enhancing drugs. References in the cover lines to articles on cholesterol, blood pressure, preventing injury, healthy eating and THE GLYCAEMIC INDEX—MYTH OR MAGIC? address a reader engaged with health issues and popular medicine.

In their analysis of *Flex* magazine, White and Gillett (1994: 26) noted the tendency of text in advertisements to 'speak to the male reader in an authoritative and commanding voice, implying that the reader is lacking in control and is in a position of relative powerlessness'. This strategy is discernible within the style of cover line used by *Men's Health*. The central image of a muscle-bound male is surrounded by imperatives, powerfully reinforced by the use of large block font and exclamation marks: SCULPT YOUR BODY IN JUST MINUTES A DAY! POWER UP YOUR DIET! LOOK YOUR BEST NOW! The male figure is also positioned so that he appears to be looking down from a position of authority on the reader.

Stibbe (2004) drew attention to an anomaly within the discourse of *Men's Health*. Stibbe suggested that

> It is written for men who are most exposed to and have most to gain from the ideals of hegemonic masculinity, and it has an openly admitted agenda of promoting 'the traditional male view'. On the other hand, traditional masculinity has been shown to involve a large number of negative health behaviours, such as excessive alcohol consumption and risky behavior. (p. 35)

This makes the magazine's address to the reader extremely complicated. Stibbe (2004) argued that the magazine actually endorses behaviour which may be injurious to health (e.g. refusing to see red meat consumption as anything other than positive because of its connotations of masculinity). The UK cover of *Men's Health* included lines such as BE A PUB GENIUS! and THE 6-PACK PIZZA!, arguably endorsing both drinking and eating fast food as a means to health.

Men's Health addresses its readers by combining an image of a self-assured, muscular male with textual commands to get in shape. The slim, controlled body has been associated with the middle-class office worker who benefits professionally from appearance (Cook 2000). Stibbe (2004: 34) suggested that the *Men's Health* readership forms a class 'and it is the class most to gain from the reproduction of male domination'. Nevertheless, emphasising appearance and bodily display has long been associated with femininity, which threatens to trouble the masculine identity of the readership. In addition, the magazine's voice of authority seems to shout orders to lose weight, get fit, get better at sex and stop being stressed. All of this constructs an address to the reader that is based on a fragile identity, one that desires the hegemonic masculinity of the cover image but does not yet identify with it. *Men's Health* tells readers to step into their desired identity by reading the magazine.

Cover lines on *Women's Health* construct a different kind of address. While there remains a focus on body shaping, slimming, sex and stress, the magazine appears to promise all these without effort: FLAT ABS NO CRUNCHES; EASY STEPS FOR LESS STRESS; LOSE WEIGHT WITHOUT FEELING HUNGRY. Bordo (1990) has discussed the paradox of consumer capitalism that wants us to possess controlled 'producer' bodies but encourages us to consume limitlessly. The magazine promises to resolve the paradox by seeming to suggest that in the act of consuming *Women's Health*, we will attain the controlled body we desire.

The address of the magazine is the result of the intertextual combination of signifiers. The central image and the cover lines work together to construct a viewing position for the reader to step into and make sense of the signification. For example, the cover of *Health & Fitness* uses turquoise and fluorescent orange lettering. The central image of a woman occupies half of the cover space lengthwise, and the colour of her bikini picks up the orange of the text. The words 'Health and fitness, SLIM WITHOUT THE GYM, Stuck in a food rut?, ARE YOU SABOTAGING YOUR HAPPINESS' take up the other half of the cover. The text is physically linked with the image as the ends of words run over the body of the woman. The additional use of yellow to highlight certain words (e.g. HOT LOOKS, in a bubble positioned in the centre of the page, overlapping the model's chest) is reflected in the yellow bikini trim. Over the model's hips are the words 'Help me stop snacking' and 'I hate my big bottom!' (references to reader makeovers), and the words 'Nell McAndrew Back in shape after her baby' are printed on top of the model's flat stomach. In these ways, the image is integrated into the textual messages, and the reader is asked to make a connection with the promise of the magazine's contents and the joyful, slim woman depicted.

The Editorial

Magazines often have an editorial column, which presents a direct address to the reader presumed to be from the magazine's editor. Analysing the editorial enables us to elicit the characteristics pertaining to the imagined speaker (the voice of the magazine) as well as the addressee (the reader). The editor's letter in *Zest* starts with 'Want a better body? Me too.' The female editor makes it clear that dissatisfaction with one's body is the normal experience of femininity, shared by the producers and consumers of the magazine. By acknowledging this commonality, the magazine neatly constructs a sense of community with its female readership. The conversational tone underlines this connection.

The editorial of the UK version of *Men's Health* uses a range of references that are likely to be shared among the readership to construct an imaginary universe for the consumer. The editor assumes readers' knowledge of laddish radio DJs and pre-miership footballers, giving markers that he is talking to youngish, single men: 'If, like 10.5m others you tune into Radio 1 (7 million listen to Chris Moyles alone!).' Heterosexuality (and lack of experience) is also assumed—an article on football links to one about women: 'what makes him [footballer Thierry Henry] tick … find out what makes *her* tick, with a magical mystery tour inside the female brain.'

Ultra Fit's editorial interestingly assumes a shared horror of female bodybuild-ers amongst its readership of '"normal" female fitness weight trainers'. While gym membership is taken for granted among the readers of *Ultra Fit, Health & Fitness* magazine's editor assumes that the magazine's readership is more interested in a fit lifestyle than a commitment to training. Her use of contemporary idiomatic phrases mimics the readers' speech style to enforce the seeming naturalness of her persona and its relationship to the expected community of readers: 'When it comes to work-outs, I'm more of an outdoor girl than a gym bunny.'

The Contents

Magazines are characterised by their variety of contents—a range of features, inter-views, regular items, advertisements, guides to products and self-help. The way items are constructed indicates how the magazine conceives of the interests of its readers. Inside *Zest*, for example, is a page devoted to explaining '6 reasons Zest loves Septem-ber!' The text is boxed in the centre of the page in a seamless paragraph. Key phrases summing up the six reasons are highlighted in larger font in aqua blue and leaf green, picking out the colours in some of the images that surround the text, particularly the blue of a swimming pool and the green of a tropical shower. The soft colours and images of shower products and smiling women swimming and showering construct a feminine subject position. Within the arrangement of words and images on the page is a highlighted key phrase, 'The Rugby World Cup kicks off this month', an image of a magenta and blue short-sleeved rugby top, a rugby ball and rugby players in a scrum. The inclusion of these references to rugby alerts us to the inscription of positionality within the contents of magazines. In considering the address of the article to the read-ers, it is not enough simply to take account of which words and images are used, but the way they position the reader. While the item suggests that the reader should be interested in the rugby, the text positions her as a heterosexual female, whose interest is secondary to that of her male partner's ('but don't let your man watch alone!'). The magazine incorporates rugby into the wider discourse of consumer fitness by suggest-ing that 'watching your team on screen can boost heart rate to workout levels' (allud-ing to an unreferenced study of football supporters). Finally, the magazine gives the Web address of the sportswear retailer Canterbury, so the reader can 'look the part in a gorgeously girlie Canterbury rugby shirt'. As a result, the reader's interest in rugby is framed in terms of appearance-orientated, heterosexualised femininity.

The contents of *Men's Health* magazine are similarly assembled and presented in a particular style of address to the reader. Benwell (2004) dated the launch of men's lifestyle magazines in the United Kingdom to 1986, pointing to the strategies that were quickly deployed to cajole men into 'the explicit adoption of the feminized role of the consumer' (Benwell 2004: 4). The tone that was used was very different from that of women's lifestyle magazines. Instead, the magazines were constructed to communicate 'strident aspiration, unassailable confidence, a lack of intimacy, and an objectification of women' (Benwell 2004: 4). Benwell went on to argue that this style has evolved in a complex way to negotiate between the competing demands of consumerism and hegemonic masculinity.

In the United Kingdom, a particular form of men's magazine has been associated with 'the new lad': a media-driven variant of masculinity that emerged as a backlash against the politically aware new man of the early 1990s. The British Broadcasting Corporation News Online's E-cyclopedia describes the 1990s as the decade of the new lad, unashamedly into football, drinking and women ('Our Decade' 1999). The magazine that catered most directly for 'laddish' masculinity was *Loaded*. Benwell (2004) has pointed to the similarity between the contents of *Loaded* and other consumer magazines: letters pages, advice, handy hints, features, interviews, advertising and, like women's lifestyle magazines, fashion, health and beauty. What marked out the lad's magazine as different, she argued, was the tone: 'invariably light and jocular, and even when it is not, the tone militates against anything being taken too seriously (personal advice pages, for instance, are present but only in satirical form in *Loaded*)' (Benwell 2004: 5).

The style of the UK version of *Men's Health,* in particular, needs to be understood in this context. An article, for example, on muscle is titled THE LAZY MAN'S GUIDE TO GROWING MUSCLE and features an image of a supine male collapsed into an armchair, naked but for his shorts, with clearly defined muscle tone and Homer Simpson slippers at his feet. Each of the article's five steps to growing muscle start with TAKE IT EASY and encourages rest between sets, rest between exercises, more time in the shower, more massages and more time asleep. The inset reads 'Memo to self. 73%. THE AMOUNT MORE LIKELY YOU ARE TO BE OBESE IF YOU SLEEP UNDER FOUR HOURS A NIGHT.' This research is credited to University of Chicago Medical Centre. Below the main article is another smaller one—a series called SECRET MUSCLE focusing on the rhomboid. This article's title asserts that you can FIX YOUR CAVEMAN STANCE BY PUMPING YOUR BACK UP and suggests that slouching at a desk may be one cause of hunched shoulders, as well as too much time spent under the bench press. This jokey presentation of health and fitness advice enables the magazine to feed the reader's anxieties and desire for a better body while reassuring him that his resistance to exercise is also a sign of masculinity.

Benwell (2004: 13) suggested that 'magazine masculinity is defined by a continual oscillation between different masculine identities, namely a form of heroism and antiheroism.' Movement between these positions results in a particular kind of irony in the tone of the magazine. The humour of the text described previously resides in the way it characterises the masculinity of the reader as both heroic and antiheroic. Benwell (2004: 14) argued that heroic masculinity could be understood as 'active, rational, professional, autonomous, knowledgeable and authoritative'. The muscular male is the epitome of heroic masculinity since he is literally a self-made man, having exerted mind over matter to create armour from muscle (Easthope 1990). The emphasis on muscle in this article (and throughout *Men's Health* magazine) conceives of the reader in the terms of heroic masculinity. However, the positioning of the reader as lazy, really just wanting to 'take it easy', and the representation of him as the opposite of active—asleep in an armchair—corresponds to antiheroism: 'resolutely and good humouredly self-deprecating. Antiheroism is associated with ordinariness, weakness, and self-reflexiveness' (Benwell 2004: 14).

The subject position offered by the article, therefore, is an unstable one, and for Benwell (2004), the ironic tone of much men's magazine writing is part of the ambiguity surrounding this conceptionalisation of masculinity. For example, the SECRET MUSCLE item addresses the reader as an unfit office worker with hunched shoulders and as a bodybuilder at the same time. The reference to a caveman stance might position the reader as lacking a body beautiful, but it simultaneously accords him excessive masculinity. The use of irony in men's health and fitness magazines could be seen as a resolution to the confusion of gender identity occasioned by asking men to step into the ostensibly feminine address of consumer culture. It enables the producers of magazines to accommodate and capitalize on the anxieties of their readers (Benwell 2004).

This chapter has argued that the address of sports and fitness magazines is not simply confined to an interest in sport and fitness. The title, image, cover lines, editorials and contents of the magazines combine to hail readers as socially situated subjects. In particular, class and gender were seen to be central to the direct and indirect address of the magazines. As Abrahamson (2007) noted, magazines use techniques to build close connections with their readership. The remainder of this chapter focuses on two case studies of specialist sports magazines: *Climber* and *Crush*. The magazine covers, editorials and contents are explored to consider the ways that the magazines attempt to address their ideal readers within the different sport cultures of climbing and golf. The case studies highlight the degrees of journalistic distance between the producers and consumers of the magazines and their differential emphasis on 'serious sport' or 'sporting lifestyle'.

Case Study: *Climber*—a Specialist Sport Magazine

Climber is a glossy magazine characterised by its use of stunning outdoor photography of climbers set amid scenic and awe-inspiring spaces. The dramatic image on the cover of a lone climber on the side of a sheer precipice is compelling and impressive. The shot is taken from above the climber and slightly angled, emphasising the verticality of the grey, jagged cliff face and the long drop to the water below. The shirtless white male climber looks strong, focused on his next move, with fingers and toes clinging to small crevices in the cliff face.

The title of the October 2007 issue of the magazine *Climber* is written in large, white letters across the top of the magazine, accompanied by a smaller strapline in yellow print: 'Britain's leading climbing magazine'. The title and picture suggest the seriousness of the magazine and its specialised target audience. The various cover lines indicating the content of the magazine reinforce the impression that the magazine aims to provide information of interest to those who climb. Three of the cover lines focus on stories introducing specific climbing routes: 'NEW SERIES! Mid-Grade Crag Tour NO 1: Castell Helen', 'Black Rocks: Fearful, fierce & fabulous!', and 'Culm coast classics: the big adventure starts here'. The excitement of the routes is highlighted by the use of exclamation points and adjectives relating to adventure or challenge. The remaining two cover lines highlight a climber profile, 'Nick Bullock: he dares, he wins', and a book review, 'Harrer: Big New Autobiography'. Along the bottom edge of the magazine cover is a list of other items in very small print: 'Young Guns: Katy Whittaker, Short Haul: Jersey, Stone Circles: Curbar, Gear: Fred Report, Masterclass: stamina'. The serious, informative tone of the cover differs from the ironic or humorous messages found in some men's magazines. The simple white and yellow font and titles are designed to entice climbers who wish to learn more about where to climb and read about experienced climbers. In addition, information about gear and technique are promised in the small print below. This package presents an image of the ideal reader as someone who climbs with some proficiency and who may travel to different places to attempt different climbs.

The editor is a climber who writes informally, sharing his experiences of climbing with the community of climbers. He uses climbing jargon to describe his trip to the Dolomites: 'you think—that looks like a juggy wall, and there's a fine crack line, but the jugs are ledges and the cracks huge chimneys and the "crag" you're eyeing-up is twenty pitches high' (Newman 2007: 3). The use of *you* emphasises this sense of community and communicates that the editor and reader share a similar perspective. The editorial closes with a signature, followed once more by an exclamation point reemphasising the excitement of climbing. Beneath the editorial is a picture of the magazine's Web page, where readers are urged to 'get involved' by sharing their 'photographs and climbing tales'. On the Web site, *Climber* advertises itself as a magazine written by and for climbers, again emphasising the lack of journalistic distance between consumers and producers.

Landscape and Nation in Reader Address

The magazine bills itself as Britain's leading climbing magazine, and the articles inside focus primarily on British climbers and locations. This further defines the ideal reader of *Climber* magazine in terms of national identity. The update section focuses on news and events of interest to climbers in Great Britain. There is a report on the completion of a Hard Rock Challenge by two climbers, local news from the Lake District and Scotland, two obituaries, and announcements about upcoming mountain festivals. These articles have a personalised tone. For example, the Lake District news includes a list of new routes that have been developed in the area, the 'altrustic' efforts of climbers who replaced old bolts on some routes, and a request for readers to get in contact regarding routes in the area. In addition, the stories about climbs that are announced on the cover are all found in Britain: the new series announced on the cover is a tour of the best crags in Britain, 'seeking our top quality mid-grades that are guaranteed to inspire you'; 'Culm dancing' features climbs on the north sea coast of Devon; and the Black Rocks are in the Peak District. The editor states that this was his first time visiting the (Italian) Dolomites in forty years of climbing, reinforcing the British address of the magazine.

Articles on places provide a description of the climb, the surroundings and practical arrangements relating to travel, accommodation, gear and guidebooks. Within articles are discussions of the appeal of an area such as its beauty, uniqueness and climbing qualities as well as very specific information on different routes and their levels of difficulty. Summaries of climbing areas highlight some of the key ways that locations are assessed. An article on Black Rocks in the Peak District concludes, 'Black Rocks is simply one of the most compelling grit crags. It is a place to test yourself, to put into context your triumphs at other crags, to experience climbing at its most basic' (Horscroft 2007: 59). Specialist language permeates the description of the Devon landscape (Pickford 2007):

> An unreconstructed spirit of wilderness climbing saturates the Culm Coast at every level, from long runouts on open slabs, to hidden tidal zawns filled with driftwood, and to clifftops covered in thrift where ragged blackthorn grows. For the adventure-seeking climber, there is no better place in England to go exploring. (p. 45)

Individuals or pairs of individuals climbing are the primary subjects of images throughout the magazine. Often these are large photographs indicating the scale of the climb and the sense of the lone or paired individual making a difficult ascent. In addition, they may portray a particularly challenging aspect of the climb. For example, the cover photograph is described inside as 'Gavin Symonds making the first ascent, ground up, without inspection ... This DWS features a wild dyno to a flared slot at two-thirds height—this was a move that eluded him on the first ten attempts!' A later photograph is captioned, 'Dave Birkett, on the first ascent, reaches for the tiny crimper from where he could place a high No. 4 wire which was effectively the first good piece of protection on the route.' The emphasis on the individual and the mountain is part of the depiction of climbing, while the address is to the community of climbers, and the images emphasise the individuality of the pursuit and the climber's technique.

Us and Them: Insider and Outsider Views of the Climber

In a book review of climbing stories from the *Guardian* newspaper titled 'Us & Them', the author, Perrin, distinguishes between climbers (us) and the press (them). Part of his differentiation relates to the tendency for some newspapers to sensationalise climbing stories, accentuate risk and identify heroes. Perrin (2007: 27) suggested that the *Guardian* has a more positive approach to reporting climbing stories, extolling their 'scrupulous, mediating and insightful gaze'. Robinson (2004: 120) contrasted the media representation of climbers as 'obsessive thrill seekers' involved in 'a risky, even crazy leisure' pursuit with the everyday experiences of climbers who may seek excitement and challenge but who may also try to minimise risk. She used the concept of 'mundane extremities' to describe the ways that extreme experiences in climbing have to be worked through the mundane activities that are also part of the everyday life of the sport (Robinson 2004: 120). The magazine focuses on preparedness, rather than risk, by providing information for the climber that will help in the planning and execution of ascents. The deemphasis of discourses of risk is echoed in the interview with an elite adventure climber, who discusses his prioritisation of preparedness and planning. He attributes this level of care in part to a serious injury that occurred when he was a young man.

Both men and women are included on the editorial staff and are featured in articles and photographs. The articles do not specifically address issues around gender, and male and female climbers are discussed in similar terms. An interview called 'young guns' features eighteen-year-old climber Katy Burke and focuses specifically on issues related to climbing such as highlights, favourite style, favourite climbs, projects, plans, training and sponsorship. The article is accompanied by four photographs of Katy in action at the British Bouldering Championships and in the Peak District. Bouldering is considered to be a relatively low risk style of climbing. Even though women climbers are depicted as serious climbers in the magazine, there seems to be an implicit sense that the most desirable image is the male climber, who is more likely to be portrayed as tackling exceptionally difficult and risky climbs. For example, the other interview in the magazine is a 'man with an awesome cv' who is associated with 'bold first ascents in major mountain ranges', some of which are listed with their level of difficulty, and who 'exemplifies the current generation of super-alpinist' (Spancken 2007: 48). Stories refer back to the accomplishments of previous as well as contemporary male climbers, with depictions of first ascents and details of the development of particular routes, pioneering techniques and admirable moves.

Climbing and Style

Drawing on Lacan's work, Erikson (2005) discussed the idealisation of style in climbing and its association with whiteness. He argued that 'style is a mode of accessing a climbing identity, reminiscent of the mirror stage, whereby I become a climber by accepting certain rules that distinguish me from other (non) climbers' (Erikson 2005: 383). Style refers to the classification of bodies within the context of climbing and risk and relates to the difficulty of particular ascents, the danger of falling and the ways that protection is used (Donnelly 2003; Erikson 2005). Arguably, the most desirable examples of 'style' on display for readers in the magazine are those attached to images and descriptions of the accomplishments of white male bodies.

A 'gear update' section features reviews of the latest climbing gear. This edition reviews five of the latest jackets using Gore-Tex and a gadget called the 'tadpole' that enhances the effectiveness of a karabiner. Again, these are all very focused on the functional needs of climbers, rather than on appearance or fashion. For example, the jackets are evaluated in relation to factors such as weight, durability, flexibility and protection. The only advertisements in the magazine feature climbing-related products such as ropes, helmets, harnesses, karabiners and clothing, reinforcing its address to a specialized and knowledgeable reader.

The final sections of the magazine focus on improving stamina through circuit training on climbing walls and a tutorial on climbing slopes. The need for preparation underpins two individual profiles that highlight the acetic lifestyle and intense training of the climbers. This again accentuates the serious tone of the magazine and provides insight into the ideal reader, the 'sporting "elite"' climber who is 'openly obsessed with training regimes, dietary habits, and body image' (Robinson 2004: 118). The emphasis on body and training is reinforced in photographs throughout the magazine which portray climbers as lean, fit white men and women who are serious and focused.

Who is the imagined reader of *Climber* magazine? The address is situated in relation to British climbers seeking to explore less populated but challenging and beautiful climbs in the country. Photographs depict individuals on difficult climbs against a backdrop of dramatic scenery. The information in the articles is designed for serious climbers and addresses the appearance of the location and the range of potential climbs and existing routes as well as the popularity (a negative) of the destination. Although it is clear from the photographs that challenge and risk are factors, the articles emphasise planning and preparation and matching the difficulty of the climb to the climber's capabilities. However, words like *adventure, difficulty, challenge, fear* and *bravery* do play a factor: 'a certain amount of technical improvisation, and an ability to stay cool well above gear is usually required on the harder slab routes of the Culm. It goes without saying that aficionados of Llanberis slate will feel at home on these adrenaline-inducing climbs' (Pickford 2007: 44).

A different kind of address is discernible in the second magazine case study. Ostensibly another specialist sport magazine, the design and contents of the first edition of *Crush* magazine focused more on the lifestyle associated with women's golf, rather than the sport.

Case Study: *Crush*—Luxury, Lifestyle and Women's Golf

Crush was an official magazine publication of the Ladies Professional Golf Association (LPGA) launched in 2004. It was described by the LPGA as a glossy magazine printed on high-quality paper in two sizes: a full-sized 'luxury' version and a more compact version for LPGA tour events. The premiere issue contained articles about LPGA players and items on fashion, finance, golf accessories, beauty, food and travel.

The cover of the first issue of *Crush* featured the golfer Annika Sorenstam set within a blurred landscape beneath a cloudless blue sky. The picture on the cover depicted Sorenstam in profile at the end of a golf swing, her gaze seeming to follow the trajectory of the ball. Sorenstam was wearing specialist golf clothing—visor, sunglasses, polo shirt and belted black pants—which gave her a streamlined, athletic look. Her sponsor's Kraft logo was clearly visible on the back of her shirt. The overall impression of the image was one of professionalism and focus.

The title of the magazine ran across the top of the page in white lettering. The title was embossed with a glossy finish and was positioned next to the LPGA logo, which depicted, as a white silhouette against a black background, a female golfer in a position similar to Sorenstam's. Four separate font styles were used on the cover. The font for the title, CRUSH, used thick capitals with flourishes at the ends of the letters. This font appeared again in a smaller version in the sell lines at the bottom of the page in both white and shocking pink. The same magenta was used in the large, rounded, sans serif letters underneath the cover image, which announced 'annika!' in lower case, and another cursive handwriting font declared the magazine to be the 'premier issue' just below on the right. Despite the variety of styles, the lettering was consistently decorative, friendly and feminine. However, even with the attention to typography, the words on the cover gave little information about what was inside, being confined to vague hints, for example, 'Girls Vs. Boys', 'Viva Ochoa' and 'Is Golf Sexy?'

The look and feel of the cover connoted wealth and femininity. The lack of informative text and multiple font types indicated that the design of the cover was attempting to address the readership in terms of style more than substance. The weight and texture of the paper suggested class and status.

The strong, sporting pose of the cover image, combined with the pink and white decorative lettering, signified an idealised reader who aspired to be physically active within the context of conventional, heterosexual femininity. This reflects a continuing tendency by the media to represent sporting female bodies within the confines of acceptable norms of female physicality (Bernstein 2002; Billings and Eastman 2002; Daddario 1998; Duncan and Messner 1998; Spencer 2003).

Characteristics of the ideal reader were discernible in the type of goods and services on offer throughout the magazine. The magazine contained advertisements for fine alcohol, high-specification electronic goods, home wares, health care plans, invitations to invest in gold and upmarket resorts. The advertisements addressed

ANALYSING *CRUSH*

Crush was an unusual magazine that appeared to be attempting to blend aspects of women's lifestyle magazines with women's sport. In addition, it was also a promotional item for the Ladies Professional Golf Association, giving them a space to showcase female golf celebrities. One of the distinctive features of the magazine was its size and texture. As a result, we considered the look and feel of the magazine as an object before moving on to analysing its content as text. We paid attention to the significant features of the cover, analysing the way that markers of the ideal reader were encoded into the title, the font, the colours, the layout, the central image and the cover lines. Inside the magazine, we identified the direct and indirect forms of address to the reader within the editorial. We noted the content of the magazine, including feature articles, smaller items and advertisements. We considered the way that articles framed issues to address the concerns and interests of the reader. We took account of the types of products advertised and identified factors that suggested the lifestyle of the target consumer (wealth, gender, age, marital and parental status, sexuality). Finally, we reflected on the way that the sport of golf was interwoven with the lifestyle orientation of the magazine.

the reader as leading a luxury lifestyle with an interest in home and family. A pool chlorinator, for example, was described as enabling owners to play golf on holiday and have their pool chlorinated in their absence. A luggage express service allowed golf clubs to be shipped on ahead of their owner's arrival. The implied lifestyle of the reader is underpinned by the position of golf as a predominately white upper- or middle-class sport that necessitates affluence for membership in country clubs, equipment and green fees.

Us and You: Crush *and Journalistic Distance*

Unlike many specialist sport magazines, *Crush* revealed a journalistic separation between its production team and its anticipated readers, indicating that *Crush* was written for, rather than by, female golfers. As a result, stylistic features revealed an uneven construction of intimacy and distance in the address to the reader. In a 'Publisher's Letter' (Squire and Redmond 2004: 10), the male publishers positioned themselves as interested in women's golf and the LPGA, but not as part of this community. Focusing on the growth and success of the LPGA tour, and mentioning some notable female golfers on the LPGA tour, the letter invited the reader to 'enjoy the magazine. We hope it adds as much to your life as it does to your game.' The use of the term *your* indicated that the publisher did not identify with the group that the magazine was targeting. Moreover, the publisher understood the magazine to be as much about lifestyle as sport. Nevertheless, the letter was signed by two first names, attempting to create a familiarity with the reader despite the publishers' lack of group membership.

The letter summarised the characteristics of their imagined reader as 'athletic, golfing women' who were 'diverse, fashionable, intelligent, active and well-traveled—just like the players [the magazine] celebrates'. The literary writing style that prevailed throughout the magazine could be understood as part of an indirect address to this well-educated, middle-class, female reader, who would be comfortable with sophisticated language constructions.

So, while the magazine sought to appeal to a specific group of female readers, it attempted to do so by flattering women, rather than by identifying with them. For example, the editor's letter (Tilley 2004: 13) began with a quote from Margaret Thatcher: 'if you want something said, ask a man. If you want something done ask a woman.' The column, written by a man, then discussed the various types of women who were involved in the production of the magazine. This slightly patronising tone achieved a further distancing of the writer from golfing women among its readership and workforce, whilst effectively interpellating them as politically conservative by praising Thatcher's bon mots.

The various contributors to the magazine were profiled on the page facing the editor's letter. They included one female golfer, a collection of male golf writers from various newspapers, non–golf specialists in sport, health and fitness and a fashion photographer. The biographical detail was written in a joking, tongue-in-cheek style, as if sharing a joke. For example, the magazine's New York–based fashion photographer was considered to 'still be having the full New York experience' despite not possessing a cat, a little dog or a bathtub in her kitchen. The tone indicated an attempt to express a shared cultural understanding which included, but also went beyond, the golf world.

Golf, Consumption and Femininity

An attempt to construct a broad address to women interested in playing golf and the lifestyle associated with golf continued throughout the features. The magazine's use of banter sometimes countered the seriousness of sport. For example, an overview of different types of grass to be found on a golf course was presented in a humorous manner, mixing technical information with jokes about losing the ball or blaming the grass for a bad putt. The profiles of golfers within the magazine covered a range of different ages and levels of experience from amateur to professional, including Michelle Wie, Annika Sorenstam, Kathy Choi-Rogers, Hilary Lunkes, Betsy King and Patricia Meunier-Lebouc. More explicit lifestyle-focused articles included one profiling different golf shoes, one on a disc Frisbee vacation package, another on golf dating on the Internet and one titled 'Summer Stuff', which highlighted the latest golfing gear, including sunglasses, gloves and clubs, golf carts, covers, clothing and golf bags. Golf's associations with wealth and luxury underpinned these articles. For example, an article called 'Teefany's' focused on designer golf-themed items available at Tiffany's. The reader is thus addressed as belonging to an upper income band. So, while there are references to more modest lifestyles (e.g. an item on 'cross golf', a form of urban golf for people 'with a couple of clubs and no cash'), these are treated as entertaining curiosities, rather than the norm.

Crush was ostensibly targeted at strong, active sportswomen as the official magazine of an organisation that claims to be the longest-running women's sport association in the world. Nevertheless, *Crush* reinforced the differences between men and women by distancing the male producers from the female readership, who were then hailed as conventional feminine subjects. This was achieved through heavily gendered codes of pinks and decorative lettering in the colour scheme and design, flippant lifestyle articles and the focus on consumer goods. The address to a politically conservative, affluent reader accorded with the LPGA's stated intention to distribute the magazine 'complimentarily in VIP airport lounges, including American Airlines' Admirals Clubs, and on private jets, at LPGA International, select LPGA tournaments and through the LPGA Fan Van' (http://www.lpga.com). The magazine appeared to be more about lifestyle and conspicuous consumption than women's sport.

CHAPTER SUMMARY

- Magazines are a distinctive media form in their close connection to the social lives of consumers
- The lack of journalistic distance between the producers and consumers of specialist sport magazines creates a sense of community for their readers
- A combination of signifiers construct sport and fitness magazines' direct and indirect address to their ideal reader, often playing on the reader's assumed anxieties and sense of lack
- The magazine cover's central image, cover lines, typography and layout work together to construct an idealised image to which the reader aspires
- Subtle differences in the mode of address in sport and fitness magazines position the reading subject in ways that relate to variants of social identity, attitudes to sport, consumption and lifestyle

---

Suggestions for Analysis

Specialist sport magazines are targeted at specific audiences, and often there can be very little journalistic distance between the producers and consumers of the magazines. However, a number of more generalist sport magazines exist, for example, *Sports Illustrated* or *The Observer*'s *Sport Monthly* supplement. Explore the ways that the identity of an ideal reader may be inscribed in the magazine's use of visual and linguistic signs. Consider the content of the magazine: which sports are included? Which issues? Consider also the way the content is being represented: how is the reader's gaze directed? What markers of gender, race or class can be identified in the address of the magazine?

Further Reading

Abrahamson, D. (2007), 'Magazine Exceptionalism: the Concept, the Criteria, the Challenge', *Journalism Studies,* 8: 667–70.

Benwell, B. (2004), 'Ironic Discourse: Evasive Masculinity in Men's Lifestyle Magazines', *Men and Masculinities,* 7: 3–21.

Cook, J. (2000), 'Men's Magazines at the Millennium: New Spaces, New Selves', *Continuum: Journal of Media and Cultural Studies,* 14: 171–86.

Holmes, T., ed. (2008), 'Mapping the Magazine', *Journalism Studies,* 8/4 [special issue].

Markula, P. (2001), 'Beyond the Perfect Body: Women's Body Image Distortion in Fitness Magazine Discourse', *Journal of Sport and Social Issues,* 25: 158–79.

McCracken, E. (1993), *Decoding Women's Magazines from Mademoiselle to Ms,* Houndsmill: Macmillan.

Robinson, V. (2004), 'Taking Risks: Identities, Masculinities and Rock Climbing', in B. Wheaton, ed., *Understanding Lifestyle Sports,* London: Routledge.

Sarup, M. (1996), *Identity, Culture and the Postmodern World,* Edinburgh: Edinburgh University Press.

White, G., and Gillett, J. (1994), 'Reading the Muscular Body: a Critical Decoding of Advertisements in Flex Magazine', *Sociology of Sport,* 11: 18–39.

6

Sport in Advertising

KEY CONCEPTS

Persuasiveness	Currency of sport goods
Consumer capitalism	Distinction
Translation of meaning	Absence and identity
Sport as sign	Jokes

> This chapter proposes that sport advertisements sell us something more than the product advertised; they sell us ourselves by creating a structure in which we and the consumer goods associated with sport become interchangeable. The chapter demonstrates how the power of sport advertisements lies in the gaps between what is shown and the meanings the audience supplies to complete the picture. The importance of difference for advertisers selling their products is explored in relation to the way audiences seek social distinction through their consumption of advertising imagery. The case studies for the chapter consider the narrative in a commercial created for Super Bowl XLII in the United States and advertising sequences broadcast during the 2007 Rugby World Cup in the United Kingdom.

The Pervasiveness of Advertising

Advertising is everywhere. Dyer (1982: 1) even claimed that the omnipresence of advertising made it 'the "official art" of the advanced industrial nations of the west'. While the most recognisable form of advertising is commercial consumer advertising, which occupies space throughout the environment, from newspapers, magazines, and cinemas to billboards, television and the Internet, techniques from advertising are used by a multitude of noncommercial organisations and institutions to promote themselves and their services. Increasingly, as individuals, we are asked to draw on our familiarity with the principles of advertising to market ourselves to potential employers (or even partners using the plethora of online dating sites). Goddard (2002: 8) suggested that we should adopt a broad understanding of advertising to 'encompass the idea of texts whose intention is to enhance the image of an individual, group or organisation'.

The relationship between advertising and the mass media is very complex. Advertising does not just use the media to reach consumers; it is intrinsically integrated into every aspect of it. There is a symbiotic relationship between editorial control of media content and the advertising industry. Within the women's magazine industry, advertisers as well as readers are considered to be primary customers whose needs and interests must be considered (Gough-Yates 2003). Gough-Yates (2003: 135) used the term *advertorial* to capture the infusion of product promotion into editorials and celebrity interviews as well as features on travel and food.

The media endorses a way of life that hinges on the consumption of products being advertised. As early as 1974, Williams argued that advertisements are part of the flow of television, rather than an interruption to it. Advertising has been just as successfully integrated into the business of sport, changing its character irrevocably. The ever-present imprint of advertising on sport equipment and clothing means that it is difficult to engage in sport without encountering advertising. Advertising is also the channel that brings the media into the live sport experience. As you sit in the stadium during a break in the action, chances are that you will be treated to an array of advertisements around the field, in your programme and on the big screen. You might even find that products for sale in the stadium are being advertised to you as you consume them.

Major sports events offer a particularly compelling resource for advertisers due to the 'conventions of iconography, procedure, ceremony, media coverage, and of course, the deep emotional current of national pride and lifelong affiliation with a team or sport' (Coots 2007: 28). Jackson, Andrews and Scherer (2005: 8) argued that sport has an appeal for the marketing divisions of transnational corporations 'that stretches beyond the field of sport per se with sporting themes, images, narratives and celebrities located within and across a complex and increasingly global system of intertexual promotional cultures including movies, art, fashion, music and politics'. At each major sport spectacle, advertisers are poised to convert mass audiences into consumers. La Monica (2006) reported that thirty-second commercial spots during the 2006 Super Bowl were selling for $2.5 million. The appeal of such events to advertisers is clear: 'a gigantic audience is virtually guaranteed regardless of which teams are playing. More than 86 million people watched the Super Bowl [in 2005] in the U.S. according to Nielson Media Research' (La Monica 2006: para. 6).

Advertising and Consumer Capitalism

Advertising may be both ubiquitous and accepted as part of our daily lives, but nevertheless, it has always faced harsh criticism from those who insist that it creates 'false wants' and encourages 'the production and consumption of things that are incompatible with the fulfilment of genuine and urgent human needs' (Dyer 1982: 3). From this perspective, advertising tricks us into believing that our happiness lies in the personal possession of the products promoted, making us selfish and materialistic in our outlook. Dyer (1982) drew on Williams (1980) to show that the paradox of advertising is that it demonstrates that we are not materialistic enough: 'if we were, the presentation of the objects being sold would be enough' (Dyer 1982: 7). A pair of new trainers would be purchased solely for their utility as footwear, without reference to social or symbolic meanings. However, as Jhally (1990) cautions, the utility of goods cannot be separated from their symbolic affiliations. Advertising requires goods to be associated with magical qualities that make them appear to fulfil our personal and social aspirations. It is for this reason that Williamson (1978: 12) suggested that advertising does more than simply sell things to us: 'it creates structures of meaning.'

In her now classic work, *Decoding Advertisements,* Williamson (1978) examined the process of advertising, arguing that we can only understand what advertisements mean by discovering how they make things mean something to us. Williamson (1978) acknowledged that this is far from easy. It is difficult to detach ourselves from the pull of advertisements. In the foreword to her book, Williamson (1978) positioned herself as being simultaneously drawn to advertisements, whilst wanting intellectually to be critical of them. She suggested that this is the power of ideology: 'feelings (ideology) lag behind knowledge (science)' (Williamson 1978: 9). Her argument is that our very selves become implicated in the advertisement, and to understand this process, we need to pay attention to how advertising works. This chapter will focus on a number of Williamson's (1978) analytical techniques and insights to consider how they might help make sense of advertising surrounding sport.

How Does Sport Advertising Work?

According to Williamson (1978), 'advertising-work' involves levels of translation from one world to another. To persuade us to buy a given product, an advertisement needs to show how that simple object can fulfil our rather more complex human needs. To do this, Williamson (1978: 12) showed that advertisements provide a structure capable of transforming the language of objects into that of people, and vice versa. A familiar example is the long-standing romantic symbolism of diamonds. To understand a diamond in its own terms, as a mineral, is to see it as an extremely hard, highly refractive crystalline form of carbon. However, in human terms, it is a sign for eternal love. An advertisement for the diamond merchants Kingston comprises a large image of a diamond-encrusted ring next to the text

SHE LOVES YOU
SHE LOVES YOU NOT
SHE LOVES YOU
SHE LOVES YOU

The advertisement appears to promise that any doubt about the sincerity of our partner's love can be quashed by the gift of a diamond ring. As we become used to the transformation of object language to human language, we forget that the translation has taken place. Instead, we take the object for what it stands for: the diamond means love and endurance. Then we begin to translate in the other direction, thinking that what we want is a diamond because the diamond means love. As Williamson (1978: 12) said, our complete immersion in this discourse means that we 'skip translating altogether: taking the sign for what it signifies, the thing for the feeling'.

It is important to understand, therefore, that advertisements are always involved in selling us something more than a product or service. Williamson's (1978) work enables us to see that advertisements provide a structure in which we and consumer goods become interchangeable. In doing so, Williamson (1978: 13) argued, 'they are selling us ourselves.' As Sarup (1996) observed, there has been a shift in ways of thinking about identity and the self. No longer is it assumed that someone has a core identity, in place from birth throughout the lifespan; rather, identity is widely considered to arise in interaction with others, and academic thought has focused on the processes by which identity is constructed. In contrast to the idea that people have a coherent, fixed identity, 'the more recent view is that identity is fabricated, constructed, in process' (Sarup 1996: 14). Advertising steps into this gap and encourages us to identify ourselves with what we consume.

Translating Meanings in Sport Advertising

Williamson (1978) argued that part of the myth of advertising is that it is transparent, that it is merely saying what it claims to say. While we can think of advertisements as containing a message ('buy this book'), we need to consider not just the content of advertising, but its form. The surface meaning of an advertisement is only one level of signification. The way the advertisement is constructed also has a meaning. The watch brand Tag Heuer has used images of celebrities from sport and film in a series of advertisements carrying the strapline 'What are you made of?' One of the advertisements that appeared in the press features the golfer Tiger Woods. The full-page advertisement contains two images of equivalent size, each vertically occupying half of the page. On the left is an image of Tiger Woods in a position that indicates he has just completed a golf swing, twisted, holding his golf club over his shoulder and across his back. He is side on to the viewer, facing towards the other half of the page, his gaze focused in the distance. An image of a metallic watch takes up the rest of the page, beneath which is the Tag Heuer logo and brand name. The images are not touching and no obvious connection is made between them. However, the colours and shapes in the advertisement link the images and ideas. The position of Woods's body mirrors the shape of the watch, with the widest part of each occupying the same plane. The images are placed against a plain background of silver and grey. The metallic grey of the watch is slightly lighter than the background, and Tiger Woods's clothes are also grey. Both images are lit from the side so that there is a shine on the surface of the watch and the side of Woods's body. The light also makes the golf club gleam with a metallic glow, and there is a reflection on Woods's face (see http://www.tagheuer.com for similar advertisements).

Williamson (1978: 21) made the observation that 'colour tells a story'. In the Tag Heuer advertisement, the play of colour and light connect the product to the image of the golfer. Qualities associated with Tiger Woods are transferred to the watch, and in reverse, qualities of the watch are transferred to Woods. The emphasis on metal connotes machinery and perseverance (mettle). The shine connotes glamour and prestige. The advertisement suggests that the watch performs like Tiger Woods, and that Tiger Woods performs like the watch. Yet the 'message' of the advertisement is not in its content, it is in the form. Importantly, the message is not complete. The strapline 'What are you made of?' is an open challenge to the consumer to find the answer. The advertisement asks consumers to step into the gaps between the elements of imagery and connect Tiger Woods, the watch and themselves. 'What are you made of?' could refer to your character, your physicality or your class. The consumer is asked to finish the advertisement, providing its meaning. The consumer imbues the object with the qualities of the person and thinks of the person in terms of the object.

The Object and the Sport Sign

Colour in advertisements can connect *objects with other objects, objects with a lifestyle or a social world,* or an *object with a person.* These sets of relationships can be seen in the advertising arising from the electronics firm Samsung's sponsorship of the English Premier League football club Chelsea. The blue of the Chelsea kit is mirrored in the blue of Samsung's logo so that it becomes unclear whether Samsung is advertising Chelsea or Chelsea is advertising Samsung. Advertisements for Samsung digital cameras featuring the Chelsea footballer Joe Cole assume an association between a sporting body and an electronic product despite their lack of inherent connection.

Joe Cole is well known for his adaptability on the soccer pitch. Within various soccer formations, he is able to play left or right in a midfield four, left or right in an attacking front three, or he can take on the playmaker role behind the front two strikers. A Samsung advertisement, split into three horizontal sections, depicts the footballer's different skills. The top panel features three images of Joe Cole controlling the ball, making an overhead kick and heading the ball. The middle panel features Cole taking a shot on goal (the goalkeeper's black leather glove is just visible to the right of the scene). In the bottom panel, Cole is featured dribbling the ball, leaving exasperated defenders in his wake. The explicit connections to the Samsung product are minimal. There is no image of the product (Samsung's NV camera series) within the advertisement. The only reference to the camera series is made in small text beneath each set of images: 'Like Joe Cole, the NV3 is a multitalented performer', 'Like Joe Cole, the NV10 takes a great shot' and 'Like Joe Cole, the NV7 is always in control'. Yet, clearly, a camera and a footballer are not very like each other at all.

The connections that the advertisement seeks to make belong to another sign system in which Joe Cole is a celebrity footballer, epitomising the glamour and success of Chelsea. As a result, the more subtle connections to the product are made visually, predominately through colour. The background is a dark blue landscape, featuring sea and a turbulent, cloudy sky. The ball is a dark, silver-grey sphere, surrounded by a bright blue glow, with a transparent blue tail like that of a comet, lending the scene as a whole, and the ball in particular, a mystical, almost religious quality. The colours of the ball are those of the product. The connections are made with an absent product by colour association.

The advertisement uses an existing sign system, the aura of Chelsea footballer Joe Cole's 'body language', and translates it into another system: the world of electronic consumer goods. As Williamson (1978: 25) said, 'advertisements are constantly translating between systems of meaning, and therefore constitute a vast meta-system where values from different areas of our lives are made interchangeable.' Samsung does not invent a meaning for the camera, but translates meaning for it by an already existing sign system that consumers understand (the significance of Joe Cole).

What a Feeling: the Currency of Sport Goods

Advertisements enable the transfer of emotions to products. Williamson (1978) suggested that the product is constructed as an intermediary currency to buy a positive feeling: love, happiness, success, popularity. While money cannot buy love, it can buy a commodity, which appears to get you what you want. By purchasing the Tag Heuer watch, the advertisements suggest that you are buying the status and success of Tiger Woods. An advertisement for a Ford Focus sports car presents fast-moving scenes of empty roads by day and night, suggesting that the purchase of the car will get you the thrill and sense of freedom of driving for sport along roads laid out like a racetrack. As Williamson (1978: 38) observed, 'the product not only represents an emotional experience, but becomes the experience and produces it.'

The connections that advertisements make are often visual, without linguistic explanation or justification. The Tag Heuer watch is simply placed next to Tiger Woods. The logic of the advertisement relies on the connection being made by the consumer. Knowledge about what sport stars like Tiger Woods or Joe Cole mean is necessarily supplied by the consumer. It is not Joe Cole's body that is important, but what his body signifies in the sign system of celebrity football. But the consumer is not necessarily aware that he or she knows what Joe Cole or Tiger Woods means until they encounter the advertisement and recognise the meaning. Our involvement in the advertisement brings those meanings into being.

Sport, Advertising and Distinction

Advertisements' lack of explicit narrative links between objects is part of their effectiveness as ideology. If they do not make explicit their claims, they cannot be questioned. If they present connections by juxtaposition, leaving us as consumers to fill in the gaps, we become implicated in the advertisements ourselves. We construct the meaning for the product on the basis of what we already know. The perceived truth of the advertisement is thereby unassailable. Yet this is not all—we are also created as particular kinds of subjects by the meanings we make of the products in the advertisements. To achieve this, the marking of difference is a vital part of advertising.

Advertisers must market their goods as distinctive with particular, desirable features. There may be very little real difference between brands of products within any one category: washing powder, sneakers, cars, drinks. Very often, two or more brands that appear to be in competition with each other are manufactured by the same company. For example, Lifebuoy, Lux and Dove soap are all brands of the company Unilever; nevertheless, these products are sharply differentiated for us in advertising campaigns.

Nike, Adidas and Reebok are all well-known brands of sport shoes, clothing and equipment. Advertising strategy for these brands constructs an identity for each by marking it as different from the others. Nike style is constructed as different from Adidas style or Reebok style. In the United Kingdom, all three manufacture boots (cleats) for soccer. Many things are common to all three lines: the function of each boot is the same; the sport is the same; all are associated with global football celebrities playing in the English Premier League. However, the advertising strategy for each brand draws on existing meanings of soccer and soccer stars in the United Kingdom to differentiate its product. Nike has tended to use players with controversial reputations such as the French footballer Eric Cantona, who gained notoriety for launching a kung fu–style kick at a Crystal Palace fan while playing for Manchester United in 1995. Nike has run advertising campaigns that feature a new, faster, more efficient version of soccer, transferring the associations with edginess to their product. In these advertisements, soccer is framed as rationalised, postnational entertainment.

Meanwhile, Adidas advertising campaigns have focused on the idiosyncratic nature of soccer customs and meanings in the United Kingdom. One advertisement series from 2005 featured a narrator questioning the logic of traditions associated with British grass roots football, accompanied by the song 'Sound of the Suburbs' by the 1970s British punk band the Members. The song detailed the banality of English suburban life. Nostalgia and an emphasis on the local in the context of global football differentiate the Adidas product from Nike. By contrast to these aesthetically styled campaigns, Reebok campaigns have emphasised everyday football integrity on the part of celebrity players such as Ryan Giggs, with straplines such as 'I am what I am' and 'true football'.

As we engage with the meaning systems of the advertisements and make our choice of product, we, too, become differentiated into Nike, Adidas or Reebok consumers. The relationship between choice and personal and social identity can be linked to broader social relationships. Jhally (1990: 6) stated, 'Goods always mean something within a social context where different interests are being played out.' Our interests may be shaped by our sense of who we are and how we perceive the world. Bourdieu (1979) argued that our 'tastes' or 'manifested preferences' were largely shaped by our class identities or habitus. For Bourdieu, *habitus* refers to the ways that individuals develop their ideas about the world, their values, desires and ambitions. He argued that consumer and lifestyle choices reflected a conscious and unconscious impetus towards creating and maintaining class-based distinctions. Our choice of products represents an expression of 'class, background, and cultural identity. Hence the connection between taste, identity, and everyday acts of consumption' (Paterson 2006: 37). The associations between class and taste have implications for maintaining inequitable power relations and social hierarchies. Later work has challenged the centrality of class structures in determining taste, arguing that consumption can better be represented as more fluid, contingent and fleeting in the context of ongoing social changes and groupings (Paterson 2006).

Williamson (1978) also linked social structures to product differentiation. She drew on Marxist insights into the operation of ideology to suggest that this process of creating difference between objects, relying as it does on the sign value attached to the products, imposed systems of social difference over real, structural differences between people. While groups such as the low-paid single parents and the elderly (and many more) exist in society with genuine interests in common—groups that would benefit from self-recognition to unite in campaigning for fair treatment and equal rights—these are not the differences between people that we see in advertising. Instead, we imagine that the differences between us lie in our choice of consumer goods. One of the paradoxes of advertising is the need to address each consumer as unique—you are different, but so is everyone else. Slogans such as the recent strapline for the UK food and fashion retailer Marks and Spencer, 'exclusively for everyone', make the contradiction clear.

Absence and Identity in Advertisements

The address of advertisements, therefore, is to a unified subject differentiated from others who do not consume the product advertised. However, theories of identity drawing on Lacanian psychoanalysis argue that the unitary subject is a myth: "the subject is split; but an ideological world conceals this from the conscious subject, who is supposed to feel whole and certain of a sexual identity" (Sarup 1996: 34). Lacan argues that the mirror stage is a vital part of identity formation, when the child misrecognises itself in its reflection as more complete and powerful than it feels (see Chapter 5). Advertisements present to us ideal images of coherent selves constituted through the consumption of a product resulting in a similar process of misrecognition. Advertising depends on this being achieved through the consumer's engagement with a complex sign system. Since identity is fragmented, rather than unitary, advertising offers us images of the different facets of the self. A Nike-Women.com print advertisement with the strapline THE ART OF CONTRADICTION AT NIKE-WOMEN. COM featured an image split into two: the top half of the advertisement showed female hands (signified by a silver bracelet) pulling on the handles of exercise equipment, which merged into the bottom half of the advertisement, showing a corkscrew attached to a cork. The advertisement presented dual faces of femininity: the gym-goer and the hostess. The traditional feminine art of conversation is morphed in the art of contradiction by a vigorous workout. The consumer was invited to step into this split and ease the contradiction by cracking the joke. Once the consumer gets the play on language and imagery, she steps into the place of the whole subject, becoming the mirror offering the coherent reflection back to this seemingly fragmented self.

Jokes require something to be left out. Absences, puzzles or jokes in advertisements include gaps that need to be supplied by the consumer. However, our conscious, active involvement with deciphering the oblique reference or absent meaning distracts us from the realisation that we already engaged in constructing the meaning of the advertisement. Advertising presents itself as if it is a reflection of reality (we already know the meanings it draws on and connects to its products). By supplying the meanings of the advertisement, the consumer is tied into the assumption that the advertisement simply represents the world as it is. Yet advertisements are creative constructions: interpretations of the world, not reflections.

Advertisers may also play on their perceptions of consumer self-awareness and ability to get the joke to create a sense of shared perspectives on the world. Goldman (1992: 181) discussed the 'knowing wink' approach used in a series of Levi's advertisements which drew on popular critiques of 'consumer conformism'. Viewers were encouraged to adopt a self-reflexive subject position that connected them to the advertisements' message that Levi's unshrunk jeans are designed to accentuate individuality as they shape themselves to the body of the wearer. The message was reinforced by the characters, who were portrayed as real-life individuals, rather than slick-looking models. Viewers were encouraged to connect with the characters and the product through a shared world perspective constituted by an ironic stance about mass consumer culture and a valuing of nonconformity.

McKay (2005) argued that Nike advertising should be understood in terms of its articulation of myths. Myths are '*partial* truths that accentuate particular versions of reality and marginalize or omit others' (McKay 2005: 83). Nevertheless, myths are presented to us in advertising as obvious and enduring. Drawing on the work of Barthes (1973), McKay suggested that Nike advertisements present a mythic universe in which the 'naturally' strong compete against the weak, minimising structural inequalities which might privilege some over others. McKay considered advertisements which extend the famous 'Just Do It' slogan into all areas of social life, implying social advancement is a matter of individual free will. Nike advertisements consistently leave out references to social realities which mitigate against success. For example, they feature athletes from marginalised ethnic groups and present a rags-to-riches narrative apparently achieved through strength of character. McKay (2005: 87) pointed to the overwhelming evidence that success in sport is an unobtainable dream for the majority, not mentioning the 'social inequalities of class, race, age, and gender that pervade sport itself and the global exploitation of labor undergirding the production and consumption of these companies' advertising slogans'. These constitute the absences of the advertisement.

Case Study: Meaning between the Gaps—Humour and Identity in Rugby Advertisements

Advertisements are often created specifically to tie into major televised sport spectacles. The car manufacturer Peugeot sponsored the 2007 Rugby World Cup as broadcast on the UK television station ITV. Peugeot created a sequence of short advertisements announcing its sponsorship of the event to play at the beginning and end of commercial breaks during airtime. The advertisements featured a group of white male rugby fans driving around France, the host nation for the tournament, comprising an Englishman, a Scotsman, an Irishman and a Welshman. Each character wore his national team's rugby shirt and was coded with national stereotypic signifiers (e.g. while the others wore shorts, the Scotsman wore a kilt). No rugby was shown during the advertisements, but their location at the start and end of broadcasts of live rugby meant that rugby was intertextually referenced by its absence. The absent-presence of rugby provided the underlying meaning of the advertisement, justifying the depiction of a group of men driving around through the French landscape, but it was a meaning supplied by the viewer. The viewer, therefore, was complicit in getting the joke, which hinged on the intimate homosocial environment created by the four disparate identities inhabiting the space of the car.

The introductory advertisement began with an extremely close shot of the Welsh character ostensibly adjusting the camera before returning to join the others by the car posed for a group shot. The narrative, therefore, presented the sequence of advertisements as a 'home movie' documentation of their road trip to the Rugby World Cup. The body language of the Welshman—frowning with concentration into the camera lens, running back to the group in an ungainly manner, grinning broadly at the camera and being the first to introduce himself—connoted an eager, unrefined personality, well intentioned but lacking in poise. The other characters are presented as more self-controlled (e.g. the Welshman's hair was uncombed and his beard unshaven, while the others were much neater). Placed in front of the group, the Englishman's stance was open and relaxed, while the Irishman was squeezed between the Welshman and the Englishman and introduced himself with hesitancy, connoting shyness or self-effacement. The Scotsman was the tallest of the group and was

---

ANALYSING THE PEUGEOT RUGBY WORLD CUP ADVERTISEMENTS

Television advertisements last only a brief time but require a great deal of resources to produce. Advertisers, therefore, make each detail count. To analyse the series of advertisements created to mark Peugeot's sponsorship of the 2007 Rugby World Cup, we applied techniques for analysing television (see Chapter 3) to each advertisement. We considered it to be even more necessary, however, to take account of every tiny element of activity in each of the five channels of communication: graphics, image, voice, sound effects and music. As with television, this required us to repeatedly replay the advertisements to note all the communication. The signification was described for the individual advertisements at the level of denotation. After that, the connotative associations of the signs with the advertisements were explored. In particular, absences and gaps in meanings were identified, where the television viewer was expected to supply missing knowledge to complete the narrative. Since the advertisements were in a series, we reflected on the way the continuous narrative required the viewer to fill in gaps between each of the advertisements. In this way, we were able to point to the way that the viewer supplied the meanings to enable the advertisement to do their work.

positioned next to the car, his hand on his hip, physically occupying more space. The names of the characters, Gavin (Welsh), Ben (Scots), Reece (English), and Connor (Irish), carried varying associations with nationality and sophistication.

Within the group, Reece, the Englishman, was presented as the most adult and dependable, being the car's driver and the group leader. Gavin, the Welshman, by contrast, was the group's most childlike character. Many commentators have pointed to a hierarchy within the group of nations that constitute Britain and Ireland. For example, Davey (1999: 6) argued that the overarching identity of Britishness has simply concealed the dominance of Englishness with the multinational state of the United Kingdom: 'the Scots, the Welsh and the Irish may have dual identifications, but for the Anglo-British, Britain serves as another name for the ambitious and self confident England that has existed as a nation state since the fourteenth century.' Within the Peugeot advertisements, the English character was positioned as quietly, but obviously, in charge. In British popular culture, the other nations have been made the butt of jokes. In recent years, anti-Welsh jokes made by high-profile celebrities have drawn media attention. For example, in 2001, Anne Robinson, the presenter of the British Broadcasting Corporation quiz show *The Weakest Link,* caused much controversy with her anti-Welsh comments. The Peugeot advertisements continued this thread, making the Welsh character's confusion a focus of the humour.

Along for the Ride

In one of the sequences, lasting only nine seconds, the camera was positioned as if being held by someone in the back seat of the car, capturing shots of the backs of the heads of Gavin (Welsh) in the front passenger seat and Reece (English) in the driver's seat as well as traffic in a French city street, visible through the windscreen. A reflection in the driver's mirror of eyes shaded by sunglasses reflected back a gaze, uniting the viewer's perspective with that of Reece, the source of the reflection. The focus of the short sequence was a snippet of seemingly ongoing conversation. Gavin's words started the sequence: 'I came out to watch the rugby, boys', greeted with 'Oh really' from Reece. Realising the potentiality of his statement to be read as homosexual desire, Gavin quickly attempted to clarify his meaning: 'Not "watch the rugby boys"'. Uproars of laughter from the others caused him to try again: 'I came out to watch the rugby. Full stop. Boys', before the sequence ended.

In another sequence, the characters were featured ordering food from a French waitress at a roadside restaurant. The scene opened with Reece ordering in French, 'Le Chateaubriand, s'il vous plait.' As the waitress turned to Gavin, 'Monsieur?' Gavin responded with, 'Chicken tikka, please toots.' Gavin's lack of cultural sensitivity is exaggerated by ordering a meal typically consumed in Britain by groups of men after a night in the pub. Gavin's infantile character, in contrast to Reece's maturity, was a constant theme. In one sequence, Reece called him 'an idiot' for delaying them because of a 'dodgy crêpe'. In another, Gavin was depicted constantly asking 'can I drive now?', in an echo of children irritatingly enquiring 'are we there yet?' throughout a car journey.

Reece was always shown behind the wheel, despite the other characters moving between the front and back seats. Gavin had moved to the back of the car for the second of two sequences involving hitchhiking backpackers. In the first, unable to tell the sex of the hitchhiker from behind, the car was shown slowing to offer a lift to a backpacker, only to drive on when he turned out to be male. The second hitchhiking sequence showed Gavin eagerly opening the car door for a female backpacker, saying, 'I can budge up' and making a stereotypic assumption about her nationality (using Australian slang for a female): 'Good day, Sheila'.

Getting the Joke: Stepping into Meaning

The differences between the characters in the advertisements are presented to the viewer without any other comment than laughter or derision targeted at Gavin, enabling viewers to similarly distance themselves from his character. As a result, the world appears as depicted, rather than as an interpretation of reality. The fragmented and contradictory national identity of British sport viewers is represented by the different national characters in the small space of the car. The viewer is asked to supply the absent meaning that Gavin's behaviour is embarrassing, but familiar and well meaning, to get the joke running throughout the sequences. As a result, the viewer provides a mirror to reflect back a unified national identity, sealing the fissures between the different nations. This idealised view of the nation/nations of Britain was constructed as a cosy community of heterosexual men. In one sequence, all four were heard singing Kenny Rogers's 'The Gambler', adopted as an unofficial anthem by the English rugby team during the World Cup, indicating that the Britishness that the viewer is asked to reflect back is one that incorporates the other nations within an expanded notion of Englishness. Other contradictions within the sequence focused on sexuality. The potential of homosexual desire in men watching other men play sport was made into a joke to diffuse that tension. In getting the joke, the viewer was required to supply the 'obviousness' that rugby fans are not homosexual. To underline the message, the characters were depicted as heterosexual predators, only picking up female hitchhikers. Gavin's naivety and childlishness was deployed to undermine any negative readings of the situation.

The sequence of advertisements translated the meaning system of heterosexual masculinity and national identity onto an object: 'the new Peugeot 308'. By interspersing the broadcast of the sequences throughout the rugby, the narrative became interwoven into the sport spectacle. The gaps between the sequences, which were shown as if they were moments of an unfurling story, were completed by the viewer supplying the missing reference to the drama of the World Cup competition moving from stadium to stadium throughout France. As a result, the advertisement organised an exchange of meaning between the people and the car through an absent reference to sport. Sport fans, waiting for the game to recommence, were asked to transfer the magic of the Rugby World Cup to the Peugeot 308.

Case Study: Super Bowl Advertising— Bigger Than the Game?

Advertising has become a central feature of the National Football League (NFL) Super Bowl (Horovitz 2008). Approximately fifty-four commercials were shown during Super Bowl XLII in 2008. A pregame survey by Hanon McKendry found that 57 per cent of US adults who planned to watch the Super Bowl were watching for the advertisements as much as (or even more than) for the game itself (Reuters 2008). After the game, *The New York Times* reported that 'the commercials "got a higher audience than the game" in homes with the TiVo video recorder service' (Elliott 2008). During the game, the announcers reminded viewers that they could access any commercials that they missed on MySpace. In addition, viewers were able to vote for their favourite advertisement on a number of different Web site polls, including *USA Today's* real-time ad meter, MySpace, and AOL. Super Bowl XLII proved to be an exciting game watched by 97.5 million viewers in the United States, and the outcome, an unpredicted loss for the previously unbeaten New England Patriots, hinged on the final play.

One of the themes present in the build-up to Super Bowl XLII was the pursuit of perfection evidenced in the New England Patriots' pursuit of a 'perfect' record, a whole season without losing a game. During the pregame show, there was an NFL promotional narrated by Russell Crowe that focused on perfection. Amidst a back-drop of images of iconic paintings, such as the *Mona Lisa,* and famous individuals, such as Martin Luther King, Einstein and Amelia Earhart, Crowe's voice-over ex-tolled the pursuit of perfection and the ways that it is embodied in the Super Bowl— not only in the Patriots' goal of a season without any losses, but in the New York Giants' desire to be perfect on the day. The piece concluded, 'Be inspired by the pursuit of perfection you will see today. Whatever it means to us, whether it's to be better at our own job, to be a better friend, to be a better parent because if they can strive for it, in our own way maybe we can too' (*Fox Super Bowl Sunday Pregame Show* 2008). Themes of working hard, pursuing success and striving for perfection were echoed within the broadcast as well as within one of the most popular adver-tisements that ran during the game.

Hank the Horse and the Spirit of Rocky

The favourite advertisement during the Super Bowl, according to the *USA Today* ad meter 2008, was a *Rocky*-themed spot by Budweiser featuring a Clydesdale horse named 'Hank' and a Dalmation. The spot began with a country scene, with sunlight streaming through the trees. Two horses stood facing another small group of horses, accompanied by two men in red Budweiser caps. One of the men announced, 'The final horse for this year's team is Thunder.' The horse identified as Thunder walked over to the group, leaving its companion on its own. The remaining horse was consoled by the man: 'Maybe next year, Hank.' A close-up of Hank was accompanied by slow, sad music as the rejected horse watched others that had earned places on the team preparing to pull the Budweiser wagon. The scene ended with a barking Dalmatian running over to the horse, as Hank whinnied his response. The dog trotted away, and Hank followed behind.

The next scene opened with the dog running down a dirt lane, with Hank behind him, to the sound of the *Rocky* theme tune. A series of training scenes followed, as Hank was shown getting stronger and faster through the course of a year. Hank was depicted hoisting a bale of hay up to the loft of a barn with the dog perched on top and going though tough night exercises as the dog watched in the pouring rain. In the light of day, Hank was then shown pulling an empty flatbed of a freight train against a mountain backdrop. Amidst autumn leaves, the pair continued to train, and in a winter landscape, Hank was shown completing weaving manoeuvres through birch trees in the snow. The final training scene returned to the railroad, as Hank was shown finally capable of pulling a fully loaded freight car down the track. The scene revealed Hank's new found speed and strength as the *Rocky* song reached its climax, recalling Rocky's triumphant run up the steps of the Philadelphia Museum of Art. The words 'One year later' appeared on the screen. Heraldic music played as Hank whinnied, emerging from the barn, in full harness, led by a Budweiser employee. The man who rejected him before announced, 'Welcome aboard, Hank.' The Dalmation barked and was shown lifting a paw to give Hank a high five. The final scene showed the full cart with Hank on the team, as the Budweiser logo and strapline appeared on the screen, 'The Great American Lager'.

Sport, Animals and Ideology

The advertisement drew on familiar themes of hard work and meritocracy that are often associated with sporting practices and US national identity as the 'land of opportunity'. The appeal of the advertisement was attributed to its positive, heart-warming message during a time of political and economic unrest in the United States. According to Lachky, the chief creative officer for Anheuser Busch, 'it is a spot about tradition, about the little guy succeeding' (Horowitz 2008). The story was invested with connotations of blue-collar or working-class codes. For example, the Dalmatian is associated with the profession of firefighting, and the Clydesdale is a strong working horse. The Clydesdale is known in popular imagery as a symbol of Budweiser, serving as a nostalgic reference to the past, when horses, rather than trucks, delivered Budweiser beer. The familiar music from *Rocky* worked intertextually by invoking the film's themes of working-class struggle, the pursuit of success, hard work, emotion, humility, determination and perseverance. The appeal of the spot also mirrored the themes of the sporting event—striving for perfection—and the emotions associated with triumph and success after hard work and sacrifice. Kelley and Turley (2004) suggested that the infusion of emotional appeals within Super Bowl advertisements succeeds in part because of spectators' expectations of experiencing emotional and affective feelings during the game. The narrative of the advertisement intertextually referenced the themes, emotions and values associated with sporting spectacles, without making explicit reference to either the film *Rocky* or the game itself.

Rocky (1976) and its numerous sequels have been used in a range of advertisements, and the films maintain an ongoing and powerful presence within US popular culture. Elmwood (2005: 56) suggested that the Rocky films provide a particular understanding of US national character through recalling a 'Revolutionary heritage', with its ideals of civic engagement and democracy, while simultaneously underplaying the presence of societal tensions around race and gender. These absences are also echoed in the Budweiser advertisement. The spirit of meritocracy in the advertisement obscures evidence that mobility in the United States is lower than in other comparable industrial nations ('Land of Opportunity?' 2007). It also underplayed the well-recognised difficulty of achieving social advancement through sport (Nixon 1984). Ironically, Hank's achievement was symbolically portrayed by being harnessed to the wagon along with the rest of the team, which, in another context, could be associated with Marxist critiques of capitalism and issues of 'alienated labour' and worker exploitation. Instead, the mythology of the American dream is associated with the 'Great American Lager' in a feel-good story of achievement reinforced by its positioning within the spectacle of the Super Bowl.

CHAPTER SUMMARY

- Advertisement is an omnipresent feature of advanced capitalism, and we are increasingly asked to understand ourselves within the discourse of advertising
- Sport offers a compelling resource for advertisers because of the meanings and passion that consumers already invest in teams and players
- We can only understand what advertisements mean by unpacking the ways they make things mean something to us
- Advertising involves translating one system of meaning onto another, connecting products with desirable people, objects, lifestyles or a social world
- Meaning is made through absences in the narrative of advertisements, and the consumer completes the circuit of meaning by 'getting the joke'
- Sport and sport events may not be explicit in the narrative of advertisements but are often referenced intertextually, invoking the host of associations that circulate around sport in society

---

Suggestions for Analysis

Advertisements have become an inseparable feature of the mediation of sport spectacles and megaevents. Advertising campaigns are often specifically created to air during a sport event. Even when the advertisements may not explicitly contain sport-related content, they often reference the event by its absence. The viewer understands that the advertisement is part of the flow of the event and supplies that knowledge before it can make sense. The sport event may be what sustains a narrative across a number of advertisements, without any sport being shown. Record the advertisements broadcast during a sport megaevent, such as the Federation Internationale de Football Association (FIFA) World Cup, and consider the way sport is referenced by its presence and absence. Television advertisements may only be one part of an advertising campaign that embraces newspapers, magazines, the Internet, the sportscape and the clothes of performers, billboards and other aspects of urban architecture. In what ways do advertisers use the variety of media forms at their disposal? What connections are made between them?

Further Reading

Andrews, D. L. (1996), 'Introduction: Deconstructing Michael Jordan: Reconstructing Post-industrial America', *Sociology of Sport Journal,* 13: 315–18.

Cole, C., and Hribar, A. (1995), 'Celebrity Feminism: Nike Style Post-Fordism, Transcendence, and Consumer Power', *Sociology of Sport Journal,* 12: 347–69.

Dyer, G. (1982), *Advertising as Communication,* London: Methuen.

Hillyard, D. (1994), 'Televised Sport and the (Anti)Sociological Imagination', *Journal of Sport and Social Issues,* 18: 88–99.

Jackson, S., Andrews, D., and Scherer, J., eds (2005), *Sport, Culture and Advertising: Identities, Commodities and the Politics of Representation,* London: Routledge.

Jhally, S. (1987), *The Codes of Advertising: Fetishism and the Political Economy of Meaning in the Consumer Society,* London: Routledge.

Scherer, J., and Jackson, S. J. (2007), 'Sports Advertising, Cultural Production and Corporate Nationalism at the Global-Local Nexus: Branding the New Zealand All Blacks', *Sport in Society,* 10: 268–84.

Silk, M., and Andrews, D. L. (2001), 'Beyond a Boundary? Sport, Transnational Advertising, and the Reimagining of National Culture', *Journal of Sport and Social Issues,* 25: 180–201.

Williamson, J. (1978), *Decoding Advertisements: Ideology and Meaning in Advertising,* London: Marion Boyars.

7

Sport, Media and Visual Culture

KEY CONCEPTS

Spectacle	Panopticon
Materiality	Power/knowledge
Performativity	Apparatus and technologies
Flâneur	Subjectivities
Exhibitionary complex	Strategies and tactics

Guy Debord (1994) claimed that we live in a society of the spectacle, referring the importance of the field of vision in making the world meaningful to us. Contemporary culture foregrounds visual experiences: we interact with visual texts and signs, we are stimulated and entertained by still and moving images, and we are surrounded by objects and places designed to be seen and appreciated in three dimensions. Technologies allow us to see more and more: endoscopic medical procedures are able to image the inside of the body, surveillance cameras monitor people without their knowledge, and biometric devices are able to identify people by scanning the retina of the eye. It is possible to say, therefore, that we live within a very visual culture, and imagery associated with sport has begun to permeate more and more aspects of our lives.

Media sport is not confined to watching the game on television, or reading about it in a newspaper or magazine. Advertisements on billboards pepper our cities' transport networks, featuring sports stars or sports images in association with all manner of goods and services. Big screens are erected in public spaces to show sports events, sports shows sell televisions in shop windows, portable video game consoles let you play simulated sport on the go, and passers-by are regularly adorned with the logos of sports clothing brands. Going to a live sport event entails engagement with a variety of mediated sport experiences, including the programmes, newspapers and scorecards you collect on the way, the advertisements in the shops and bars you pass by, the logo on the ticket you show, the big screen in the stadium and the advertisements on the scoreboard. While the majority of these experiences are dominated by the visual, they also intersect with other sensory experiences, like touch, smell, taste and hearing as in: drinking a beer in a cup emblazoned with the logo of your team, smelling the food of the people behind you, feeling the heat of the sun, and listening to the crowd singing. Watching a game is a visual spectacle, but the total experience is also an intersensory one.

Materiality and Performativity

There is no shortage of objects that we can associate with media sport. Cars, balls, shoes, bags, toys, replica team shirts, mobile phones, all resonate with meanings, discourses and mythologies constructed through the sport media and within advertising campaigns. Often they remain imprinted with logos, traces of the global, and the media-driven economy of consumer capitalism. A *Chelsea* soccer shirt, for example, is a media object: it retains its links to the team's media celebrities that are seen wearing it, and it carries three logos, media signifiers of the club and its sponsors: *SAMSUNG MOBILE* written across the chest, the circular *Chelsea Football Club* logo above the left breast, and a smaller *Adidas* logo underneath the collar. But the shirt is not simply a representation. It has three dimensions: it is an item that exists in the world in a concrete form; it combines imagery with physicality; and, its weight and volume, the way it looks and feels, its shape and texture. Rose (2007: 219) suggested that these sensual qualities of the object can be understood as their 'materiality'. Objects, however, are not simply material things, they are reflections of the wider lives of communities and individuals. People have social relationships with things:

The things that we relate to have embodied within them the social relations that gave rise to them through their design, the work of producing them, their prior use, the intention to communicate through them and their place within an existing cultural system of objects (Dant, 1999: 2).

Objects have a context; they become meaningful as people use them and give them meaning. For Rose (2007: 220), this can be understood as their performative dimension. An object or image 'may have a range of potential meanings, but they are latent until mobilized in a specific context'. As they engage with visual culture, individuals themselves come into being through their use of things. Rose (2007) gave the example of a person gazing at a painting in an art gallery. Only in this context does the painting become art and the person a connoisseur. What we do with things, the way we display them, store them, archive them and catalogue them, gives them the meaning they have. The arrangement of sporting objects in a museum display or a shop window can construct them as interesting curiosities, objects to revere or desirable possessions. Simultaneously, the person responsible for the arrangement is constructed as a museum curator or a window dresser, and the onlooker as a cultured museum visitor or a shopper. In this sense, the object can be understood as a performance, resulting in the 'co-constitution of image and observer' (Rose 2007: 220).

Ambient Television Sport

It is possible to see this dual concern with the materiality and performative dimensions of the media object in McCarthy's (2001) study of televisions located outside of the home. McCarthy (2001: 1) was interested in analysing televisions placed within the public sphere: 'the store, the waiting room, the bar, the train station, the airport'. Her aim was to trace how the positioning and meanings attached to television in public places 'blend with the social conventions and power structures of its locale' (McCarthy 2001: 2). This kind of cultural geography of the city draws on Benjamin's (1983) reflections of the figure of the flâneur in nineteenth-century Paris.

Benjamin was fascinated by the metropolis, writing a series of reflections on European cities in the 1920s and 1930s. In 1927, he began an analysis of the Parisian shopping arcades in the nineteenth century, called the 'Passagenarbeit', or 'Arcades Project'. The project was not finished in his lifetime and remains a collection of notes, drafts and quotations (see http://www.othervoices.org/gpeaker/Pas sagenwerk.php). A long section is concerned with the writings of the poet Charles Baudelaire. Benjamin was interested in a figure from Baudelaire's poetry, the flâneur, the gentleman of leisure strolling through Paris. The flâneur's deliberate distancing of himself from the crowds allowed him to perceive the city as a spectacle of delights for his entertainment.

Like the flâneur, contemporary consumers are presented with a series of spectacles as they traverse the city. Signs, screens, events and window displays all have the effect of discursively positioning them as subjects, sometimes as shoppers, sometimes as commuters, sometimes as tourists. McCarthy (2001) argued that the location of public televisions constructed subject positions for viewers. Television screens are a regular feature of many different public places. They can appear in bars and restaurants, beside the queue in shops and libraries, in train stations, at bus stops, by the security guard in public buildings. Their function can range from distraction and entertainment to information or interdiction. Silent screens showing news channels, for example, address us as intelligent, busy people interested in current affairs and world finance. The locations of such screens in airport lounges position the viewer as a business traveller, rather than a holiday maker. The screens appear above head height with the sound muted and the subtitles displayed in a clear response to the exigencies of the situation—they need to be out of the way of foot traffic and the noises of an airport mean that the volume is not an option. Yet these two features also give the news channels a position of authority to which a viewer must look up, and make the news a literary event to be read, rather than heard. By contrast, the location of a giant sport screen in a public park addresses viewers as a community fascinated by the spectacle of the event.

McCarthy (2001) suggested that some of our earliest images of spectators watching television in public are groups of wide-eyed and open-mouthed men (and some women) watching sport shows in bars and taverns. Despite the diverse clientele of such establishments, McCarthy (2001: 32) argued that a myth arose about the 'tavern audience as a masculine, sport-viewing collectivity in the postwar years'. In turn, this belief that the industry knew its spectators was part of a general cultural anxiety about working-class leisure patterns. The arrival of television screens in taverns was viewed as altering the social relations within them. The democratic space of the bar was argued to be giving way to a commercialised, privatised space, and there were concerns that televised sport would attract children to bars and detract spectators from the live game. While watching sport on television at home was thought to make viewers yearn for the stadium, watching in a bar appeared to offer a preferential 'live' experience. McCarthy (2001) suggested that is possible to see the same issues surrounding the rise of the sports bar. While the tavern was accused of taking from stadium audiences, sports bars were charged with stealing regular television audiences for sport.

Media Sport in Three Dimensions

McCarthy (2001) offered points of consideration for studying the mediated visual culture of sport. Firstly, television has a materiality. McCarthy (2001: 118) observed that those people who would dismiss the television set as just another household appliance fail to understand that 'appliances, like all commodities, are complicated discursive objects'. Secondly, McCarthy (2001) was interested in the way that televisions communicate as objects by studying where the TV set is located in a public space like a restaurant, a retail store or an airport. She argued that 'tracing its physical relationship to other signs and objects, can tell us something about the parameters that are defined for public personhood in such spaces' (McCarthy 2001: 119). Finally, McCarthy highlighted the different modes of address that can be encompassed by the positioning of television screens in public. The visual culture of sport provides opportunities for official, mass spectatorship and more intimate, unofficial viewing. McCarthy (2001) discussed the giant TV images at a baseball game as well as her observations of New York Yankees fans attending a baseball game in the stadium while watching a live basketball game on portable TVs.

The mediation of sport is performed though a combination of two-dimensional images and three-dimensional visual displays. Media sport embraces the objects, places and spaces of sport. Sport museums bring together texts, objects, images and sounds of sport and arrange them according to a logic of display. Porter (1996) argued that by 'reading' the museum, it is possible to make sense of the many layers of meaning that reside in

> the exhibition themes; the physical layout of space and design; the sources and choices of objects, images, texts and other materials; the position, condition and presentation of these elements; the lights, movements, sounds and smells created in the exhibition. (p. 114)

Porter (1996) also observed that meaning was made at the point where visitors enter the exhibition. The way visitors move around the space of the museum, the expectations they bring with them and the way they engage with the exhibits is all part of the production of the exhibition. The next section considers ways to unpack the mediation of sport through museum displays.

The Sport Museum

Sport museums mediate meanings of sport, constructing perspectives for the masses on what is valuable and interesting about sport through the display of artefacts. The 'exhibitionary complex' (Bennett 1995: 59) has the effect of ordering, not just the objects on display, but the public who come to inspect them. As Dicks (2003: 146) put it, 'museums are powerful agencies for defining culture to the public, and for the public to define itself through the viewing relations they embody.'

In tracing the history of the museum, Bennett (1995) showed that museums in the nineteenth century reflected a connection between the new techniques of display and the principles of classification found in emerging disciplines: history, art history, archaeology, geology, biology and anthropology. In contrast to the private, chaotic collections of rare and exceptional artefacts that characterised the 'cabinets of curiosity' of previous centuries, the new museums were rationalised, ordered and underpinned by a logic of historical development which moved chronologically from the past to a triumphant present (Bennett 1995: 2). The museum became a 'showcase for key modern ideas about the hierarchical ordering and logical progression of knowledge, identity and culture' (Dicks 2003: 147). Museums enforced the logic of colonialism by displaying the transition from 'simple and traditional to complex and modern societies, propagating the message that "traditional" societies were colonized for their own good in order to modernize them' (Dicks 2003: 147). These hierarchical displays of other cultures created the viewing public as knowing subjects, complicit in the ordering of the world according to the rhetoric of imperialism.

Simultaneously, museums made visitors aware that they were the subject of surveillance themselves. Bennett (1995) argued that the exhibitions of the nineteenth century were also part of the disciplinary society. The Crystal Palace, built to house the Great Exhibition of 1851, in London, was designed so that 'while everyone could see, there were also vantage points from which everyone could be seen, thus combining the functions of spectacle and surveillance' (Bennett 1995: 65). Instruction booklets sought to discipline the potentially troublesome working-class visitor into appropriate behaviour by advising on dress and demeanour (Bennett 1995: 73). The location of museums was also part of a strategy to civilise the masses. Bennett (1995: 87) noted that museums were typically placed at the centre of cities, standing there as 'embodiments, both material and symbolic, of a power to "show and tell" which, in being deployed in a newly constituted open and public space, sought rhetorically to incorporate the people within the processes of the state'.

Power–Knowledge and the Museum

Rose (2007) suggested that the following concepts derived from the work of Foucault (1977) were useful in approaching the analysis of museums: the panopticon, surveillance, institutional apparatuses and institutional technologies. The panopticon was Jeremy Bentham's design for a revolutionary new prison architecture in 1791. He suggested that it could be used as model for all kinds of institutions such as hospitals, workhouses, schools and madhouses. The prison consisted of a tall tower surrounded by cells whose single occupants were always visible from a central tower. While occupants of cells could be seen, the officers in the guard tower remained invisible; thus prisoners could never be certain when someone was watching them. The effect of this architectural arrangement was for prisoners to internalise the gaze of the warden. The prisoners adopted a subjectivity of surveillance, altering their behaviour in a way that resulted in the production of docile bodies. Foucault (1977) argued that this internal regulation, operating through the constant fear of surveillance, has become the principal way in which contemporary societies are organised.

For Foucault (1977), there can be no power without the construction of a field of knowledge, and no knowledge without corresponding power relations. This intersection of power–knowledge can be seen in the way that powerful discourses are able to have effects in the world on the basis that their knowledge claims are assumed to be true. Discourses of the body beautiful, for example, are effectively able to discipline individuals into perpetual body modification through diet, exercise and surgery because it is assumed to be true that slim people lead better lives. Power–knowledge is imbued in a variety of ways in the constitution of institutions such as prisons and can include architecture as well as rules and regulations, timetables, scientific treatises, philosophical statements, laws and moral codes. These forms of power–knowledge can be understood as institutional apparatuses (Rose 2007). Institutional technologies are the much less formulated sets of tools and methods used to practise power–knowledge.

Bennett (1995) saw connections between the museum and the prison that was the focus of Foucault's (1977) work. While Foucault traced the history of the prison as taking punishment away from the public (where previously, the scaffold provided punitive theatre, the prison enclosed the criminal body in the state apparatus), Bennett (1995) argued that museums made public objects and bodies that had previously been enclosed and private and used them to communicate messages of power through spectacle. Bennett (1995: 63) suggested that these two sets of institutions, with their accompanying power–knowledge relations, have different but parallel histories, and adapted Foucault's work 'to unravel the relations between knowledge and power effected by the technologies of vision embodied in the architectural forms of the exhibitionary complex'. In this spirit, Rose (2007: 177) suggested that a discourse analysis of the museum should examine its institutional apparatuses and technologies and the ways that it produces and disciplines its visitors.

The Apparatus of the Museum

Attention to the apparatus of the museum requires us to consider the themes and truth claims of the exhibitions. Museums in the nineteenth century communicated their message about the hierarchical ordering of nations, for example, by establishing national collections to propagate the political identities of European countries, while ethnographic museums were arranged to make colonised cultures appear primitive and in need of 'modernisation'. Since then, however, the world order has changed, and newly independent nations have used the language of display to their own ends. Equally, as the discipline of anthropology began to acknowledge that non-Western cultures were different but not less advanced, exhibitions involved 'a gradual turning away from taxonomies of objects to displays which situated objects within their cultural and place-based contexts' (Dicks 2003: 148). These types of exhibitions, which have presented a 'window on the world' in an attempt to capture other cultures, have also been challenged for propagating a touristic view of the world as unchanging and essentialised (Dicks 2003).

While contemporary museums may be more reflexive about their role in discursively constructing knowledge about people and objects, Dicks (2003) suggested that they are also under pressure to provide visitors with what they want. The need to satisfy customer expectations becomes necessary as government policies push museums to embrace the logic of the marketplace. As Dicks (2003: 149) observed, this means that they are expected to offer views of the world which do not conflict with those of visitors and sponsors, and visitors tend to prefer 'clear cultural identities on display ... not ... reflexivity, hybridity and fragmentation'. Consideration of how museums negotiate these demands and represent the world enables us to elicit the apparatus of the institution. As Emmison and Smith (2000: 121) noted, by examining exhibitions, we can 'learn a good deal about the various discursive frameworks which are at work, not so much in the society represented, as in the society doing the representing'.

Contemporary museums are able to draw on a range of intersensory technologies to construct, not simply display, experiences. Visitors expect to interact with exhibits that deliver so-called living history with sound, smell, touch and sight. Objects are not always placed reverently in dusty cabinets, and visitors' engagement with displays is at odds with the ideal of the contemplative gaze. All kinds of media are part of the new museum experience: photographs, audio-visual films on small or large screens, audio narratives on headsets and touch-screen computer monitors as well as more traditional panels, wall displays and glass cases. While some critics have argued that the emphasis on experience and sensation may detract from the museum's role in delivering knowledge and understanding, Dicks (2003) pointed to ways that multimedia can also be used to produce rich and detailed stories.

Museums can also deliberately refuse to present clear and unambiguous interpretations of the world by adopting a postmodern, aestheticised approach to display (Dicks 2003):

> Techniques of bricologe, pastiche, montage, quotation, and so forth represent a different tendency to that of simulation. They are designed to ask questions about the nature of representation rather than answering ones about the interpretation of history. (p. 167)

Part of this approach is its rejection of fixed routes through the collections, giving visitors the freedom to make their own choices about where to go and what to see. The use of different media to deliver a range of spectacles for the visitor avoids the delineation of one single storyline in favour of multiple perspectives. A danger of this style of exhibition is its sound-bite version of knowledge, so that while these strategies may appear democratic and accessible, they may 'simply forestall engagement with the exhibition's subject matter' (Dicks 2003: 168).

Analysing the Sport Museum

The sport museum asks the visitor to understand sport in a particular way. To analyse the sport museum and the way it constructs the social subjectivities of its visitors, it is useful to consider the ways that the features discursively construct meanings. Rose (2007) discussed the importance of technologies of display, interpretation and layout in effecting meanings. These concepts provide a useful starting point for drawing out the specific characteristics of sport museums.

Apparatus

Any analysis needs to consider the architecture of the museum. The design of the building produces a specific impression of the place and its contents. For example, a flat entrance to a plain, concrete building will create different expectations in the minds of visitors that an entrance with iron gates, magnificent steps and neo-classical columns. The impressions created by the building in which the museum is housed is the first part of making the exhibition meaningful. Once inside the building, the internal layout of the exhibition is the next point of focus. It is important to identify the thematic organisation of the exhibition to begin to illuminate its discursive framing of sport. The analyst is interested in the ways the exhibits construct truth claims as well as the things they leave out or avoid. What do the displays claim to be true about sport? If they present a history of sport, what appears most important, and what is left out?

Technologies of Display

The choice between display cases or open displays creates a different relationship to the objects that make up the exhibition. Display cases create a barrier between the visitor and the exhibit, constructing a relationship of reverence towards the objects on display. Exhibits in open display can appear more familiar and encourage the visitor to take a closer look, or even touch. Sometimes museums create displays that reconstruct events or scenes. For example, the Wimbledon Lawn Tennis Museum has a reconstruction of the men's dressing room. These reconstructions can be significant to a discourse analysis because they are creating a representation of the world as if it were true. It is important to ask which scenes are depicted in this way. In a similar vein, some objects are deemed so important to the knowledge presented by the museum that even though they are not possessed by the museum, they are recreated to fill a gap in knowledge. Lidchi (1997) argued that the connotations of different display techniques created different reactions to the exhibits:

> Putting material artefacts in glass cases therefore underlines the dislocation and re-contextualisation that is at the root of collecting and exhibiting. So whereas

reconstructions may establish a context which evokes and recreates the 'actual' environment of production or use of an object, glass cases render the objects more distant; they do not merge into their context in the same way as they might if they were placed in a reconstructed site. (p. 173)

Rose (2007) drew attention to the way images are framed and hung in the art gallery and museum. If paintings are hung in a single row around the walls of a room, they invite the spectator to look at each in turn and consider each individually and thoughtfully. Rose observed that this is a twentieth-century practice—in the nineteenth century, walls of galleries would be packed with images. The arrangement of exhibits asks the visitor to look and feel in particular ways; sparse displays produce more individualised and contemplative subjects. By contrast, multimedia displays create stimulating intersensory experiences for visitors. Visitors are not only encouraged to look, but also to listen, to touch and to smell.

Technologies of Layout and Interpretation

In addition to thinking about the overall design of the building, we can consider the significance of the layout of individual rooms. How do the different elements of the room relate to each other? According to what system are things arranged together? Is a consistent narrative achieved, or are there objects that appear to stand out? The decoration of the room is important: the colours and textures of the floors, walls and ceilings as well as the type of furniture. Are visitors encouraged to sit and look or listen?

The labels, captions and other written materials that accompany the exhibits can be understood as technologies of interpretation, texts which act to tie down the possible range of meanings of the exhibit to those preferred by the museum. Rose (2007) suggested that the typical labels accompanying paintings which specify the name of the artist have the effect of making the author of the work the most important thing about the art. The way such labels prioritise certain pieces of information work against her contention that 'there are many other aspects of an image that are more important than who made it' (Rose 2007: 186). It is useful, then, to consider how the visitor is guided towards interpretation by pamphlets or catalogues that accompany the exhibition, and whether the guides make clear that they are presenting an interpretation or whether they are making claims to purport the truth.

The Subjectivity of the Museum Visitor

Museums construct subject positions for visitors to step into as they enter the exhibition. Just as prisoners are disciplined by the all-seeing gaze of the invisible warden, museum visitors are subject to disciplinary technologies. Rarely are museum visitors allowed to touch exhibits, except under very special conditions. Sight is the privileged sense, and visitors are asked to understand themselves as contemplative eyes (Rose 2007). Guards and cameras monitor visitors' behaviour, and signs tell them what they can and cannot do. The museum routes visitors in specific ways, so even though there may be no physical impediments to their walking one way or another, traffic will be encouraged to flow according to a plan. Rooms may be numbered, arrows marked on floors or walls or the features of the building design may lead visitors to entrances and exits. Benches in front of pieces the museum considers important act as cues for visitors to spend a longer time in those rooms. Lidchi (1997) argued that at every point, curators, designers and technicians must make choices about which objects to display, how to display them and what information to put on accompanying panels for the visitor to have a meaningful journey through the museum. However, she observed that these choices will always be 'in part "repressive", in the sense that they direct the visitor towards certain interpretations and understandings, opening certain doors to meaning but inevitably closing off others' (Lidchi 1997: 170).

Divisions between the producers and consumers of knowledge are also built into the fabric of the museum. There are partitions between the public displays and private areas for stores and archives, offices and service areas. Visitors are expected to keep to their place. The positioning of the shop or café also constructs the subjectivity of the visitor in a particular way, shifting his or her identity from that of a spectator within a public institution to that of a privatised consumer. There are often continuities within the display of goods in a museum shop and the display of artefacts within the museum itself, making the identity shift appear seamless.

Museums construct ways of knowing particular worlds. As a result, they construct the visitor as someone who is charged with understanding that knowledge. It is no coincidence, therefore, that museums appeal to those whose educational background makes them confident in this environment, and Dicks (2003) has discussed the numerous studies that show that museums appeal most to people with elevated educational qualifications. Fyfe and Ross (1996: 133) suggested that museum visiting is, in fact, a strategy 'by which some people accumulate cultural capital and others do not'. This observation echoes the study conducted by Bourdieu and Darbel in the 1960s which found that 'working-class visitors to art museums experience them as a test—which they fail—of their cultural capital, and hence learn to devalue their own taste' (Dicks 2003: 161). The way the exhibition is constructed makes assumptions about the knowledge, educational background and tastes of the visitors, making some visitors feel included and others excluded. Sport museums, however, make an interesting case in this regard. Knowledge of sport has not been regarded as high culture in the way that the arts have been revered. As a result, sport museums may be more interested in addressing a wider community of visitors than most. Nevertheless, sports are strongly coded by class, gender and race and construct cultural competence along these dimensions. The types of sport featured in the museum also inform the interaction between visitors and the museum's exhibitions. An analysis of museums, therefore, must incorporate strategies for unravelling the perspectives and frameworks embedded within their apparatuses and technologies as well as exploring the potential subjectivities afforded to the visitor.

Case Study: The Apparatuses and Technologies of the National Football Museum

> Football is an important part of England's heritage, our way of life and sense of identity. The National Football Museum collects, preserves and interprets this unique heritage for the public benefit.

> —*Souvenir Guide*

The football museum is attached to Deepdale Stadium, the home of Preston North End Football Club, the 'first winner of the world's first professional league in 1889'. It is visually and materially connected to the contemporary world of football through this external architecture as well as through a viewing area inside that overlooks the inside of the stadium. This connection is also embedded within its invitation to the visitor: 'you are about to embark on a fascinating journey through the history of England's national sport, charting its progress from humble beginnings to a present day national obsession.'

The museum is separated into two halves, discursively replicating the temporal dimensions of the game. The first half is a gallery providing the history of football. Visitors are directed down a corridor taking them on 'an emotive journey back in time'. The left side of the corridor is called 'The Big Picture' and focuses on images of the social context within historical decades back to the late nineteenth century. Opposite, on the right side, is a display titled 'A Fan's Life', documenting the fan's perspective within each historical period.

The journey, therefore, begins by inviting the visitor to share the subject position of the present-day fan—which may provide a feeling of identification with the images and issues on display. At the end of the first section, the visitor to the museum has moved back in time to the early days of the sport and an exhibit called 'In the Beginning', which looks at ancient ballgames which prefigured football. At this point, the visitor is directed towards the second part of the gallery. On the right-hand side, 'The Greatest Game' provides a 'narrative history' of the development of football through time using 'stories, pictures, objects, film and sound'. The left-hand side houses 'The Real Things': a glassed-in display of artefacts that is reportedly 'the length of a football pitch'.

Visitors experience an overflow of images, sights and sounds as they move through the space of the corridor. The walls are a collage of images and quotations, embedded cabinets containing artefacts and TV screens playing matches and newsreels. The pastiche of quotes, facts, brief stories, displays and interactive exhibits invites visitors to engage with whatever they wish. Occasional holes in the wall allow the visitor glimpses of other sections of the gallery. It is a departure from museums that display individual, carefully labelled, ordered and interpreted exhibits. The images displayed on 'The Big Picture' side are large, framed individually, and separated from each other. They are illuminated from behind and glow brightly first in colour and then, in earlier eras, in black and white. The other displays in 'A Fan's Life' and 'The Greatest Game' are a montage of sights, sounds and artefacts. There is no space between pictures; images overlap; quotations, stories and labels are imposed across the images; occasionally, there are displays in glass cabinets within the walls; and TV screens play famous moments from football history. While the walls show a degree of organisation within historical periods, the themes, issues and events are interspersed. Different music or snippets of broadcasts play as you move around the space, sometimes overlapping as you walk between sections of the exhibit.

The segment of 'The Big Picture' display which presented the social context of the 1990s incorporates the following images: British Prime Minister Tony Blair and former England football manager Kevin Keegan standing together with each heading

---

ANALYSING THE NATIONAL FOOTBALL MUSEUM

Our analysis of the museum focused on the ways that apparatuses and technologies are used to create and display the museum's version of the past and present of football. Prior to visiting the museum, we developed a guide to analysis which detailed a range of features of apparatuses and technologies of museums that we could observe and consider. These included the broad categories of apparatuses, technologies of display, textual and visual technologies of interpretation, technologies of layout, spaces behind displays, shops/café and the visitor. We also detailed specific characteristics within each of these broader categories. For example, within textual and visual technologies of interpretation, we identified the following subcategories: labels and captions, panels, catalogues, multimedia/intersensory experiences, visual technologies and audio technologies. Each of these subcategories was also explicitly defined. A fundamental aspect of the analysis was to try to understand how social subjectivities and claims to truth were produced through the use of apparatuses and technologies. To contextualise our findings, we also considered preferred meanings, examples of intertexuality and silences.

We used a combination of note-taking, photographs and documents to analyse the museum. The data collection began with the exterior of the museum and then an exploration of the interior design and layout. We started by walking through the museum following the prescribed route and taking brief notes about the displays, the organisation, the images, objects, sounds and texts in relation to our identified analytical categories. We also observed other visitors and the way that they moved through the space and engaged with the exhibits. After walking through the museum and experiencing the melange of images, artefacts, audio-visual displays and interactive exhibits, we went to the museum café and discussed our impressions and notes in relation to the characteristics of technologies and apparatuses. We decided to focus our case study on the first half of the museum and went through again, taking photographs and detailed notes about the exhibits.

a ball; a woman participating in London's Notting Hill carnival; a picture of murdered teenager Stephen Lawrence's parents seated in front of his portrait; stacks of flowers laid in front Diana Prince of Wales house after her death; Nelson Mandela; a video of the Spice Girls; rowers Matthew Pinsent and Sir Steve Redgrave; and students working on a computer. Across are displays from 'A Fan's Life'. The displays offer no explanation of the significance of the objects and images, and the visitor must supply his or her own interpretation of the depicted events and issues. There are, however, recurring themes that resonate with particular versions of the story of the English fan throughout the exhibit, including seating, ticket prices, ruffians and hooligans, safety, stadia or playing fields and commercialisation. Along the bottom of the display, a banner with pictures of England fans throughout history runs the entire length of the 'A Fan's Life' exhibit.

The 1990s section includes a range of images and objects. A sky blue board displays a quotation from author Nick Hornby: 'televised football has become like music. It's on all the time and you can tune in or not. And most of it isn't any good'. There is no reference to the fact that Hornby wrote the book *Fever Pitch,* which portrays events in the life of a dedicated Arsenal fan. Also on the board are pictures of the SkySports Blimp, a Sky Dish and a photograph of a group of fans, one of whom is wearing an England shirt, with expressions of tension and excitement as they watch a televised match. In contrast to 'The Big Picture', the images are not framed but positioned unevenly on the board, with the edges of the blimp and the Sky Dish cut off. A glass display cabinet has a blue seat from Deepdale, which is labelled as 'typical to those used in all seater stadiums'. The historical link to the tradition of standing in the terraces that ended in most grounds after the Hillsborough disaster is not explained here. Next to the seat is a large photograph of a bride and groom walking across a football pitch. A picture of a modern stadium illustrates the floodlights, huge green pitch, large seating capacity, partial roof, massive crowds and security at a Premier League night game. In one corner, there is a darkened picture of a football crowd, some of whom are raising their hands in a Nazi-style salute, with the date '15/02/95' in large letters across the top. Again, there is no description or explanation, even though the photograph refers to a specific historical event and makes intertextual reference to connections between football's history and far Right politics.

The exhibition creates a preferred meaning that implies more than just a reporting of events. For example, there is an ambivalence towards the 'modernisation of football': a picture of empty stadium seats is overlaid with the following quotation:

> The heart and soul of British football, going way back to when the game emerged from the grimy backstreets of the Industrial Revolution, is being ripped out and the clubs don't care … the clubs could see money coming in from better 'clientele' and they did not stand in the way of progress. Leicester City Fanzine, *The Fox.*

Nearby, a reproduction of three large ticket stubs refers to ongoing discourses about increasing ticket prices: 1992 (£8), 1994 (£12) and 1998 (£20). These images, texts and artefacts link the exhibit to social issues emerging from the sensibilities and experiences of the working-class spectator who has traditionally been associated with British football.

The exhibits 'The Big Picture' and 'A Fan's Life' allow the visitor to immerse himself or herself in a range of visual, aural and tactile images, objects and sounds associated with football's history. The lack of labelling and organisation encourage the visitor to supply his or her own interpretations of the significance of images and objects on display. The story of the fan and the images portrayed in 'The Big Picture' refer to football's political and social history in particular ways. Some narratives, themes and perspectives are emphasised, while other potential issues, such as racism, sexism and homophobia, are present but peripheral. Some aspects of some fans' lives remain unaddressed. It is, therefore, possible to gain a sense of the political sensibilities underpinning the museum's choice of 'narrative' and the presence of an imagined fan or visitor. The National Football Museum occupies a particular space within mediated culture, using particular forms of apparatuses and techniques to relate the story of football to its visitors.

The Spectacle of Sport in the Space of the Stadium

The spaces in which sport takes place are designed for people to inhabit in particular ways—to enter and exit at designated points, to occupy numbered seating and to observe certain standards of behaviour. Nevertheless, sports stadia are filled with sensory stimuli in the form of signs, directions, posters, advertisements, television screens, scoreboards, food stands, team colours and logo-laden clothing on spectators, stewards and athletes. The copious channels of communication combine to create a complex affective event, evoking sometimes unpredictable emotions, behaviours and meanings. In his discussion of the artist Julie Mehretu's paintings of stadia and spectacles, Chua (2007: 10) observed that space often fails to behave in the way it is designed: 'there is always someone walking the wrong way down the corridor, always a disturbance on the playing fields, always a disaster impeding the smooth flow of traffic'. Chua (2007) suggested that there is a sensual excess that is produced in the spatial forms of modernity. Chua argued that Mehretu's paintings attempt to capture the way stadia are composed of sediments of meaning from architectures of the nineteenth and twentieth centuries. Imperial relations were encoded into modernist architecture, for example, the colonial railway system in India had toilets marked for 'gentlemen' and 'Indians' (Chua 2007: 11). Residues of such meanings are part of the experience of contemporary architectural spaces. For Chua, Mehretu's art draws attention to the importance of sport architecture in the construction of the modern public sphere, the way that work and leisure were allocated times and spaces within 'the built environment of the colony and metropole' (Chua 2007: 12). Stadia in this account can be understood as repositiories of memories of the past.

Mehretu's triptych *Stadia* combines elements of the nineteenth-century Panathinaiko Olympic Stadium and the Wukesong Olympic Cultural and Sports Center, which, at the time, was being built for the 2008 Olympic Games in Beijing. A circular field is discernible at the centre of the paintings, but Chua (2007) argued that the gaze is drawn elsewhere, to the visual activities in the surroundings:

> In *Stadia,* the eye's habits are guided by the force of sensuality. The stray marks in the center of the field interest us only in the way we're told to watch the spectacle that has been staged for us in the center of the arena. What is as interesting is everything that is happening in the stands as well. There is a disorienting force created by a clash of gestures: the shapes that resemble banners that occupy part of the foreground of the painting, the marks that seem to explode in uncountable directions across the edges of the stadium, the counter-structures that form on its periphery and in its very center. (p. 14)

Mehretu's layered imagery conjures up a host of historical and geographical connotations of the architectural spaces of stadia. Stadia, according to Chua (2007: 15), provide places where 'members of a nation, an empire, or a community can recognize one another physically, bounded by time and space'. The spectacle of sport in the space of the stadium resounds with meanings constructed by its mediation through multiple sensory channels. Within the three-dimensional spaces of sport, meaning is made both through the architecture and people's engagement with the resulting structure.

De Certeau and the Practice of Everyday Life

The work of the sociologist de Certeau is useful to explain the active part played by the consumer in making sense of the places he or she encounters in everyday life. De Certeau (1984) was interested in what consumers did with the products of capitalist society. He argued that it is not enough to study, for example, images broadcast on television, but it is also necessary to think about what cultural consumers make or do with these images. De Certeau (1984: xii) tried to avoid the passive connotations inherent in some accounts of consumption and considered consumers to be creative users of cultural products, including 'urban space, the products purchased in the supermarket, the stories and legends distributed by the newspapers, and so on'. In this sense, consumption can be understood as another stage in the production of meaning. De Certeau (1984: xiii) argued that the task for analysis was to illuminate the manipulation of culture by 'users who are not its makers'.

For de Certeau, everyday life was characterised by numerous, miniscule acts of creativity, as people manipulate the products of society to suit their own ends. While Foucault focused on the operation of disciplinary regimes that keep people in their place, De Certeau (1984: xv) proposed that consumers are involved in a micro-level 'antidiscipline' as they reappropriate culture in clandestine and makeshift ways. These 'ways of operating' amount to a series of 'tactics' which consumers use to resist the 'strategies' of the official producers of culture (de Certeau 1984: xix). Many everyday practices, such as talking, reading, moving about, shopping and cooking, can be understood as tactical operations, and as such are 'victories of the "weak" over the "strong"' (de Certeau 1984: xix). In contrast to the tactics used by the 'weak', the 'strong' use strategies to keep themselves in power. Institutions, enterprises and organisations are able to use strategies because they have an official place in society from which they are able to operate and generate relations with those outside (competitors, clients, target groups). While a strategy depends on 'a place that can be circumscribed as *proper*' (a title, a place, a building, an address), a tactic has 'no base where it can capitalize on its advantages, prepare its expansions, and secure independence with respect to circumstances' (de Certeau 1984: xix).

The strategies of the powerful are, therefore, associated with place. They establish places and master them through sight: dividing places up so that the people that inhabit them can be seen and controlled. De Certeau referred to this as a panoptic practice. Strategies attempt to create the conditions for continued existence and expansion. Companies use strategies to reduce the variability of consumers so that they all buy the same product in the same way. Ritzer's concept of 'McDonaldization' provides one explanation of the organisational strategies that transnational organisations employ, including predictability, calcuability, efficiency and control. Consumers going to McDonald's, IKEA, Disney World or Starbucks receive the same or very similar product and style of service throughout the world (Paterson 2004). This allows the corporation to consolidate resources in the manufacturing of a limited number of items. While on the surface, these strategies appear designed to provide customers with a quick and dependable product, they also provide a way of controlling the consumer. In the case of McDonald's, consumers may develop a taste for potentially unhealthy food, which may also be sourced from industries that are reliant on environmentally unfriendly production techniques employed to meet the high demand of a transnational corporation (Paterson 2004). Consumers may adjust their demands to the expectations of the industry, accepting long waiting times, crowded environments and 'do it yourself' aspects of the service (e.g. flat-pack furniture, self-service grocery store scanning) to attain the desired object or experience.

Tactics, however, are associated with time, waiting for opportunities and seizing chances as they arise. Tactics also involve manipulating events to turn them to advantage. De Certeau (1984) observed that power was limited by its very visibility. Institutions want to be seen to possess legitimate status, and as a result, they cannot engage easily in trickery or deception. These arts, therefore, have become the purview of the weak. De Certeau's (1984: 25) example of *la perruque* brings together the joyful trickery of the tactic and its manipulation of time over place. The French term *la perruque* translates literally as 'the wig' and refers to employees doing their own work on the company's time, sending personal email on the company computer, checking the latest score or booking a flight on the Internet. De Certeau observed that the worker engaging in *la perruque* is not stealing anything of material value, but instead is diverting time towards his or her freedom and creativity and away from profit. This illicit work is done in the full glare of the disciplinary mechanisms of the workplace (although occasionally, employers attempt strategies to stop it, like banning access to certain Internet sites) and in the official place of employment. Tactics, therefore, involve waiting for propitious moments to arrive, when the chance can be taken to recreate the situation to one's own advantage.

The Visual Culture of the Sport Stadium

Sport stadia represent a space for observing the strategies associated with providing a desirable experience to a large number of consumers and the tactics of those who engage with the space. The sport geographer Bale (1994: 67) argued that the rationalisation at the heart of much sport architecture expressed the principles of modernism: 'modern space is objective space ... nowhere more apparent that in sportscape'. Boundaries are everywhere in sport space—demarcating space between sport and nonsport spaces. The enclosure of the field of play by straight lines separating the playing space from the spectators was a marker of the emergence of modern sport. Spatiality is inherent to sport. The distinction between sport and other recreational activity is to be found in the spatial designation of where sport can take place, the restrictions on behaviour and circumstances, the exact measurement of distance. Bale (1994) suggested that there were parallels between Foucault's (1979) account of the disciplinary architecture of the prison and the way power and control are inscribed into the spatial segmentation of the modern stadium. Bale (1994) argued that the increasing spatial rationalisation of sport can be seen in the changing architecture of the baseball stadium. Modern ballpark design typically employs geometric standardisation, compared to classic asymmetrical stadiums such as Fenway Park.

A greater degree of segmentation of spectators, not just from the field of play, but from each other, has also occurred during the development of the stadium. Bale (1994: 82) referred to this as the 'increasing territorialisation of the spectating areas of sports grounds' resulting in the confinement of individuals to specific spaces, separated from each other. The placing of each person in a seat and subjecting the person to close-circuit television has led to the 'stadium analogue to Foucault's panopticon', in Bale's (1994: 83) terms. Bale cites the historical use of stadia as secure places of containment (e.g. the Parisian Vélodrome d'Hiver was used to incarcerate Jews in 1942) as testament to their effectiveness in the discipline of society.

Bale (1994) suggested that sportscapes may generate either *topophilia* (love of place) or *topophobia* (fear of place). Visual pleasures associated with a place, and the intersensory experiences of being there, are an important part of topophilia. Much is in the detail: 'landscapes of sports possess many elements often rather small features which are taken for granted by those who daily pass them by, which are ... icons for the sports fan' (Bale 1994: 135). The noises, smells and sounds of sportscapes are part of the sense of place experienced by fans: 'often the sound of sport greets the fan before the sight of it' (Bale 1994: 139).

Case Study: Strategies and Tactics in Fenway Park

It comes back to why the ballparks matter to us—because exactly comparable people played a comparable game in this ballpark for generation after generation.

—George Will

The Red Sox baseball franchise can be conceived of as a strategy in de Certeau's terms for the club to manage relations with its competitors, adversaries and clienteles. Strategies can be understood as dynamic ways that specific enterprises define, demarcate, identify and sustain themselves. Strategies of sport organisations work in part though their capacity to exercise some element of control over the fans, encouraging particular forms of behaviour and creating a commitment to and consumption of a place and its products. The Red Sox franchise has been highly successful in this regard. Filling their stadium, Fenway Park, for each home game (eighty-one games) is a sign of a club's success and an ongoing task for the owners and operators of Major League Baseball's thirty ballparks. The Boston Red Sox have successfully sold out all of their games for eight seasons in a row and hosted over 400 consecutive sell-out games ('MLB Shatters' 2007). In 2007, 2,970,755 fans watched the Red Sox play in home games. Successful strategies have also been required to manage these high attendance figures.

In response to organisational strategies, Red Sox fans may be said to engage in tactics, the activities of the less powerful who nevertheless exercise their own forms of resistance and appropriation of spaces. Tactics refer to those moments when the weak are victorious over the strong and when they can manoeuvre and take advantage of opportunities to act in their own interests, express their views and incorporate their own needs within spaces. Fans do not simply act as passive, obedient consumers, but engage in resistant practices that may subvert or deviate from the intentions of the Red Sox management. Tactics involve cleverness, trickery and quick thinking, as fans are subject to the panoptic gaze of the more powerful strategic enterprise. An exploration, based on observation, of the sensory, mediated experience of the journey to Fenway Park on game day can help to illuminate some of the strategies and tactics of the Red Sox and their fans.

On Game Day

On game day on 4 July 2007, the packed trolleys were full of people travelling to Fenway Park. Fenway is one of the few ballparks in the United States that are still primarily accessed by public transport. The morning newspapers highlighted the Red Sox' loss the previous night and reported on the injury list and pitching line-up for the game that day. Lugo was in a slump and out of the starting line-up, as was the injured Crisp. Around two-thirds of the passengers were attired in clothing bearing Red Sox logos. The sea of bodies alighting at Kenmore station was not uniform, however, as the T-shirts and jerseys they wore were in a range of styles. Both men and women were wearing shirts with players' names on the back such as Ortiz, Ramirez, Schilling, Youkilis, Daisuke and Papelbon. The consistent displays of Red Sox merchandise, logos and news worked together as a strategy defining the sites and sounds of the space as belonging to the Red Sox experience.

Kenmore station was imprinted with signifiers relating to the Red Sox interwoven with advertisements or indicating the direction of the ballpark. Miller Lite billboard advertisements covered the walls of the exit to the street with the strapline 'Season after Season Greatness is in Reach', linking the beer with baseball. A sign comprising the Red Sox traditional emblem (two red socks with white heels and toes) alongside an arrow indicated the exit. A poster featuring a cartoon of a grinning Red Sox fan with hat, jersey, ball and bat advised travellers to buy their return ticket before leaving the station to save time after the game. The presence of posters and signs fixed on the walls of the station extended the boundaries of the Red Sox enterprise to the modes of transport bringing fans to their celebrated destination, the 'nirvana of ballparks', Fenway Park.

Upon exiting the station, passengers were offered the *metro GAMEDAY,* an official publication of the Boston Red Sox that contained team news, a scorecard, a K card (to wave when the pitcher strikes out a batter) and advertisements. The walk from the station to the ballpark was crowded with people heading towards the stadium. Restaurants, cafés and bars decorated with Red Sox paraphernalia were full of people eating and drinking. An array of vendors punctuated the journey, selling programmes (with free Yoooouk! bumper stickers after the player Youkilis) and newspapers (*The Boston Globe,* featuring an image of World Series star David Ortiz) and distributing K cards sponsored by the local radio station, alongside individuals selling tickets, buskers and religious evangelists. Neon signs announced names of pubs like 'Game On'; banners for the Beth Israel Deaconess Medical Center, the 'official hospital of the Boston Red Sox', adorned lamp posts; and billboards with images of players from Hispanic, Japanese and US origins welcomed fans to Fenway Park and the 'Red Sox Nation'.

Immediately surrounding the stadium were an array of souvenir stands and stores as well as food concessions. The surroundings were crammed with businesses, merchandise and advertisements featuring the Red Sox label juxtaposed with their own logos, decors, displays and products. Part of the Yawkey Way side of the stadium was cordoned off and accessible only to ticket-holders. The official team store, a statue of Ted Williams and banners representing stars of the past were key points of interest outside the stadium. The walk to the ballpark, therefore, became part of the experience of game day at Fenway Park. The overload of Red Sox images and information combined to form part of the dominance of space surrounding the stadium and the overwhelming visibility and presence of the enterprise.

Not all of the sights, sounds and products, however, were official Red Sox creations, as a range of people can access the primary routes to the ballpark and appropriate these spaces to their own ends. Religious evangelists, ticket 'scalpers', restaurateurs, panhandlers, newsagents and shopkeepers may have their own ways of profiting from the events of game day.

Strategies for manoeuvring the 38,000 plus crowd on game day included the use of multiple entry points. Tickets indicated which of the five entrances should be used to enter the stadium, thus dividing the crowd. A sign advertised a separate private entrance:

Nation's Way: Exclusive 2006 Red Sox Nation Member Entrance redsox nation.com.

The members club served as a further admittance point for a select group. Tickets provided information about the location of the holder's assigned seat designated by section, box, row, and seat. The tickets were also imprinted with details of teams, time and place as well as outlining key rules, including no smoking, no reentry and no large bags. The back of the ticket was covered in small print with further detail about rules and the rain check and refund policies. The 4th of July ticket had a nostalgic photograph of two former players and was bordered by the dates when Boston was the World or American League champion. At the gate, bags were checked and tagged by security staff and tickets were scanned before entry through the turnstile. The crowd was, therefore, controlled and monitored through a combination of security checks, filtering techniques, rules and regulations. These strategies were generally accepted by the crowd, who were encouraged to behave in particular ways that maintain order, allowing the franchise to reassure fans that they are attempting to promote a particular type of atmosphere and experience.

Through Gate C, there was a concourse filled with people patronising the many stalls selling food, beer, souvenirs and memorabilia. There were numerous markers of tradition throughout the historic ballpark. The font used in signage from beer sales to restrooms was evocative of the early part of the twentieth century, when the park was built, as were the black and white photographs, beer sold from barrels, the pastoral green of the decor and the lack of modernisation. The historic elements of the ballpark form part of the Red Sox brand as one of America's oldest and 'most beloved' parks. The Red Sox brand is also linked to the food. For example, 'Fenway subs' offered sandwiches named after baseball terms such as 'triple play', 'curve ball' and 'bench warmer', and a neon Budweiser sign was displayed alongside a jersey. Television screens showing the game were abundant so that fans buying food and drink would not miss the action, and the sounds of baseball permeated the space.

While the branding of the space in these ways may be understood as part of the Red Sox management strategy, fans have used tactics to actively create their own meanings that are occasionally in opposition to the official stance. The fans' commitment to the nostalgic, historical and traditional aspects of the Red Sox image led to a massive protest against owners' announced plans to build a new stadium that would seat more spectators. The plan prompted *Sports Illustrated* columnist Rich Reilly (1998: 3) to question the strategy: 'let me get this straight. We're bulldozing real vintage ballparks like Tiger Stadium and Fenway Park to put up fake vintage ballparks?' The protests ultimately served to help save Fenway Park from destruction.

Entering the stadium, there was an overwhelming sense of green covering the field, walls and seats, reinforcing a pastoral sense of times gone by. The famous Green Monster, one of the most renowned architectural components of any ballpark, loomed over left field. This historical branding has been one of the Red Sox' most successful strategies and encompasses the size and shape of the stadium, the red seat marking Ted Williams's home run, the Pesky Pole, vintage souvenirs and the manual scoreboard, which is still operated by hand. The historical space merged into the contemporary with massive scoreboards displaying video clips, messages and images of players and spectators. Loud music filled the air and vendors roamed up and down through the aisles as spectators located their seats. Huge billboards for Ford, Dunkin' Donuts, Volvo, Bud Light, and Sports Authority were situated around the edge of the ballpark, and there was a large neon Budweiser sign. Smaller advertisements adorned the scoreboards, and the names of advertisers written in old-fashioned white script appeared on the older, manual scoreboard.

Rules for fan behaviour were announced, including no trespassing, cleaning up the space, language, respect for all fans, cell phones, sitting in allocated seat and no smoking. Anyone who spoiled the enjoyment of others was subject to ejection. Signs throughout the park highlighted other rules:

PATRONS ENGAGED IN THE HANDLING OF INFLATABLE OBJECTS, OR IN ANY WAY INTERFERING WITH THE ENJOYMENT OF THE GAME BY OTHERS WILL BE SUBJECT TO IMMEDIATE EJECTION FROM THE BALL PARK

FANS WHO ATTEMPT TO INTERFERE WITH BALLS IN PLAY WILL BE EJECTED

Crowds were ordered through entrances; even the restrooms had in and out entrances to help organise people. Lines for food and drink were less structured, although the fans seemed to impose order on themselves.

The fans engaged in the events of the game in a range of ways. Some dutifully followed the play, completing the scorecard, while others talked to each other, ignoring much of the game. Couples (lesbian and heterosexual) sat with their arms around each other, kissing and holding hands. A fan for the visiting team, the Texas Rangers, was teased, '*T* is for time to go home.' Many spectators wore team shirts of current and past players. Some fans altered the official shirts or wore homemade ones. One had former player Johny Damon's shirt with masking tape over the name (former Boston hero Damon transferred to the Red Sox' most hated rivals, the New York Yankees). Fans smuggled in illegal food, used banned language, performed the 'wave', shouted rude comments to visiting players, got in each other's way and even fell asleep. They also cooperated—passing food and money down when fans purchased food from vendors, singing and chanting together and adjusting to allow people to leave and return to their seats.

The events, sights, sounds and smells of game day were in part orchestrated by the franchise to create an overwhelming Red Sox presence before, during and after the game. The permeation of media throughout the spaces within and beyond the stadium was designed to create a particular image of the Red Sox and Fenway Park to sustain its popularity and appeal to current and potential fans. While strategies are employed to organise and control consumer behaviour and deliver a consistent and expected event, fans engage with the happenings and with each other in a range

---

CHAPTER SUMMARY

- We are surrounded by the visual culture of sport, and our analysis of media sport needs to take account of this three-dimensional experience
- Media sport has materiality when it takes the form of objects and performativity when the objects are given meanings in use
- The different locations of television screens in public spaces create ways for the contemporary flâneur to engage with the spectacle of sport
- The sport museum mediates meanings of sport, discursively constructing ways of knowing our sporting past and present
- Analysis of the technologies of display, interpretation and layout and their role in effecting meanings can illuminate the way a museum frames sport
- Sport organisations use strategies to manage the fan experience through manipulating the visual culture of sport, while fans use tactics of creative consumption, making their own use of the mediated experience of sport

of ways, creating their own experiences and meanings within the sportscape of Fenway Park.

Suggestions for Analysis

The experience of live sport is inevitably mediated in some form. Fans approach the event with preexisting knowledge of the sport and its stars gained from consumption of the sport media. Attendance at the event itself involves multiple encounters with mediated sport, including newspapers, programmes, posters and advertisements, logos on fans' and players' clothing, big-screen TVs and music played into the stadium. Select a sport event and consider how the 'live' sport experience is mediated through the spatial environment. How do aspects of the media impact the experience of sport as you travel to the event? What audio-visual stimuli greet you? How is music used to sonically brand the players and the event?

Sport museums can be said to mediate the meaning of sport by framing and delimiting visitors' understanding of a sport's past and present. In addition, the sport media itself often makes up a large part of the museum displays. Newspaper cuttings, events that received media attention and old television and film clips are common features in sport museums. Visitors are encouraged to interact with exhibits through multimedia displays. Select a sport museum and explore the effect of the technologies of display on constructing the visitor's understanding of sport. How do the architecture and the interior design invite the visitor to move through the museum? How are objects labelled, organised and explained? How are visitors encouraged to interact with exhibits? Consider whether museums focused on specific sports have a tendency to construct the past, present and future of that sport in a particular way.

Further Reading

Bale, J. (1994), *Landscapes of Modern Sport,* Leicester: Leicester University Press.

Bennett, T. (1995), *The Birth of the Museum,* London: Routledge.

De Certeau, M. (1984), *The Practice of Everyday Life,* Berkeley: University of California Press.

Dicks, B. (2003), *Culture on Display: the Production of Contemporary Visitability,* Maidenhead: Open University Press.

Foucault, M. (1977), *Discipline and Punish: The Birth of the Prison,* London: Penguin.

McCarthy, A. (2001), *Ambient Television: Visual Culture and Public Space,* Durham: Duke University Press.

Mehretu, J. (2004), *Stadia II & Stadia III,* North Carolina Art Museum, <http://ncart museum.org/exhibitions/citysitings/cs/Arts> accessed 4 April 2008. [painting]

Mehretu, J. (2004), *Stadia III,* Virginia Museum of Fine Arts, <http://www.vmfa.
state.va.us/collections/2006_1.html> accessed 12 April 2008. [painting]
Rose, G. (2001), *Visual Methodologies,* London: Sage.
Vertinsky, P., and Bale, J. (2004), *Sites of Sport: Space, Place, Experience,* London:
Routledge.

–8–

New Media Sportscapes: Branding and the Internet

KEY CONCEPTS	
Interactivity	Pleasures and identities
New media object	Hyperlinks and narrativity
Brandscape	Websphere
Multimedia and multimodality	Communicative experience
Multivocality and multilinearity	Global consciousness

This chapter explores the construction of the sport experience through new media objects and spaces constituted by the sport brand and the Internet. Developments in interactive technologies have expanded the potential for consumers to tailor media sport to their own requirements. Simultaneously, the dynamism of the brand has enabled advertisers to reconfigure the relationship between producers and consumers of sport goods. Flagship stores like NikeTown have become brandscapes delivering three-dimensional multimedia experiences that rival the movies. These interactive environments have the potential to shift the power dynamics of media sport, as the capacity of consumers to produce their own meanings has become impossible to ignore. The chapter considers how users are invited to navigate through the virtual spaces of Internet sport sites. The many faces of the global Web site http://www.adidas.com are analysed to explore the way the brand experience is tailored to users located in different geographical locations.

Branding the Experience of Sport

On the tenth day of the tenth month at 10:10 CET, Adidas kicked off its biggest ever global football marketing campaign to date, which focused on the idea of teamwork. Their '+10' campaign was launched globally at http://www.adidas.com/football and involved a wide range of marketing elements. Coots (2007: 28), the Chief Marketing Officer for one of the advertising agencies who developed the campaign, suggested that major sports events offer a particularly compelling resource for advertisers due to the 'conventions of iconography, procedure, ceremony, media coverage, and of course, the deep emotional current of national pride and lifelong affiliation with a team of sport'. She further declared that the Adidas campaign 'breathed life into every aspect of the World Cup' (Coots 2007: 28).

The extent of the campaign was enormous, incorporating print, Web, merchandising, spectacular urban architecture, tournaments and roadshows. A new match ball '+teamgeist' (team spirit) was unveiled, and over 15 million were sold. The ball was launched in New Zealand in a 'Be the Ball' campaign, where consumers who purchased a ball could go on a bungee-like thrill ride called the Sky Screamer that had been transformed to look like an Adidas World Cup football. An in-ball camera recorded the experience, and the resulting video was put onto a DVD that people could take away. The ride was situated across from New Zealand's then largest billboard, featuring England player Steven Gerrard.

The outdoor advertising was particularly striking and included an enormous Sistine Chapel–style fresco (800 metres squared) of football players at the Central Train Station in Cologne and a colossal billboard of Oliver Kahn stopping a goal that stretched across four lanes of the Autobahn in Munich. In addition, Adidas sponsored a range of tournaments throughout the world, in which young people competed to win the right to play in a tournament on the Adidas World Football pitch in Berlin

(Coots 2007). Mobile interactive 'Adidas +10 World Cup Tours' provided fans with opportunities to play on an inflatable pitch, attend a coaching clinic, watch amateur games and compete on an Xbox. Fans could also become members of the +10 Society. Adidas attempted to dominate the sportscape and paid to shut Nike out of all advertising during televised World Cup matches in the United States ('Adidas World Cup' 2006). They also worked with the Federation Internationale de Football Association (FIFA) and host cities to ensure that official sponsors gained privileged access to potential desirable outdoor spaces.

Members of the Clean Clothes Campaign (CCC) were also present in the sportscape. The CCC is an international group focused on improving working conditions within the global garment and sportswear industries. They focus on issues such as low wages and human rights violations. The CCC campaign included a speaking tour throughout Germany, protests at Adidas directors' meetings, street theatre, an interactive Web site, videos and the handing out of postcards with which individuals could submit comments to Adidas. They adopted the campaign slogan 'Fair P(l)ay', a twist on the FIFA fair play code.

This multimedia extravaganza used the Adidas brand to bring fans and football together in numerous interactive ways, managing even to embrace consumer opposition to the brand itself. Considered in this way, the brand is not simply something that the media advertises; rather, it is a medium in its own right. Sport is increasingly mediated through the brand. To unravel the ways it is able to do this, it is necessary to focus on the features that define the complex entity of the brand.

The Sport Brand as New Media Object

Lury (2004) considered the multilayered character of the brand to constitute it as a new media object. She argued that despite our tendency to name it as such, the brand is far from being a single thing. For Lury, brand is a site of interactivity, organising a dynamic, two-way exchange of information between consumers and producers. The brand does not simply mediate cultural meanings, but has a legally recognised identity as a trademark. Logos make possible brand recognition across multiple, shifting product lines. A successful logo is dynamically linked in the mind of the consumer with a host of associations, capable of highlighting one facet of the brand image, then another. Lury (2004) argued that it is the incompleteness of the brand that makes it so effective as a mode of capital accumulation and so interesting to consumers and sociologists.

In *No Logo,* Klein (2000) argued that brands have propelled the work of advertising into new realms:

Advertising and sponsorship have always been about using imagery to equate products with positive cultural and or social experiences. What makes nineties-style branding different is that it increasingly seeks to take these associations out of the representational realm and make them a lived reality. (p. 29)

Along similar lines, Lury (2004: 18) argued that 'the contemporary brand marks a new stage in the mediated relationship between producer and consumer.'

Lury (2004) traced the development of the brand back to the maturation of the discipline of marketing in the 1950s and 1960s. Information technology and the increase in self-service systems in retail outlets enabled the brand to act as a silent salesman coordinating selling through promotion and packaging. The view that emerged at this time saw the relationship between producer and consumer as an exchange, rather than as stimulus–response. This insight gave rise to so-called creative advertising in the 1980s and 1990s, which utilised new forms of consumer research to construct imaginary lifestyles around products.

Another change was the branding of whole product ranges, rather than isolated products. Lury (2004: 26) described this kind of brand object as having three dimensions: *width* (the number of product lines), *depth* (the number of products within each of the lines) and *consistency* (the degree of relatedness of the product lines 'in end use, production requirements and distribution channels'). Branding organises these connections. For example, the Web site of the sportswear company Umbro (http://www.umbro.co.uk) presented three product lines: performance, football and fashion. Each line contained a number of products, for example, the performance line included SX soccer clothes and boots, the football line included the official England team kit and the fashion line included the Umbro by Kim Jones menswear collection. The Umbro brand organised the set of relationships between these products, differentiating them from competing brands such as Diadora or Hummel.

Changes in contemporary production processes of capitalism have moved away from mass production, enabling goods to be channelled to rapidly changing, specialised markets (Harvey 1990). Within this environment, brands organise the flexible range of products being developed and distributed to the shifting consumer base. Trademark law protects the role of the brand as a mark to indicate the consistency of the products. However, test cases have shown that brands can be protected even when product confusion is unlikely to arise, for example, in the use of a similar brand name for very different products. For example, Olympic symbols and terminology are trademarked, which forbids their use on goods, in business names, in advertising and in myriad circumstances completely unconnected to the Games. The London 2012 Web site explained this prohibition as follows:

If anyone could use the 'Games' Marks... for free, or otherwise create an association with the Games, sponsors and merchandise licensees would not want to invest in the Games. Similarly, uncontrolled or free use of the brand could damage its reputation and prestige. ('Using the Brand' 2008: paras 7–8)

Lury (2004: 27) concluded, therefore, that the brand is 'a mechanism—or medium—for the construction of supply and demand... It is not simply an add-on, a mark to identify an origin that is fixed. Instead, it is an abstract machine for the reconfiguration of production.'

Positioning the Sport Brand

Lury (2004) argued that traditional approaches to advertising—persuading someone to buy something—have been superseded by brand positioning. Consumers have been conceptualised as in search of meaning, which the brand supplies. Advertisers no longer take consumers' conscious accounts of their needs and desires as good indicators for predicting their future behaviour. As an example of this trend, Lury cited an account of the story of Sony's successful launch of portable television, followed by the Walkman personal stereo. On the basis of market survey results, a similar product was previously rejected by General Electric on the grounds that consumers said that portability was a low priority. Sony, however, looked at consumer behaviour in their homes and anticipated that portability would suit existing usage patterns (Julier, as cited in Lury 2004).

Something similar could be seen to be at work in the launch of Nike's campaigns to target female consumers. In Britain in the early 1990s, the market for women's sporting footwear was dominated by sales of aerobics/fitness shoes, with Reebok having the vast majority of the market share (70 per cent) followed by Nike (8 per cent; Boydell 1996). Gender differentiation of product lines was made primarily by colour, which, for women's shoes, was 'white with pink, purple or lilac trim', and for men, 'black, navy blue, green and red' (Boydell 1996: 123). In both the United Kingdom and the United States, female consumers represented the largest upward trend in the market for sporting goods in the 1990s (Boydell 1996; Goldman and Papson 1998). To take advantage of this upsurge of interest, Nike developed advertising strategies that did not simply attempt to sell goods to women on the basis of what market research indicated they wanted to buy (pastel-coloured aerobics shoes). Instead, Nike branded female sport participation by transferring desires for physical liberation onto their sporting goods.

Goldman and Papson (1998) documented Nike's 'Empathy' campaigns, which attempted to tap into women's anxieties about their bodies and traditional, restrictive gender identities. Text from advertisements in the United States presented contradictions in women's relationships with conventional femininity: 'you do not have to be your mother' (Goldman and Papson 1998: 127). An advertisement in the United Kingdom presented a group of naked women standing together with the strapline, 'It's not the shape you are, it's the shape you're in that matters' (Boydell 1996: 128). By completing the circuit of the advertisement's meaning system, the female consumer acknowledged that insecurities were the perpetual domain of feminine identity. Nike, however, provided the solution by presenting their brand of liberatory sports participation: 'Just do it'. Many commentators have pointed out that this version of highly individualistic, commodity 'feminism' reduces the struggle for gender equity to the highly constrained exercise of consumer choice (Macdonald 1995; Cole and Hribar 1995).

Logos and the Frame of the Sport Brand

The logo functions as the face of the brand so that the brand can be seen. If a brand is to be successful, brand awareness (being able to recall an example of the brand such as Coca-Cola or Nike) must be connected to a brand image. The logo is central to the brand image, and repeated exposure to the logo is the key to brand awareness.

The logo can be understood as an indexical sign of the producer of the product. Sometimes logos are simulated signatures purporting to be that of the producer (Betty Crocker, Paul Smith), having the effect of implicating 'the organisation as if it were an individual' (Lury 2004: 80). Sometimes logos personalise the corporation, not as a mark of origin, but as an iconic sign of the brand (e.g. the life insurance company Scottish Widows' living logo, a beautiful woman in a mysterious cloak). The personality of the brand may be embodied in a person (real or fictional), but it can also be a blend of characteristics. The mobile phone company Orange used consumers' positive associations with the colour orange to brand its range of products (Lury 2004).

Logos are dynamic and are able to move across products, functioning as a frame of activity, in much the same way as the frame of a movie screen (Lury 2004):

> This movement or relay between frames across media is further extended in the dynamic framing activity of the logo. Think here of the relation between figure and ground, with the logo as the figure and the (dynamic) frames or screens being sites in media as diverse as a poster, a window display, a television advertisement, a film, a sponsored event, as well, of course as products. In these cases, the logo may acquire a face, but it is also a sign of a liquidity that flows through old and new media, across windows, products, signs, screens and (computer) interfaces. (p. 94)

For example, the insinuation of Nike logos on clothing transforms everyday life into a framed event. Lury (2004: 95) observed that the placing of insignia on the back of clothing creates them as moving communication, where a Swoosh on the back of a shirt means 'you still have a face when your back is turned'.

The Celebrity Face of the Sport Brand

Lury (2004) argued that the use of the logo as a face or personality for the brand transforms the relationship between producer and consumer from a one-off interaction to an ongoing relationship. The established fan appeal of sport celebrities means that their image and qualities are often associated with particular brands or sponsors. Nike, for example, regularly associates the qualities of the brand with an individual sportsperson or a team. Lury (2004) cited Hatfield's account of the design of a shoe for Bo Jackson:

> Bo reminded me of a cartoon character…his muscles are big, his face is big— he's larger than life. To me he was like Mighty Mouse. So we designed a shoe called the Air Trainer that embodied characteristics of Bo Jackson and Mighty Mouse. Whenever you see Mighty Mouse, he's moving forward. He's got a slant to him. So the shoe needed to look like it was in motion, it had to be kind of in- flated looking and brightly coloured, and its features had to be exaggerated. That's how we came up with the larger-than-life, brightly coloured Stability Outrigger and the similarly coloured, inflated-looking tongue top. (p. 90)

But Nike's Swoosh logo is not associated with a real person. Lury (2004: 91) argued that the Swoosh can be understood as an abstract personification of Nike: 'the desire for success, and then of its realisation, success itself'.

To broker a lucrative sponsorship deal, athletes must distinguish themselves through their play or their character. This was illustrated in the film *Jerry McGuire* (1996), in which football players developed distinctive touchdown celebrations after a good play to ensure that companies could recognise them. However, there are risks involved in giving a brand the face of a sport celebrity. Increasingly, the public has access to a range of information about sport celebrities' lives through blogs, home tours and fanzines. According to Rein and Shields (2007: 69), new technologies can foster 'electronic intimacy and fan adoration', but they can also make athletes 'more vulnerable to situations that can significantly impact their image'. Sponsorship con- sultants Redmandarin suggested sport crises such as tabloid scandals, drug use, un- popular public statements and equipment problems can pose a threat to 'sponsors' most valuable assets, their brands' (Barrand 2005: para. 1). An article on managing crisis in sport in their newsletter claimed, 'The national press is filled to the brim with sports stars dragging the image of their employers—and the sports they represent— through the proverbial mud' (Barrand 2005: para. 2). If an athlete is shown to fail using the product range, the brand suffers:

Tiger's Lost Ball, 2003

Nike entered the golf market with a five-year £90m deal with Tiger Woods. It came unstuck at the first hole of the 2003 Open Championship at Sandwich. Using the new Nike driver, Woods lost his ball with his first shot. He later reverted to his old driver, made by rival Titleist. (Barrand 2005: para. 21)

The vulnerability of athletes' bodies can also lead to crisis. Manchester United football player Wayne Rooney broke his right foot during a match while wearing Nike's Air Zoom Total 90 Supremacy soccer boots (cleats). The incident prompted speculation about the design and safety of the footwear. Another Manchester United player, Gary Neville, caused public relations problems for Nike when he claimed that the company was commercially benefitting from football's antiracism initiatives with their 'Stand Up, Speak Up' campaign in 2005 ('Nike Just Doing It' 2005).

Brandscaping: NikeTown and Retail Entertainment

Branding has become a three-dimensional experience. Architects have attempted to capture the spirit of the brand in the fabric of buildings. The process of shaping architecture and interior design to become 'primary instruments of customer-oriented brand communication' has been termed 'brandscaping' (Riewoldt 2002: 7). Brandscaping aims to deliver 'backdrops for experiences with a high entertainment value, from flagship stores to corporate theme parks, from customized modular shop systems to innovative mall concepts' (Riewoldt 2002: 7). Riewoldt (2002) argued that the age of information technology has, paradoxically, made physical locations more important because they can do something that virtual brand experiences cannot—stage and enact concrete encounters in real places.

Brandscaping creates affective brand experiences: 'we can experience the manifestation, the messages and the emotions of the brand in company with the products themselves, in unadulterated, unusual and unique style' (Riewoldt 2002: 8). By creating a flagship store, the brand is given its own location on the tourist map. It becomes an attraction in its own right. This was the marketing philosophy behind Nike's placement of NikeTown stores at the centre of cities like New York, Honolulu and London. The former Global Creative Director for Nike Brand Design, John Hoke (2002: 103), argued that the Nike brand experience is based on 'brand seeding' or 'sowing the seed of a memory in your customer's mind, so that you can draw on that memory again—"harvest" it—weeks, months or even decades later'. According to Hoke, NikeTown stores are successful in getting customers to keep coming back because the space is constantly changing, offering new products, messages and meanings (Hoke 2002).

The multimedia-saturated experiences offered by NikeTown borrowed heavily on the entertainment industry, 'the Broadway stages in New York City, the cineplexes' (Hoke 2002: 108). Hoke argued that consumers want the retail experience to provide an escape from everyday life: 'they want to react very strongly, both physically and emotionally' (Hoke 2002: 108). Retail entertainment aims to create a fascination with the brand, 'to get the customer to identify with the world of the brand, creating a brand awareness and providing it with a deep-set emotional anchor' (Riewoldt 2002: 10). Designers of the London NikeTown aimed to create an experience reflective of the uniqueness of the city by drawing on the idiosyncrasies of London architecture and sporting history: 'the store has its own "Town Square"... streets, town plans and street signs' (Nike Brand Design 2002: 23). London NikeTown was designed as a place 'to come for inspiration, information, opportunities to play, first-class service and the very best sports products' (Nike Brand Design 2002: 22). Hoke (2002: 107) argued that that the immediacy of NikeTown was the company's 'highest form of expression... Our customers experience NikeTown live, not on a screen.' As a brandscape, NikeTown does not just compete with other stores, but with cinemas, theme parks and other fantasy experiences.

Brandscape physical experiences contrast with the virtual experiences made available through information technology, but the flexibility and complexity of the brand enables it to encompass consumers' interactions with sport in both environments. The Internet is increasingly important for advertisers, who measure the success of campaigns during live sport events like the Super Bowl by the number of hits on their Web sites. Traffic to major advertisers' Web sites peaked at a combined 782,679 hits per minute immediately after Super Bowl XL, compared with 50,000 hits per minute on a typical Sunday (Richard K. Miller and Associates 2006). The Internet enables a different kind of engagement with the sport experience than that offered by traditional media. It is necessary, therefore, to identify some of the features that are most characteristic of this new medium.

Sport and the Internet

Just after the NBA's All-Star break, the league's official site launched a project that lets fans put together their own highlight videos, complete with editing tools, logos, and music. Don't laugh, you TV types. This is the momentum of YouTube and MySpace rolled into one, because the Internet generation has already decided the printed word is basically good for nothing but lining the cat box.

NBA fans can go to http://MyVideo.NBA.com and turn into digital editors with a 2-minute registration and a 30-minute practice.

Highlights from recent games (and there are more being added all the time) are categorized as three-pointers, assists, blocks, buzzer-beaters, and (of course) dunks. There's also a team-by-team index for stand-by-my-team types and one collection of video simply called LeBron James that is worth watching just to see a viewer's jaw hit the table.

—King (2007: 37)

In recent years, the Internet and information technologies have profoundly altered many people's relationship to work and leisure, transforming both business and private life. Mautner (2005) has argued that the Internet now has a privileged status as the primary information source in the public sphere. The Internet has changed the way people contact and communicate with each other. It has 'created new channels for advertising...for government...and the articulation of the self' (Mautner 2005: 812). Digital technologies have had a major impact on traditional media, changing existing practices and extending possibilities. Trend (2001: 1) argued that mediation is now one of the defining characteristics of the new digital culture, 'an age in which cyberspace has transformed much of material culture into a vaporous cloud of signal and code'.

Sport is a central part of the new media, becoming 'one of the most important thematic areas on the internet' (de Moragas 1999: 18). Changes are happening fast as more and more people are growing accustomed to the new media: http://www.ESPN.com, for example, received 18.8 million hits in September 2005, 21 per cent more than in the previous year (Richard K. Miller and Associates 2006: 64). It is essential, therefore, that any contemporary analysis of media sport take account of the Internet and its associated technologies. Critical media analysts have begun to identify ways that the new medium differs from the old, and these insights can be applied to the transformation of sport via the Internet.

The Characteristics of the New Media

The first stage in an analysis of the Internet is to reflect on its distinctive characteristics. Research on digital culture has stressed certain qualities that belong to the new media. These can be summarised as multimodality, permanence and ephemerality, unboundedness, intertextuality, multilinearity and multivocality. These features will be considered in turn.

Multimodality

Commentators such as Trend (2001: 53) have echoed MacLuhan's (1964) observation that 'the content of any new medium is frequently the old medium that it replaces'. A perusal of sport Web sites will confirm that they are a distinctive assemblage of a range of familiar media: written texts, animation, music, radio and live or recorded television and video. In addition, a Web site may be a digital version of a printed magazine, newspaper or fanzine, reconfiguring existing formats for the new media. The Web is, therefore, a multimedia space, yet it is this defining feature that has been most neglected in analysis (Pauwels 2005; Mautner 2005). Words are important signifiers on the Web, but so, too, are graphics, colours, sounds and movement. In addition, technological interfaces with the Internet can range from keyboard and mouse to touch screens and voice recognition. The Internet, therefore, enables different modes of interaction. Referring to these features, Mautner (2005: 821) has argued that 'the unique semiotic potential of the web creates new challenges for the analysis of multimodality.'

Permanence and Ephemerality

Another characteristic of the Internet as a medium is the way that it seems both ephemeral and permanent at the same time. The Web has a sense of permanence because, unlike older media, such as TV or theatre, it needs to exist in permanent form for it to be transmitted. But a Web site may destroy its content when it updates. Schneider and Foot (2004: 115) suggested that an analogy would be 'as if each day's newspaper was printed on the same piece of paper, obliterating yesterday's news in order to produce today's'.

This means that Web content also seems ephemeral because it cannot be expected to last. Updating can happen all the time. For example, the results of a football match or other sport events can be posted in real time. Every time the Web page refreshes, its content can change. This ephemeral quality can lead users to feel frustration when they come upon outdated information on a Web site, for example, if an announcement for an upcoming event remains after it has occurred. In this, Schneider and Foot (2004) have observed that the Web has something in common with other 'performance media' like TV, radio or theatre. Once Web content is presented, it needs to be reconstructed to preserve it. By contrast, nothing needs to be done to archive older media like film, print or sound recordings. This is a feature that can cause problems for a researcher—a Web site visited one day may have changed radically by the next. The analysis of Web sites, therefore, presents new challenges to researchers. For example, we may need to download all their constituent files and reassemble them, rather than simply copying the URL of a Web site that may change.

Unboundedness

Another feature of the Internet that distinguishes it from previous media is its unboundedness. While Williams (1974) originally proposed the notion of flow to characterise the experience of viewing television, where one programme merges into an evening's viewing, this concept can be seen to have even greater resonance for the Web. Where does a Web site begin and end? By following links, users can travel infinitely across the Internet. If a team's official Web site has a link on a sport news site, then by following that link, a user's journey makes both sites inextricably intertextually connected. This characteristic also presents a challenge for a researcher wishing to analyse a Web site. As a result, Schneider and Foot (2004: 118) preferred to think of Web sites as taking part in a Websphere. They proposed the term *Websphere analysis* for the analysis of 'communicative actions between web producers and users over time'. They conceptualised a Websphere as 'not simply a collection of websites, but as a hyperlinked set of dynamically-defined digital resources that span multiple websites and are deemed relevant, or related, to a central theme or "object"' (Schneider and Foot 2004: 118).

Intertextuality

The form of organising text that is characteristic of the Internet, known as hypertext, allows for this high degree of intertextuality. In traditional media, 'demarcation lines between texts are easily drawn' (Mautner 2005: 818), but hypertext links create intertextuality and render Web sites borderless. Hypertext is, therefore, one of the Internet's most important features. Landow (2001: 99) described hypertext as 'text composed of blocks of words (or images) linked electronically by multiple paths, chains, or trails in an open-ended, perpetually unfinished textuality described by the terms *link, node, network, web* and *path*'.

Landow (2001) observed that this organisation of text matches exactly that conceived of by Barthes (1974) as an ideal 'writerly' text, the antihierarchical open text where readers are able to make their own meanings, rather than being restricted in their capacity for interpretation by the structure of the text. The nonsequential, interactive hypertext allows the user to make choices, creating his or her own trail of knowledge.

Multilinearity

Critics such as Landow (2001) have suggested that the open architecture of the Internet accords with the desire of poststructuralist philosophy to decentre meaning and embrace multilinearity. The development of hypertext foregrounded users' capacity to modify the text, changing fonts, making annotations, choosing their own route. Laurel (2001: 110) has argued that it is possible to compare computer users to theatrical audiences, but they are 'like audience members who can march up onto the stage and become various characters, altering the action by what they say and do in their roles'. Of course, this means that the user ceases to be, in fact, a passive observer of the performance provided by the computer, and instead becomes an actor in his or her own right. As a medium, then, the Internet gives users unprecedented agency, encouraging critics like Rowe (2004a: 204) to augur the transformation of 'the passive sports media consumer' into an 'all powerful media auteur'.

Multivocality

An internet text constructed out of an interaction of multiple voices is the encyclopaedia Web site Wikipedia (http://en.wikipedia.org). Wikipedia describes itself as being written collaboratively by volunteers from all over the world. In addition to writing, users can, and are encouraged to, edit existing pages. Links to other pages are placed throughout articles so that pathways through the encyclopaedia are individualised to the search requirements of users. In doing so, users are constantly shifting the centre or focus of their investigation. In many ways, therefore, Wikipedia is an example of a multivocal, intertextual, decentred text. As a result, analysts have argued that 'on the web, connectivity matters as much as content' (Schneider and Foot 2004: 117).

The Pleasures of the Internet

Considering these features, we can ask if there is a different kind of pleasure to be gained from new media. Kerr, Kücklich and Brereton (2006) have pointed to the commonly held belief that new media offer more fun than traditional media. They argued that the pleasure of old media (e.g. a television drama) is seen to derive from both immersion in a fictional world and an appreciation of textual strategies that bring it life. However, the characteristics of new media mean that the textual pleasures they provide will be different. In traditional media theory, a reader or viewer is argued to adopt a (human) subject position inscribed in the text. However, with computer simulation games, the gamers' pleasure is in their identification with the computer itself, understanding the logic of the game from the perspective of the machine (sport games). In addition, new media are not fixed in the same way as traditional, analogue media. Instead, digital media are in constant flux. The database form characteristic of much new media enables them to offer a new experience each time the user engages with them. With traditional media, while you can interpret them in many ways, what you see is what you get. With new media, each user can see a different thing, depending on the route he or she navigates through a Web site or the multimedia components he or she chooses to play.

While the new media may provide new pleasures, and a much wider variety of voices are to be heard on the Web than in traditional media, other commentators have been more careful in celebrating the Web as a new egalitarian community. Despite widened access to the media, Mautner (2005: 821) has argued that 'web content remains biased against those disadvantaged individuals, groups and communities.' The Internet's capacity to transcend limitations of space and distance has led to it being seen as a manifestation of globalisation. Yet, while national and cultural boundaries can seem irrelevant to the Internet, Orgad (2006: 878) has argued that online spaces do not exist in isolation from social and cultural processes and institutions, pointing to the way that 'cyberspace is fundamentally embedded within specific social, cultural and material contexts.'

Writing in 1999, De Moragas showed that only a few countries (United States, Canada, Japan and Western Europe) accounted for 90 per cent of the world's Internet use. De Moragas (1999: 5) argued that the inequalities stemmed not from the Internet, but from the world's technological and economic inequalities as well as from the 'information, content availability and languages used on the Web'. De Moragas estimated, for example, that written information in English accounted for 60 to 80 per cent of the Web's content, despite native speakers of English representing only 8.3 per cent of the world's population. So, while the new media may have the potential to challenge the dominant cultural order by creating a new multivo-cal democracy, it is necessary to temper our enthusiasm by attending to the cost of access to the technologies. Jackson (2001: 349), for example, feared that unequal access may lead to the 'construction of enclaves of the technologically plugged-in surrounded by the plugged out'.

Identity and the Internet

The way the Internet enables individuals to construct identity has also been the sub-ject of much discussion. Nakamura (2001) summarised the possibilities provided by the Web for the performance of identity in the following way:

> Users of the Internet represent themselves within it solely through the medium of keystrokes and mouse-clicks, and through this medium they can describe them-selves and their physical bodies any way they like; they perform their bodies as text. On the Internet nobody knows that you're a dog; it is possible to 'computer crossdress' … and represent yourself as a different gender, age, race, etc. (p. 226)

Users of the Internet can participate in virtual communities, adopting any identity they wish. The ability of users to appropriate racial identity, enabling one to 'co-opt the exotic and attach it to oneself' (Nakamura 2001: 230), has led to the practice of identity tourism in cyberspace. It can be argued that identity tourism (Nakamura 2001) can provide a vacation from fixed, real-world identities and geographical lo-cales, undermining the ideology of biological essentialism which ties social identity to physical embodiment.

As a result, if we are to analyse new media, particularly Web sites, it may be useful to think about the variety of identities and experiences they offer. Consider-ing the flexibility of identity positions that the Internet presents for users to adopt, sometimes even asking the user to identify with the computer itself, and the range of navigation pathways through a Websphere, any analysis needs to take into account that there will be many ways of reading digital culture. Internet content may change and be created by multiple authors, including the users of a Web site. Nevertheless, commercial Web sites are constructed by professionals to create a particular experi-ence, albeit a malleable one. The growing number and types of sport Web sites are there to cater for a perceived demand for sport information. Our questions are, there-fore, how is the sports enthusiast asked to engage in communicative action with the Web site? What kinds of experiences do sport Web sites offer users?

Analysing Sport Web Sites

Boardman (2005) argued that Web sites had their own language, referring to the sets of meaningful conventions involving text and audio-visual elements. A consideration of these conventions will help guide our analysis.

The Narrativity of Hyperlinks

In the early days of the Internet, underlining of words was the graphological conven-tion for marking hypertext links. Contemporarily, however, any area of the page, text or graphics, is potentially a hyperlink. This has the effect of requiring users to move the cursor over every inch of the computer screen to see if there is a hyperlink to another page, making this aspect of user activity 'as routine a part of the reading process as turning the pages in a book' (Boardman 2005: 19). When verb phrases are made into hyperlinks, Boardman (2005) suggested that they act in a similar way to pull quotes in tabloid newspapers, that is, reported speech or other high-impact extracts separated out from the text by editors to sum up the whole article. Boardman (2005) maintained that the way hyperlinks are presented can make the difference between a surfer following one of the links or hitting the back button on the browser toolbar. Hover buttons or rollovers that use the dynamism of animation to lure you into clicking, or the use of imperatives (e.g. 'click here now') as links to imply ur-gency, act to move you forward in 'the hyper-narrative' (Boardman 2005: 25) as you navigate the site.

Multimedia and Interactivity

While the Internet allows users to construct their own pathways, giving them a greater degree of agency as consumers than older media forms, commercial Web sites use a range of multimedia components to engage users in communicative ac-tion on their terms. For advertisers, this presents both a problem and an opportunity. Advertisers have the ability to speak simultaneously to different interest groups, but their audiences are far from captive, and they need not move into the hypernarrative unless they choose to do so. Multimedia elements have, therefore, created narrative forms that depart from those available in traditional media, which act to make users feel they are already involved in the story. Rotating banner advertisements, for ex-ample, are common on commercial Web sites and are timed to be replaced by a dif-ferent advertisement or a different part of the same one at intervals of a few seconds. Internet users expect to begin reading at any point during the cycle. Rotating adver-tisements are one of the ways language on the Web has moved from linear to cyclical narrative form. Pop-up windows enable new windows to be opened by clicking on links instead of loading the new window in the same page, so that several windows can be open at once. This adds to the capacity of hypertext by making it 'possible to have several narrative threads on the go at the same time and switch between them' (Boardman 2005: 62).

Drop-down menus and database searching are further interactive features of Web sites that have developed in response to the growing complexity of the Web. The repeated motif of the search dialogue box at the top of the Web page enables users to short-cut hyperlink browsing and go directly to the page they require. Along with site maps, these features indicate Web sites too large for users to navigate without additional assistance or the anticipation of users whose time is short.

Web Conventions and House Style

Consistency in design across a Web site has become a convention that enables the establishment of a house style. This is achieved through the repeated use of graphical elements, for example, the use of sidebars on every page to highlight and formalise possible navigation choices. Among these, 'About us' and 'Contact us' sidebars have become a standardised feature on most institutional Web sites. These features lend an institution legitimacy in the ephemeral world of the Web. Boardman (2005: 18) argued that the 'house style is crucial in branding the company that has created it'. Domain name branding (making the URL of the site as similar as possible to the name of the organisation) and the use of a logo throughout the site is part of the aim of lending validity to the organisation by creating a corporate identity and market recognition. Boardman (2005: 25) argued that if logos are also hyperlinks, the user can explore 'exactly how this extra validity is being offered'.

Text on the Internet

A great deal of Web content is still the written word, and text style and font are important signifying elements. The absence of upper case for the initial letters of title words is 'a very pervasive typographical feature that has taken hold', according to Boardman (2005: 18). Boardman argued that this was a result of the influence of email and SMS text messaging and their corresponding 'subconscious contextual assumption that the messages need to be sent quickly, and that the monitoring of typographical patterns militates against this' (Boardman 2005: 18).

Font choice is equally significant. Boardman (2005) argued that fonts are closely linked to register, that is, the degree of formality of the text, determined by social convention. Serif fonts are identifiable by flourishes at the ends of the letter strokes, such as Times New Roman, and were the standard for centuries. Sans serif fonts are a more modern, nineteenth-century development and have no flourishes (like Arial). Word processing software gave home and small business users access to proportionally spaced typefaces, like those used in publishing, so they no longer needed to use the monospaced fonts, like Courier, which were developed because of the physical limitations of the typewriter. As a result, Courier is now associated with a retro look. A serif font at a size of around 12 point is seen now as the de facto standard for print publishing, and this has extended to software tools to create Web pages. The use of sans serif fonts is therefore often a deliberate move away from the default serif font and indicates a more contemporary, modern feel, as opposed to the established and traditional connotations of serif fonts.

Sport Web sites are often complex, multilayered, multimodal experiences. Web sites are available to a global audience, but the geographical location of the Web site user may affect the way he or she experiences the site. To analyse these Web sites, therefore, it is necessary to consider the multiple navigation routes that may be available. The following analysis explores the multiple faces of the Adidas Web site.

Case Study: The Global Consciousness of the Adidas Web Site

The Adidas Web site is a globally conscious Web site presenting different multimedia experiences according to the geographical location of the user and the navigation route the user chooses to follow. The Web site is clearly branded with the Adidas brand name and three-stripe logo, which act as a constant frame for multimedia activity to take place within. On reaching the home page, sounds and moving images play immediately within the central frame. While some elements of the Web site remain stable irrespective of the geographical location selected, this central multimedia experience changes by country, as chosen by the user (or automatically selected for the user). Among the unchanging elements of the Web site's home page is the rollover hyperlink in the top right-hand corner, displaying the user's country and the invitation to 'change location', accompanied by a graphic world map. By following

---

ANALYSING ADIDAS.COM

Corporate Web sites, such as http://www.adidas.com, exhibit many of the multimedia and interactive features that have been considered characteristic of new media. It is also a good example of ephemerality—the content and organisation of the site constantly change as the site is updated. The lack of permanence meant that our analysis needed to be undertaken on one day and required us to take screenshots and download the constituent elements of the site that we wanted to reassemble in case the site changed. We analysed the Web site on 3 December 2007.

To capture the communicative experience offered by the Adidas Websphere, we followed various hypernarratives by clicking on the links to each individual country's home page. We analysed the common features of the Web sites, for example, corporate information and menus, and noted the differences between the countries. On the day we analysed the Websphere, each country's home page contained a large, central image, often a video or animated sequence. The enormity of the Websphere meant that we had to limit our analysis to following links to the home pages, exploring the menu choices available there and following a hyperlink from the central image to the next pages. On one occasion, this led us away from the Adidas site to YouTube. While the Adidas Web site has changed its campaign, many of the videos can be found archived elsewhere on the Internet, so not everything is lost when the site changes.

We noted the ways that the Websphere displayed multimodality, multivocality and multilinearity. We considered the intertextuality that resulted from following the hypernarratives. This process enabled us to begin to conceptualise the pleasures and experiences presented to the user interacting with different aspects of the Websphere associated with geographical locations around the world.

this link, a grey and white page appears with a choice of country divided into five areas: the Americas, Europe, Asia Pacific, Middle East and South Africa, and a further global site 'if your country isn't shown'. In total, there are thirty-three different national sites, including two for Canada—Canada and Canada (French)—and a catch-all site for Latin America (Latinoamérica).

Common to all of the national Web sites is a series of larger hyperlinks running down the right-hand side of the window, each showing a clickable image of a shoe from the various product ranges, 'Performance', 'Originals' and 'Y-3', each with its own version of the Adidas logo. An additional link to the online shop appears on the home page of the US, UK, Canadian and German sites, with an invitation to select a product catalogue or a store or to 'sign up' on the remaining countries' sites. By rolling the cursor over the first link to the 'Performance' clothing line, a menu appears to the left, displaying a series of rollover buttons to take the user to the various sport collections. While this is a feature of all of the national Web sites, the options can change by country. For example, in the United Kingdom, the choices are Football, Running, Basketball, TechFit (for clothing made from technologically innovative fabric), Tennis, Cycling, Women, Stella McCartney (for the fashion designer's clothing range), Porsche Design Sport (for men's clothing designed for driving and other activities), Eyewear and Watches. On the US site, by contrast, there are fewer choices, the first of the selection being an invitation to 'Shop Performance', and the other choices extending to Basketball, Running, Women, Soccer, MLS, Football, Stella McCartney, Tennis and Golf. The Major League Soccer (MLS) button is unique to the US site and links the user to a mini site called 'represent', containing official songs recorded for MLS teams.

A consideration of the difference and similarity between the menu choices made available to users in different geographical locations begins to illuminate the Web site's attempts to coordinate the experiences offered by the Web sites to the national tastes of the users. Hierarchies appear a constant element across geographical boundaries (e.g. the product ranges are divided, always in the same ranking order, into Men's, Women's and Kid's). However, among the options available in the Performance menu, 'Women' occurs higher in the list on the US site than on the UK site. Running along the bottom of all national sites, varying sometimes by language, are a number of small and discreet links common to all legitimate businesses, including 'Help/Contact Us', 'Careers' and 'Corporate Information'. Among this list is a link to the 'Adi Dassler Fund', a charitable endeavour which lends an ethical dimension to the company. Sans serif fonts are used for all text. The most noticeable difference between the national Web sites is the varying sound and moving image sequences in the central frame of the country home pages, and the links forward into different hypernarratives that they encourage. All the Web sites carry the strapline 'Impossible is nothing' and so present themselves as interconnected threads of a shared narrative, but the specific manifestation of this narrative varies by country.

The UK Site: Urban Sports and 2012

Accessed on 3 December 2007, the UK Web site featured an animated black and white sequence of 'urban sports', accompanied by music evoking the sound of a live DJ scratching a beat and then letting it roll. White athletic silhouetted figures were depicted engaging in a series of sporting manoeuvres in a black urban landscape, with London landmarks including the Millennium bridge, a tower block, a London double-decker bus and Marble Arch, picked out in sepia tint. Text overlying the images delineated the names of the sports: BRIDGE SPRINTING; FLASH JUDO; BUS JUMPING; URBAN GYMNASTICS. The sequence ended with the London 2012 Olympic Games logo, with its urban graffiti connotations, appearing in the centre of a black paint-like splatter that echoed the 2012 logo's shape. The Adidas logo joined the 2012 logo, and the text 'official sportswear partner' appeared beneath both.

A hyperlink inviting users to 'See the Impossible' under the image was connected to an external YouTube site containing an explanation of the 'Adidas Urban Challenge' campaign, which is the theme of the home page sequence. The campaign challenged users to upload videos showing themselves engaged in an 'urban twist' on an Olympic or Paralympic event. Users were also encouraged to interact with the site by becoming subscribers or friends, sending a message, adding a comment or sharing the channel (sending the page URL to a friend). Videos that users had uploaded included stunts such as so-called urban long jump, which showed someone jumping over a car, and videos created by a South London *parkour* group.

The page also included a series of professional videos showing the staging of events on which the urban sport animation sequence is based. For example, a gymnast is shown performing underneath the London landmark Marble Arch, and a pole-vaulter performs between two London buses. Interestingly, these videos showed that the sports depicted were very far from urban and are only made to look so by image manipulation (e.g. the pole-vaulter has a traditional bar and landing mat placed between two buses, but the animated sequence makes it look like he is, in fact, vaulting a bus). The interactive dimension of the YouTube site allows for dissenting voices as well as supportive ones. Comments posted by users about the animated sequence included praise ('looks great!!') as well as detraction ('Why are the people at the 2012 Olympics trying to market the Olympics as if it's a hip-hop event?').

Meanwhile ... Soccer and Running Gear

On the same day, the home pages for Canada, Latin America, Hong Kong, India, Japan, Thailand, the Philippines, Australia, New Zealand, the Middle East and South Africa, as well as the sites for all the European countries, except for the United Kingdom, showed a sound and moving image sequence combining live action and animation.

To a sunny, Latinesque tune played on guitar, flute and bass, three soccer players, Kaká (Brazil), Gerrard (UK) and Messi (Argentina), were shown drawing stick figures of themselves on the brown cardboard interior of an Adidas shoebox. The stick figures became animated and addressed themselves to the camera, extolling their virtues as team players. For example, Gerrard stressed his power, Kaká his elegance and Messi his flair. The sequence ended with the figures of Kaká and Messi displaying fancy footwork, passing the ball between themselves, while Gerrard waited, yawning and hitching up his line-drawn sock before saying, 'Just gimme the ball mate!' and kicking it out of the box. The nonhierarchical counterpoint of the three instruments in the audio track echoed the final sentiment of the sequence, as the words FIND YOUR PLACE IN THE TEAM were displayed inside the empty shoebox.

This sequence was by far the most commonly found sequence on all of the different Adidas national sites, varying only by the language of translation in the subtitles that accompanied the spoken words of the players. Of the Web sites that did not show this sequence, the US site and the Korean site showed sequences unique to them, while the sites for Brazil, Taiwan, China and Canada (French) showed a sequence featuring items from the Adidas running range. To the thick, squeaky sound of an acoustic guitar, the sequence displayed shoes and clothing circled by felt-tip pen marks, the names of the products appearing as if pinned to a board with thumbtacks. As the audio cross-faded to filtered beats and synthesised sounds, the sequence ended with an image of a woman running, an arrow drawn by pen connecting the products to the woman.

A Site for All Nations: the Many Faces of Adidas

On the home page of the Brazilian site, a hyperlink took users to an animated landscape of Rio with a road race marked out. By following the links further into the hypernarrative from the other national home pages showing this sequence, the user arrived at the Adidas running site. This site described the clothes and shoes as having been developed through a process of Formation (which was trademarked). The font used gave the impression of handwriting on parchment paper (a wax seal was part of the design). Digital images of the products bounced when the cursor rolled over them to reveal handwriting like a scientist's notes in old-fashioned technical drawings. The overall impression combined the comfort of classic physics (categories describing the shoes were drawn from Newton's three laws of thermodynamics) with cutting-edge technology in the interactive graphics. The trendy acoustic guitar and synthesised sounds of the audio track in the home page sequence echoed this classic–contemporary feel.

The US site showed a sequence featuring Reggie Bush, National Football League running back for the New Orleans Saints. Making connections with the soccer narrative on the majority of other national sites, Bush is shown drawing a stick figure of himself trapped in a maze, extolling the importance of patience. The Korean site showed the soccer player Messi painting stick figure legs and feet on a large canvas and saying, in Korean, that disadvantage can be an advantage (referencing the idea that Messi's short stature gives him extra speed). By following the hyperlink at the end of the sequence, the user was taken to the 'Adidas Impossible Is Nothing' site. On clicking the 'enter' link (an image painted on a whitewashed brick wall), the image changed to one of Messi idly balancing a ball on his head and roaming around a sparse artist's studio. The soundscape was made of slowly morphing drones, while the cursor rolling over parts of the image created short, musical, electronic percussive bleeps and moved the image around to reveal unseen parts of the studio. The overall effect was one of artistic contemplation. On the US site, a similar background and soundscape featured Reggie Bush as the central character.

On the day we accessed the Adidas Web site, Adidas presented different home pages to individuals ostensibly located in different geographical locations. Nevertheless, every home page was accessible, wherever the user was located, simply by selecting the country from the drop-down menu. The flexibility of the brand remained able to organise the interactivity of Web users and to engage with their own versions of the Adidas experience. The constantly present Adidas logo surrounded the activity within the Websphere, bringing all its diversity into the frame of the brand. The Adidas Web site illuminates some of the potential for new interactive engagements with the sport media made possible by developments in technology. It also shows how capitalism constrains possibilities for the consumers of media sport, while appearing to promise them individual choice.

CHAPTER SUMMARY

- The brand can be understood as a new media object that organises the interaction between producers and consumers of sport goods and events
- The logo is the flexible face of the sport brand, framing and connecting diverse product ranges; sport celebrities are regularly associated with brands to create relationships between producers and consumers, but sport crises can have adverse effects on brand image
- Brandscapes like NikeTown have made brands a three-dimensional entertainment experience
- The Internet has altered the way that people consume sport, creating new opportunities for interactive engagement with mediated sport; characteristics of the new media include multimodality, permanence and ephemerality, unboundedness, intertextuality, multilinearity and multivocality
- The new media promise new pleasures and new identities, but despite the global presence of the Internet, access is still very restricted; similarly, sport Web sites can present multimedia experiences for users to navigate, creating their own meanings, but nevertheless, choice remains largely circumscribed

Suggestions for Analysis

Sport Web sites have the capacity to present the user with an interactive, multimedia sport experience. Select an official Web site of a sport organisation (such as the International Olympic Committee) and consider the way the Web site constructs the user's experience. What multimedia features are available? How interactive are the features? How free are users to make their meanings by following hyperlinked threads? How do certain features (like banner advertisements and navigation options) curtail the possibilities? Are users also producers of the Web site's content? Are users' contributions encouraged, and if so, how are they moderated and controlled?

Sport celebrities are often used as the face of a brand. Particular brands are linked to particular individuals. Tiger Woods, Maria Sharapova, Kimi Räikkönen and Yao Ming have all featured in the Tag Heuer 'What are you made of?' campaign discussed in Chapter 5. Consider what qualities and characteristics link the sport celebrities chosen to feature in advertising campaigns. In what ways are the products or brands associated with their sporting or personal identities? Are their sports, playing styles, abilities, looks or reputation involved in the transfer of meaning involved in the campaign? Which celebrities are chosen for which products? How do companies manage celebrities' sport crises, which threaten the reputation of their brands?

Further Reading

Boydell, C. (1996), 'The Training Shoe: Pump Up the Power', in P. Kirkham, ed., *The Gendered Object,* Manchester: Manchester University Press.

Goldman, R., and Papson, S. (1998), *Nike Culture,* London: Sage.

Jackson, S., and Hokowhitu, B. (2002), 'Sport, Tribes, and Technology: the New Zealand All Blacks *Haka* and the Politics of Identity', *Journal of Sport and Social Issues,* 26: 125–39.

Lury, C. (2004), *Brands: the Logos of the Global Economy,* London: Routledge.

Nike Brand Design (2002), 'NikeTown, London', in O. Riewoldt, ed., *Brandscaping: Worlds of Experience in Retail Design,* Basel: Birkhauser.

Riewoldt, O., ed. (2002), *Brandscaping: Worlds of Experience in Retail Design,* Basel: Birkhauser.

Ruddock, A. (2005), 'Let's Kick Racism out of Football—and the Lefties Too! Responses to Lee Bowyer on a West Ham Web Site', *Journal of Sport and Social Issues,* 29: 369–85.

Trend, D., ed. (2001), *Reading Digital Culture,* Oxford: Blackwell.

Making Connections: Wimbledon, Media and Society

On arriving at the All England Lawn Tennis and Croquet Club in Wimbledon in November 2007, we were escorted from the gate to the shop by one of the many members of the security staff, where we embarked on a tour of the club and a visit to the Museum. We were asked to wear green stickers imprinted with 'Wimbledon 2007 Lawn Tennis Museum' to indicate that we were legitimate visitors to the grounds. Our stickers were inspected by our Blue Badge Tourist Guide, a flamboyant, middle-aged woman with a southern English accent, green coat and bright red handbag. We were led through the outside courts and instructed not to touch the 'special grass'. We went to Henman Hill, where assembled crowds cheered on the British player on the huge outdoor television screen erected during the Championships. Our guide chatted about the rules of Wimbledon—the restrictions on advertising, the size of logos and the need for players to wear predominantly white. We were told that in total, there were just 500 members of the Club, of whom only 375 were full-time, and that the easiest way to join was to win Wimbledon. According to our guide, the members describe themselves as cutting-edge traditionalists. We were taken down to the instantly recognisable space of the press interview rooms and up to the British Broadcasting Corporation (BBC) television studio. We were invited to take photographs of ourselves sitting where commentators host shows and players hold interviews during the televising of Wimbledon.

The path leading into the Museum was indicated by a series of glass 'stepping stones' embedded into the floor. Set into the ground were scenes featuring iconic objects associated with Wimbledon, branded in its green and purple colour scheme: an official Wimbledon umbrella labelled 'play suspended', Wimbledon strawberries on green grass and a tennis ball on a patch of green and white court. The Museum itself was organised as a chronological journey through the history of Wimbledon tennis from 1555. According to the brochure, visitors to the Museum are invited to explore the game's evolution from a garden party pastime to a multi-million-dollar professional sport played worldwide. Fine objects and antique artefacts were displayed in glass cabinets and neatly arranged, numbered and labelled. Opportunities for interactive engagement with the exhibits were provided alongside. For example, it was possible to see versions of early racket sports being played. Connections between lifestyle and tennis were captured in displays such as a reconstructed Victorian sitting room with a tennis racquet–themed tea service, toast rack and sugar tongs.

Museum, Media, Tennis

The mediation of tennis was a repeated motif throughout the museum, including a display titled 'What's the Picture', featuring press photographs from 1924 onwards; a historical display of camera equipment from the 1930s to the 1970s; and an interactive display, where visitors could select and watch televised scenes from Wimbledon finals. John McEnroe, the notorious tennis player turned television commentator, appeared as a hologram discussing the game in the changing room that he once used. 'On the Circuit' featured a tunnel of overlapping still and moving images of contemporary professional tennis capturing the pace, intensity and emotion of mediated sport.

The Wimbledon tour and Museum incorporate the many facets of what has become the highly successful brand of Wimbledon. Nostalgia, tradition and English manners are incorporated into a globalised media product delivering the best in professional tennis. The width, depth and consistency of the brand enables it to extend over the space, goods, spectator experience, the two-week tournament and throughout the year. The green, purple and white logo appears on television screens throughout the world, communicating a seemingly unchanging essence of Wimbledon across a range of multiple and shifting product lines.

In 2007, television coverage of the Championships was broadcast globally for 10,211 hours, aired on 129 channels in 185 territories across Europe, Asia Pacific, Central and South America, North America, Africa and the Middle East. A staggering 748.4 million television households watched the action. The BBC broadcast 804 hours of interactive coverage through its BBCi service. Eight million users logged on to the official Web site, http://www.wimbledon.org, and the site was visited, in total, 40 million times. Live coverage of the Championships was available on the official Web site and via twenty-one other Internet providers. Ten different mobile providers enabled users to access the Championships on their mobile phones, including daily video highlights, archive content, the Official Java Scoreboard, wallpapers and ring tones (All England Lawn Tennis Club 2007).

Addressing Difference in Wimbledon's Global Broadcasts

Hills and Kennedy's (2006) analysis of the broadcasting of Wimbledon on British and American television revealed how similarities and differences in the media coverage constructed a subtly different national address. Morley (2000) observed that programmes signal to members of some groups that they are specifically designed for those groups. The coverage of Wimbledon on the BBC and by the National

Broadcasting Corporation (NBC) of the United States addressed UK and US viewers in ways that corresponded to their national settings. For example, the NBC coverage constructed an address that oscillated between the 'we' of the viewer imaginatively situated in England and the 'we' of the viewer at home in the United States. In the build-up to the start of the 2005 Williams vs. Sharapova semifinal, NBC commentary noted, 'These are the moments that you so appreciate [in] this championship—how quiet it is. None of the accessories we've been fed in American sport on centre court. Just spectators and their applause.'

The coverage of the ladies semifinals on the BBC created a montage of signifiers of Wimbledon designed to appeal to a British audience. It opened with a series of shots of an empty centre court. Rows of green seats, the entrance to the stairwell and a close-up of the scoreboard (emphasising the words *Previous Sets*) were shown over a soundtrack of courtside ambience. The voice of former British Wimbledon champion and commentator Virginia Wade entered the soundtrack: 'and believe me, Lindsay Davenport's heart is beating very fast'. Wade's voice gave way to that of Sue Barker, another former British player and the anchor of the BBC broadcast. Barker was flanked by two armed forces personnel acting as guards at the open doors of the club house. Abruptly, the music changed to the nostalgic, upbeat, big band theme tune evoking 1960s BBC sport shows. The images were a collage of past champions, the trophies, the Wimbledon logo, a Womble waving a Union Jack flag, Henman Hill and the court being covered for rain; it culminated in a shot of clouds in a blue sky, with the sun just peeping out and the recognizable BBC Sport Wimbledon 2005 graphic over the top.

On NBC, over the kind of music used to herald the arrival of royalty, the same event was announced as an exciting change from normal broadcasting. The initial images were of a tea table covered with a Union Jack flag for a tablecloth and crowded with cups and saucers, trophies and silverware, with a teapot next to a tennis ball and wooden racket. The word *Wimbledon* appeared in swirly golden calligraphy next to the NBC logo. Following a sequence of images of Venus Williams and Maria Sharapova to the tune of Madonna's 'Vogue', the tennis match was announced by a collage of tourist signifiers of London (Big Ben, Tower Bridge, Westminster Abbey, guards in bearskin caps) intermingled with images of green grass courts, the Wimbledon logo and Union Jacks. The words *Wimbledon SW19* appeared across the screen, accompanied by a medieval fanfare.

These opening sequences presented a version of English cultural nationalism through a collection of iconic sounds and images of Englishness deeply located in a specific space and time. The 1960s and 1970s nostalgia of the cosy British sports programming on the BBC, with its referencing of previous years' viewing of the Championship and its stars, invited the audience into the space of Wimbledon through its camera shots of the empty court waiting to be filled. NBC combined a more distant past of historical landmarks and medieval tournaments with the almost-contemporary sound of Madonna to achieve a similar result. For a British audience, the NBC opening sequence might appear as an overly touristic representation of a generalised London location. For a US audience, the BBC sequence is likely to be too obscure, with reference to Wombles (1970s children's television characters) and Henman Hill. The brand is able to organise the interaction between the producers and consumers of Wimbledon in different geographical locations and different national cultures.

Exclusively Mass-Mediated Wimbledon

Behaviour codes that have become part of the recognisable Wimbledon brand—the politeness and self-control of the English upper middle classes—help to create the aura of exclusivity that surrounds the tournament. Expectations that male and female players behave in gentlemanly and ladylike ways can conflict with the demands of high-performance sport. Bodies that appear out of control become marked as deviant in this context. During the 2005 tournament, the press wrote extensively about the 'grunting' of primarily female tennis players, and NBC drew on this reporting to present an item prior to the Williams–Sharapova match which ended with a shot of a woman in a floppy white Wimbledon hat with a refined English accent, who said, 'Sharapova's grunting is…appalling.' The woman's appearance and accent marked her as a Wimbledon insider, someone who knows about appropriate etiquette. The discussion of grunting included a suggestion that it should be banned from tennis, indicating the criteria by which certain bodies are judged to be unacceptable at Wimbledon. The refined, white (and definitively heterosexual) characters played by Paul Bettany and Kirsten Dunst in the romantic comedy film *Wimbledon* (2004) captured the poise and charm of the bodies coded as most acceptable.

The exclusivity of the Wimbledon brand is reflected in the design of the Web site (http://www.wimbledon.org). The sober layout in the Wimbledon colours of green, white and purple connote refinement and prestige. The Web site offers Wimbledon merchandise—'tennis and casual wear, footwear, tennis rackets, bags and balls…a select range of luxury products such as towels, fine leather goods, sunglasses, crystal, jewellery and luxury food products'—for sale and shipping anywhere in the world. Global access via the Web site means that the brand is able to combine Wimbledon's exclusivity with mass consumption. For a fee, during the Championships, the Web site also enables viewers located anywhere in the world to choose which live match to watch via the Internet. The same space that appears to exclude so many unacceptable bodies is delivered right to your door for your own personal use.

Sport, Media, Society

The mediation of Wimbledon exemplifies the dynamic interaction between sport, media and society. In the introduction to this book, we argued that the sport media illuminated important themes in sociological research in sport: the values of sport,

sport and commercialization, sport and social identities, sport and embodiment. All these concerns are part of the mediation of Wimbledon. The historical and cultural values of tennis have become part of the Wimbledon brand, broadcast around the world. 'Queuing Procedures and Code of Conduct' are available on the official Wimbledon Web site for actual or virtual participation in the event. Despite appearances, Wimbledon is a highly successful commercial enterprise. The lack of sponsorship around the courts at Wimbledon masks the effectiveness of its strategy of marketing the Wimbledon brand. The politics of social identity are firmly part of that brand: Wimbledon has been branded as a reconstruction of upper-middle-class English identity, with antiquated gender codes and a 'predominantly white' ethnic mix. The bodies, therefore, that are celebrated at Wimbledon are those that best fit the mould. The grunts of contemporary, aggressive sportswomen are frowned upon.

Nevertheless, the success of the brand and its global mediation through newspapers, magazines, television, films, the Internet, the Museum and the branded space of Wimbledon itself suggests that things are not quite as they seem. Far from exclusive, Wimbledon is available to anybody with a television or access to a newspaper, the Internet or a mobile phone. The contemporary players are not Victorian ladies and gentlemen, even if some of them are constructed as such by the media. Resistance to the anglicized, upper-middle-class behaviour code shown in John McEnroe's outbursts in the 1980s has been incorporated into the brand, as McEnroe has become one of the stalwarts of Wimbledon commentary in both the United States and the United Kingdom. New meanings are being generated in the media flows enabled by globalization, and Wimbledon's legacy of exclusivity predicated on the basis of nation, class, gender and race is destabilized through this process. The bodies of players like the Williams sisters, which populate the globalised media representations of Wimbledon, are 'other' to the white, male, upper- and middle-class English bodies who have traditionally held power at Wimbledon. Wimbledon demonstrates the interconnections between the varied elements that constitute mediated sport in contemporary society as well as illustrating the interconnections between media analysis and sociocultural issues and themes.

This book has demonstrated approaches to analyse the complex and fast-moving flows of mediated sport. Each chapter has focused on specific cases that show how to conduct an analysis of sport in film, on television, in newspapers, in magazines, in museums and stadia and on the Internet. Our aim has been to provide a toolkit with which it is possible to unpack the layers of meaning in mediated sport as it happens. We hope that readers will be inspired to apply these tools to make sense of their own experience of sport in the media. We conclude the book by asking readers to reflect on their own interaction with the sport media, transforming their consumption of mediated sport into the critical analysis of sport, media and society.

References

Abrahamson, D. (2007), 'Magazine Exceptionalism: the Concept, the Criteria, the Challenge', *Journalism Studies,* 8: 667–70.

'Adidas World Cup Shutout' (2006),<http://www.businessweek.com/magazine/content/06_14/b3978079.htm> accessed 2 May 2008.

Aitchison, C., and Pussard, H. (2004), *Leisure, Space and Visual Culture: Practices and Meanings,* Eastbourne: Leisure Studies Association.

All England Lawn Tennis Club (2007), *Wimbledon 2007 Broadcast Report,* Wimbledon: All England Lawn Tennis Club.

Althusser, L. (1970), *For Marx,* New York: Vintage Books.

Altman, L. K. (1988), 'New Breakfast of Champions: A Recipe for Victory or Disaster?' *The New York Times* (20 Nov.).

Altman, R. (1986), 'Television/Sound', in T. Modleski, ed., *Studies in Entertainment: Critical Approaches to Mass Culture,* Bloomington: Indiana University Press.

Altman, R. (1999), *Film/Genre,* London: BFI.

Anderson, D. (1988), 'The Seoul Olympics: Sport of the Times; the Smearing of the Olympics', <http://query.nytimes.com/gst/fullpage.html?res=940DE1D9163EF934A1575AC0A96E948260&sec=&spon=&pagewanted=2> accessed 5 May 2008.

Andrews, D. (1998), 'Feminizing Olympic Reality: Preliminary Dispatches from Baudrillard's Atlanta', *International Review for the Sociology of Sport,* 33: 5–18.

Audit Bureau of Circulations (2007), 'Welcome to eCirc', <http://abcas3.accessabc.com/ecirc/index.html> accessed 13 August 2007.

'Bad Luck Finally Runs Out for Our Golden Girl' (2004), *The Sunday Times* (29 Aug.).

Bale, J. (1994), *Landscapes of Modern Sport,* Leicester: Leicester University Press.

Barr, C. (1975), 'Comparing Styles: England v West Germany', in E. Buscombe, ed., *Football on Television,* London: BFI.

Barrand, D. (2005), 'Sports Marketing: When Disaster Strikes', <http://www.redmandarin.com/news/media-articles/sports-marketing-when-disaster-strikes> accessed 9 March 2007.

Barthes, R. (1967), *The Elements of Semiology,* London: Cape.

Barthes, R. (1973), *Mythologies,* London: Paladin.

Barthes, R. (1974), *S/Z: An Essay,* New York: Hill and Wang.

Barthes, R. (1977), *Image-Music-Text,* Glasgow: Fontana.

Barthes, R. (1993), *Mythologies,* London: Vintage.

'BBC Says Farewell to Boat Race' (2004), <http://news.bbc.co.uk/sport1/hi/other_sports/3514353.stm> accessed 5 May 2007.

Bell, A. (1991), *The Language of News Media,* Oxford: Blackwell.

Benjamin, W. (1983), *Charles Baudelaire: A Lyric Poet in the Era of High Capitalism,* tr. Harry Zorn, London: Verso.

Bennett, T. (1995), *The Birth of the Museum,* London: Routledge.

Benwell, B. (2004), 'Ironic Discourse: Evasive Masculinity in Men's Lifestyle Magazines', *Men and Masculinities,* 7: 3–21.

Berger, A. A. (1992), *Popular Culture Genres,* London: Sage.

Bernstein, A. (2002), 'Is It Time for a Victory Lap? Changes in the Media Coverage of Women in Sport', *International Review for the Sociology of Sport,* 37: 415–28.

Beynon, J. (2002), *Masculinities and Culture,* London: Open University Press.

Bignell, J. (1997), *Media Semiotics,* Manchester: Manchester University Press.

Billings, A. C., & Eastman, S. T. (2002), 'Selective Representation of Gender, Ethnicity, and Nationality in American Television Coverage of the 2000 Summer Olympics', *International Review for the Sociology of Sport,* 37: 351–70.

Birrell, S., and McDonald, M. G., eds (2000), *Reading Sport: Critical Essays on Power and Representation,* Boston: Northeastern University Press.

Blain, N., and Bernstein, A. (2002), *Sport, Media, Culture: Global and Local Dimensions,* London: Frank Cass.

Blain, N., and O'Donnell, H. (1998), 'European Sports Journalism and Its Readers during Euro '96: "Living without the Sun"', in M. Roche, ed., *Sport, Popular Culture and Identity,* Aachen: Meyer and Meyer.

Boardman, M. (2005), *The Language of Websites,* London: Routledge.

Bordo, S. (1990), 'Reading the Slender Body', in M. Jacobus, E. Fox Keller and S. Shuttleworth, eds, *Body Politics: Women and the Discourses of Science,* London: Routledge.

Bourdieu, P. (1979), *Distinction: A Social Critique of the Judgement of Taste,* London, Routledge.

Bower, T. (2007), 'The Big Sell Out', *Observer Sport Monthly* (29 July).

Boydell, C. (1996), 'The Training Shoe: Pump Up the Power', in P. Kirkham, ed., *The Gendered Object,* Manchester: Manchester University Press.

Boyle, R., and Haynes, R. (1999), *Power Play: Sport, the Media and Popular Culture,* Harlow: Longman.

Brohm, J.-M. (1978), *Sport: a Prison of Measured Time,* London: Ink Links.

Brookes, R. (2002), *Representing Sport,* London: Arnold.

Burns, J. (1988), 'Ban Could Cost Johnson Plenty', *The New York Times* (28 Sept.).

Buscombe, E., ed. (1975a), *Football on Television,* London: BFI.

Buscombe, E. (1975b), 'Cultural and Televisual Codes in Two Title Sequences', in E. Buscombe, ed., *Football on Television,* London: BFI.

Carrard, P. (1988), 'Telling the Game: Baseball as an AP Report', *The Journal of Narrative Technique* 18: 47–60.

Cashmore, E. (2008), 'Chariots of Fire: Bigotry, Manhood and Moral Certitude in an Age of Individualism', *Sport in Society,* 11: 159–73.

Chion (1994), *Audio-Vision,* New York: Columbia University Press.

Chua, L. (2007), 'Julie Mehretu', in MUSAC, ed., *Julie Mehretu,* Ostfildern: Hatje Cantz.

Clavane, A. (2004), 'Heaven for Kel', *Sunday Mirror* (29 Aug.).

Clough, P., ed. (2007), introduction in *The Affective Turn: Theorizing the Social,* Durham: Duke University Press.

Cole, C., and Hribar, A. (1995), 'Celebrity Feminism: Nike Style, PostFordism, Transcendence, and Consumer Power', *Sociology of Sport Journal,* 12: 347–69.

Cook, X. (2000), 'Men's Magazines at the Millennium: New Spaces, New Selves', *Continuum: Journal of Media and Cultural Studies,* 14: 171–86.

Cooper-Chen, A. (1994), 'Global Games, Entertainment and Leisure: Women as TV Spectators', in P. Creedon, ed., *Women, Media and Sport,* London: Sage.

Coots, L. (2007), 'Disrupting Official Sponsorships', *The Hub,* <http://www.hub magazine.com/archives/the_hub/2007/jan_feb/the_hub16_coots.pdf> accessed 16 April 2008.

Daddario, G. (1998), *Women's Sport and Spectacle: Gendered Television Coverage and the Olympic Games,* London: Praeger.

Dant, T. (1999), *Material Culture in the Social World: Values, Activities, Lifestyles,* Buckingham: Open University Press.

Davey, K. (1999), *English Imaginaries,* London: Lawrence and Wishart.

Davies, H., and Walton, P. (1983), 'Death of a Premier: Consensus and Closure in International News', in H. Davis and P. Walton, eds, *Language, Image, Media,* New York: St Martin's Press.

Debord, G. (1994), *The Society of the Spectacle,* New York: Zone Books.

De Certeau, M. (1984), *The Practice of Everyday Life,* Berkeley: University of California Press.

de Moragas, M. (1999), *The Olympic Movement and Information Society: New Internet Challenges and Opportunities,* Barcelona: Centre d'Estudis Olímpics, <http:// olympicstudies.uab.es/pdf/wp101_eng.pdf> accessed 5 May 2008.

Dickinson, M. (2008), 'Beckham Pledge: I'll Be Back', *The Times* (1 Feb.).

Dicks, B. (2003), *Culture on Display: The Production of Contemporary Visitability,* Maidenhead: Open University Press.

Dillon, A. (2008), 'This Will Hurt Becks Like Hell No Matter How Much He Has in the Bank', *The Sun* (1 Feb.).

Donnelly, P. (2003), 'The Great Divide: Sport Climbing vs. Adventure Climbing', in R. E. Rinehart and S. Sydnor, eds, *To the Extreme: Alternative Sports, Inside and Out,* Albany: State University of New York Press.

Donohew, L., Helm, D., and Haas, J. (1989), 'Drugs and (Len) Bias on the Sports Page', in L. A. Wenner, ed., *Media, Sports, and Society,* Newbury Park: Sage.

Duncan, M. C. (1994), 'The Politics of Women's Body Images and Practices: Foucault, the Panopticon, and "Shape" Magazine', *Journal of Sport and Social Issues,* 18: 40–65.

Duncan, M., and Hasbrook, C. (1988), 'Denial of Power in Televised Women's Sports', *Sociology of Sport Journal,* 15: 1–21.

Duncan, M. C., and Messner, M. A. (1998), 'The Media Image of Sport and Gender', in L. A. Wenner, ed., *MediaSport,* London: Routledge.

Durkheim, E. (1966), *The Rules of Sociological Method,* New York: Free Press.

Dyer, G. (1982), *Advertising as Communication,* London: Methuen.

Easthope, A. (1990), *What a Man's Gotta Do: The Masculine Myth in Popular Culture,* London: Unwin Hyman.

Eitzen, S. (2000), 'Social Control and Sport', in J. Coakely and E. Dunning, eds, *Handbook of Sport Studies,* London: Sage.

Elliott, S. (2008), 'For Marketing, the Most Valuable Player Might Be YouTube', *The New York Times* (5 Feb.).

Ellis, C., and Bochner, A. (2000), 'Autoethnography, Personal Narrative, Reflexivity: Researcher as Subject', in N. K. Denzin and Y. S. Lincoln, eds, *Handbook of Qualitative Research* (2nd edn), Thousand Oaks: Sage.

Ellis, C., and Flaherty, M. G. (1992), 'An Agenda for the Interpretation of Lived Experience', in C. Ellis and M. G. Flaherty, eds, *Investigating Subjectivity: Research on Lived Experience,* Newbury Park: Sage.

Elmer, D. (2008), 'Beijing Olympics: By Numbers', *The Telegraph* (2 Aug.), <http://www.telegraph.co.uk/sport/othersports/olympics/2489001/Beijing-Olympics-By-numbers.html> accessed 16 December.

Elmwood, V. A. (2005), ' "Just Some Bum from the Neighborhood": the Resolution of Post–Civil Rights Tension and Heavyweight Public Sphere Discourse in *Rocky*', *Film and History: An Interdisciplinary Journal of Film and Television Studies,* 35: 49–59.

Emmison, M., and Smith, P. (2000), *Researching the Visual: Images, Objects, Contexts and Interactions in Social and Cultural Inquiry,* London: Sage.

Erikson, B. (2005), 'Style Matters: Explorations of Bodies, Whiteness, and Identity', *Sociology of Sport Journal,* 22: 373–96.

Finlay, F., and Johnson, S. (1997), 'Do Men Gossip? An Analysis of Football Talk on Television', in S. Johnson and U. Meinhof, eds, *Language and Masculinity,* London: Blackwell.

Fishman, M. (1980), *Manufacturing the News,* Austin: University of Texas Press.

Fiske, J. (1987), *Television Culture,* London: Routledge.

Foucault, M. (1972), *The Archaeology of Knowledge,* London: Tavistock.

Foucault, M. (1977), *Discipline and Punish: The Birth of the Prison,* London: Penguin.

Foucault, M. (1978), *The History of Sexuality: An Introduction,* London: Penguin.

Foucault, M. (1979), *Discipline and Punish: the Birth of the Prison,* Harmondsworth: Peregrine.

Fox Super Bowl Sunday Pregame Show (2008), Fox Network (3 Feb.) [television broadcast].

Frey, J., and Eitzen, S. (1991), 'Sport and Society', *Annual Review of Sociology,* 17: 503–22.

Fuss, D. (1992), 'Fashion and the Homospectatorial Look', *Critical Inquiry,* 18: 713–37.

Fyfe, G., and Ross, M. (1996), 'Decoding the Visitor's Gaze: Rethinking Museum Visiting', in S. Macdonald and G. Fyfe, eds, *Theorising Museums: Representing Identity and Diversity in a Changing World,* Oxford: Blackwell / Sociological Review.

Gans, H. (1979), *Deciding What's News: A Study of CBS Evening News, NBC Nightly News, Newsweek and Time,* New York: Pantheon Books.

'Gazza Laid Bare' (2003), *Observer Sport Monthly* (2 Feb.).

George Best's Body (Football Stories) (2001), Channel 4 (25 June) [television broadcast].

Giannetti, L. (2005), *Understanding Movies,* Upper Saddle River: Pearson / Prentice Hall.

Goddard, A. (2002), *The Language of Advertising: Written Texts,* London: Routledge.

Goldaper, S. (1988), 'A Stellar Career Abruptly Clouded', *The New York Times* (27 Sept.), <http://query.nytimes.com/gst/fullpage.html?res=940DE4DC173EF934A 1575AC0A96E948260&scp=1&sq=&st=cse> accessed 19 February 2008.

'Golden Joy: Kelly's Historic Double' (2004), *The Sunday Times* (29 Aug.).

Goldman, R. (1992), *Reading Ads Socially,* London: Routledge.

Goldman, R., and Papson, S. (1998), *Nike Culture,* London: Sage.

Gough-Yates, A. (2003), *Understanding Women's Magazines: Publishing, Markets and Readership,* London: Routledge.

Graber, D. A. (1979), *Mass Media and American Politics,* Washington, DC: Congressional Quarterly Press.

Grossberg, L. (1992), *'We Gotta Get Out of This Place': Popular Conservatism and Postmodern Culture,* New York: Routledge.

Hall, S. (1980), 'Encoding and Decoding', in S. Hall, D. Hobson, A. Lowe, and P. Willis, eds, *Culture, Media, Language,* London: Hutchinson.

Hall, S. (1992), 'The Question of Cultural Identity', in S. Hall, D. Held, and A. McGrew, eds, *Modernity and Its Futures,* Cambridge: Polity Press.

Hall, S., Hobson, D., Lowe, A., and Willis, P., eds (1980), *Culture, Media, Language,* London: Hutchinson.

Hardt, M. (2007), 'Foreword: What Affects Are Good For', in P. Clough, ed., *The Affective Turn: Theorizing the Social,* Durham: Duke University Press.

Hargreaves, J. (1994), *Sporting Females: Critical Issues in the History and Sociology of Women's Sports,* London: Routledge.

Harris, J. C., and Hills, L. A. (1993), 'Telling the Story: Narrative in Newspaper Accounts of a Men's College Basketball Tournament', *Research Quarterly for Exercise and Sport Science,* 64: 108–21.

Harrison, D. (2004), 'Kelly's All Goold', *News of the World* (29 Aug.).

Harvey, D. (1990), *The Condition of Postmodernity,* Oxford: Blackwell.

Hayward, S. (2006), *Cinema Studies: The Key Concepts,* London: Routledge.

'Henman Caps Months of Agony' (2004), *The Sun* (1 July).

Hills, L., and Kennedy, E. (2006), 'Space Invaders at Wimbledon: Televised Sport and Deterritorialization', *Sociology of Sport Journal,* 23: 419–37.

Hills, L., and Kennedy, E. (2009), 'Double Trouble: Kelly Holmes, Intersectionality and Unstable Narratives of Olympic Heroism', in P. Markula and T. Bruce, eds, *Olympic Women and the Media: International Perspectives,* Basingstoke: Palgrave Macmillan.

Hillyard, D. (1994), 'Televised Sport and the (Anti)Sociological Imagination', *Journal of Sport and Social Issues,* 18: 88–99.

Hogan, J. (2003), 'Staging the Nation: Gendered and Ethnicized Discourses of National Identity in Olympic Opening Ceremonies', *Journal of Sport and Social Issues,* 27: 100–23.

Hoke, J. (2002), 'Brandscaping: New Dimensions in Retail Design—an Expert Roundtable', in O. Riewoldt, ed., *Brandscaping: Worlds of Experience in Retail Design,* Basel: Birkhauser.

Holmes, T. (2007), 'Mapping the Magazine: an Introduction', *Journalism Studies,* 8: 510–21.

Horne, J. (2006), *Sport in Consumer Culture,* Basingstoke: Palgrave.

Horovitz, B. (2008), 'Budweiser's Dog and Pony Show Takes Top Ad Meter Spot', *USA Today,* <http://www.usatoday.com/money/advertising/admeter/2008admeter. htm> accessed 6 May 2008.

Horrocks, R. (1995), *Male Myths and Icons: Masculinity in Popular Culture,* London: Macmillan.

Horscroft, J. (2007), 'Black and Merciless', *Climber* (Oct.).

Hughes, R. (2004), 'Wake Me Up It's a Dream Says Kelly', *Sunday Times* (29 Aug.).

Hughson, J. (2005), 'The Loneliness of the Angry Young Sportsman', *Muse,* 35: 41–8.

Huizinga, J. (1949), *Homo Ludens: A Study of the Play Element in Contemporary Civilization,* London: Routledge and Kegan Paul.

Hunter, L. (2005), 'What's Natural about It? A Baseball Movie as Introduction to Key Concepts in Cultural Studies', *Muse,* 35: 71–7.

'Inside the Mind of Roy Keane' (2002), *Observer Sport Monthly* (1 Sept.).

Irwin, M. (2008), 'Is It Any Wonder?', *The Sun* (1 Feb.).

Jackson, J. (2008), 'Heroic Howard Spells End for Liverpool', *The Observer* (17 Feb.).

Jackson, S. (1998), 'A Twist of Race: Ben Johnson and the Canadian Crisis of Racial and National Identity', *Sociology of Sport Journal,* 15: 21–40.

Jackson, S., Andrews, D., and Scherer, J. (2005), 'Introduction: the Contemporary Landscape of Sport Advertising', in S. Jackson and D. Andrews, eds, *Sport,*

Culture and Advertising: Identities, Commodities and the Politics of Representation, London: Routledge.

Janofsky, M. (1988a), 'Drug Cheaters May Be Winning the Battle of Wits with Testers', *The New York Times* (15 Sept.).

Janofsky, M. (1988b), 'At Edge of Furor, Lewis Describes Dream Come True', *The New York Times* (28 Sept.).

Janofsky, M. (1989), 'Coach Tells a Canadian Inquiry Johnson Used Steroids since '81', *The New York Times* (2 March).

Janofsky, M., and Alfano, P. (1988), 'Drug Use by Athletes Runs Free Despite Test', *The New York Times* (19 Sept.).

Jarvie, G., and Maguire, J. (1994), *Sport and Leisure in Social Thought,* London: Routledge.

Jensen, E., Gurber, J., and Babcock, G. (1987), 'Drug Abuse and Politics: The Construction of a Social Problem,' paper presented at the meeting of the Society for the Study of Social Problems, Chicago.

Jhally, S. (1990), *The Codes of Advertising: Fetishism and the Political Economy of Meaning in the Consumer Society,* London: Routledge.

Jobling, I. (2005), 'Olympics 2004', *Berkshire Encyclopedia of World Sport,* 3: 1107–11.

Jones, G. (2005), 'Down on the Floor and Give Me Ten Sit-Ups: the British Sports Feature Film?' *Muse,* 35: 29–40.

Jones, G. (2008), 'In Praise of an "Invisible Genre"? An Ambivalent Look at the Fictional Sports Feature Film', *Sport in Society,* 11: 117–29.

Kane, M. J., and Greendorfer, S. (1994), 'The Media's Role in Accommodating and Resisting Stereotyped Images of Women in Sport', in P. Creedon, ed., *Women, Media and Sport,* London: Sage.

Kaufman, M. (1988), 'Rise in Steroid Use Seen as Side Effect', *The New York Times* (29 Sept.), <http://www.nytimes.com/1988/09/29/sports/the-seoul-olympics-rise-in-steroid-use-seen-as-side-effect.htm> accessed 19 February 2008.

Kelley, S., and Turley, L. W. (2004), 'The Effect of Content on Perceived Affect of Super Bowl Commercials', *Journal of Sport Management,* 18: 398–420.

Kellner, D. (2003), *Media Spectacle,* London: Routledge.

Kennedy, E. (2000), ' "You Talk a Good Game": Football and Masculine Style on British Television', *Men and Masculinities,* 3: 56–84.

Kennedy, E., Pussard, H., and Thornton, A. (2006), ' "Leap for London"? Investigating the Affective Power of the Sport Spectacle', *World Leisure,* 48: 6–21.

Kerr, A., Kücklich, J., and Brereton, P. (2006), 'New Media—New Pleasures', *International Journal of Cultural Studies,* 9: 63–82.

Kidd, B., Edelman, R., and Brownell, S. (2001), 'Comparative Analysis of Doping Scandals: Canada, Russia, and China', in W. Wilson and E. Derse, eds, *Doping in Elite Sport—the Politics of Drugs in the Olympic Movement,* Champaign: Human Kinetics.

King, D. (2007), 'Fans Flock to DIY Video Highlights', *Information Today,* 24: 37.

Klein, N. (2000), *No Logo,* London: Flamingo.

Knox, G. (2008), 'A Happy Hending', *The Sun* (13 Feb.).

Lacan, J. (1977), *Ecrits: A Selection,* London: Tavistock.

La Monica, P. R. (2006), 'Super Bowl XL's Extra-Large Ad Sales', <http://money. cnn.com/2006/01/03/news/companies/superbowlads/index.htm> accessed 6 March 2008.

'The Land of Opportunity?' (2007), *The New York Times* (13 July), <http://www. nytimes.com/2007/07/13/opinion/13fri2.html> accessed 5 May 2008.

Landow, G. (2001), 'Hypertext and Critical Theory', in D. Trend, ed., *Reading Digital Culture,* Oxford: Blackwell.

Lapchick, R. (2006), 'The 2006 Racial and Gender Report Card: Major League Baseball', <http://www.bus.ucf.edu/sport/public/downloads/2005_Racial_Gender_ Report_Card_MLB.pdf> accessed 29 November 2007.

Laurel, B. (2001), 'Computers as Theatre', in D. Trend, ed., *Reading Digital Culture,* Oxford: Blackwell.

Lidchi, H. (1997), 'The Poetics and Politics of Exhibition in Other Cultures', in S. Hall, ed., *Representation: Cultural Representation and Signifying Practices,* London: Sage.

Lipton, M. (2008a), 'The Red Lion to Three Lions!', *Daily Mirror* (1 Feb.).

Lipton, M. (2008b), 'Snarling Cup Final', *Daily Mirror* (22 Feb.).

Lury, C. (2004), *Brands: The Logos of the Global Economy,* London: Routledge.

Macdonald, M. (1995), *Representing Women: Myths of Femininity in the Popular Media,* London: Edward Arnold.

MacLuhan, M. (1964), *Understanding Media: Extensions of Man,* New York: McGraw-Hill.

Malloy, D. (2007), 'Matsuzaka Was on the Money', *The Boston Globe* (4 July).

Massumi, B. (2002), *Parables of the Virtual: Movement, Affect, Sensation,* Durham: Duke University Press.

Mautner, G. (2005), 'Time to Get Wired: Using Web-based Corpora in Critical Discourse Analysis', *Discourse and Society,* 16: 809–28.

Mayberry, K., Proctor, M., and Srb, R. (1996), 'The Agony of Deceit: Ladies' Night at the NBC Olympics—Television Coverage of the 1996 Olympics', *Humanist,* 56, <http://findarticles.com/p/articles/mi_m1374/is_n6_v56/ai_18844573> accessed 5 December 2007.

McArthur, C. (1975), 'Setting the Scene: Radio Times and TV Times', in E. Buscombe, ed., *Football on Television,* London: BFI.

McCarthy, A. (2001), *Ambient Television: Visual Culture and Public Space,* Durham: Duke University Press.

McCracken, E. (1993), *Decoding Women's Magazines from Mademoiselle to Ms,* Houndsmill: Macmillan.

McDonald, M. G., and Andrews, D. L. (2001), 'Michael Jordan: Corporate Sport and Post-modern Celebrityhood', in D. L. Andrews and S. J. Jackson, eds, *Sport Stars: The Cultural Politics of Sporting Celebrity,* London: Routledge.

McKay, J. (2005), 'Enlightened Racism and Celebrity Feminism in Contemporary Sports Advertising Discourse', in S. Jackson and D. Andrews, eds, *Sport, Culture and Advertising: Identities, Commodities and the Politics of Representation,* London: Routledge.

McKay, J., and Rowe, D. (1987), 'Ideology, the Media and Australian Sport', *Sociology of Sport Journal,* 4: 258–73.

McLoughlin, L. (2000), *The Language of Magazines,* London: Routledge.

Metz, C. (1974), *Film Language,* Chicago: University of Chicago Press.

Miller, T. (2000), 'Men of the Game', in K. Schaffer and S. Smith, eds, *The Olympics at the Millennium: Power, Politics and the Games,* Piscataway: Rutgers University Press.

Mills, S. (1992), 'Knowing Your Place: a Marxist Feminist Stylistic Analysis', in M. Toolan, ed., *Language, Text and Context,* London: Routledge.

Mills, S. (1997), *Discourse,* London: Routledge.

'MLB Shatters Attendance Record' (2007), <http://mlb.mlb.com/news/press_releases/press_release.jsp?ymd=20071002&content_id=2245590&vkey=pr_mlb&fext=.jsp&c_id=mlb> accessed 23 December 2008.

Modleski, T. (1984), *Loving with a Vengeance: Mass Produced Fantasies for Women,* London: Methuen.

Morley, D. (2000), *Home Territories: Media, Mobility and Identity,* London: Routledge.

Nakamura, L. (2001), 'Race in/for Cyberspace: Identity Tourism and Racial Passing on the Internet', in D. Trend, ed., *Reading Digital Culture,* Oxford: Blackwell.

Newman, B. (2007), 'Editorial: Dollie Mixture', *Climber* (Oct.).

Nielsen Media Research (2008), 'The Final Tally—4.7 Billion Tunes in to Beijing 2008—More Than Two in Three People Worldwide', <http://blog.nielsen.com/nielsenwire/wp-content/uploads/2008/09/press_release3.pdf> accessed 16 December 2008.

Nike Brand Design (2002), 'NikeTown, London', in O. Riewoldt, ed., *Brandscaping: Worlds of Experience in Retail Design,* Basel: Birkhauser.

'Nike Just Doing It for the Cause' (2005), *The Guardian* (10 Feb.), <http://www.guardian.co.uk/football/2005/feb/10/newsstory.sport11> accessed 2 May 2008.

Nixon, H. (1984), *Sport and the American Dream,* Champaign: Human Kinetics.

O'Connor, A. (2008), 'Games Torch Invitation for Christie Sparks Anger', *The Times* (22 Feb.).

Ogden, D. C. (2007), 'Major League Baseball and Myth Making: Roland Barthes's Semiology and the Maintenance of Image', *Nine: A Journal of Baseball History and Culture,* 15: 66–78.

'One Day in Seoul' (1988), *The New York Times* (28 Sept.).

Orgad, S. (2006), 'The Cultural Dimensions of Online Communication: a Study of Breast Cancer Patients' Internet Spaces', *New Media and Society,* 8: 877–99.

Orvice, V. (2008), 'Don't Make Me a Leper', *The Sun* (13 Feb.).

O'Sullivan, T. (2000), 'Public Service Broadcasting', in D. Fleming, ed., *Formations: A 21st Century Media Studies Textbook,* Manchester: Manchester University Press.

O'Sullivan, T., Dutton, B., and Rayner, P. (2003), *Studying the Media,* London: HodderArnold.

'Our Decade: New Lad Rules the World' (1999), *BBC News,* <http://news.bbc.co.uk/1/hi/special_report/1999/02/99/e-cyclopedia/289778.stm> accessed 24 December 2008.

Ovett, S. (2004), 'Why We Do It', *The Observer* (29 Aug.).

Padwe, S. (1989), 'Drugs in Sports: Symptoms of a Deeper Malaise', in D. S. Eitzen, ed., *Sport in Contemporary Society,* New York: St Martin's Press.

Paterson, M. (2006), *Consumption and Everyday Life,* London: Routledge.

Pauwels, L. (2005), 'Websites as Visual and Multimodal Cultural Expressions: Opportunities and Issues of Online Hybrid Media Research', *Media, Culture and Society,* 27: 604–13.

Perrin, J. (2007), 'Us vs. Them', *Climber* (Oct.).

Phillips, M. (2008), 'Christie Torch Role Sparks Uproar in Olympic Circles', *The Guardian* (22 Feb.).

Phillips, W. (2002), *Film: An Introduction* (2nd edn), Boston: Bedford/St Martin's Press.

Pickford, D. (2007), 'Culm Dancing', *Climber* (Oct.).

Porter, G. (1996), 'Seeing through Solidity: a Feminist Perspective on Museums', in S. Macdonald and G. Fyfe, eds, *Theorizing Museums: Representing Identity and Diversity in a Changing World,* Oxford: Blackwell / Sociological Review.

Pritchard, S. (2002), 'Who Do We Think You Are?' *The Observer* (3 March), <http://observer.guardian.co.uk/readerseditor/story/0,661155,00.html> accessed 26 March 2007.

Rail, G., and Harvey, J. (1995), 'Body at Work: Michel Foucault and the Sociology of Sport', *Sociology of Sport Journal,* 12: 164–79.

Reah, D. (1998), *The Language of Newspapers* (2nd edn), London: Routledge.

Reilly, R. (1998), 'The Flip Side of What's Right about Sports', <http://64.236.22.106/features/1998/weekly/lifeofreilly/0810/index.html> accessed 23 December 2008.

Rein, I., and Shields, B. (2007), 'Reconnecting the Baseball Star', *NINE: A Journal of Baseball History and Culture,* 16: 62–77.

Reuters (2008), 'Super Bowl Ads Take Equal Billing to Game in 2008 According to Hanon McKendry Survey', <http://www.reuters.com/article/pressRelease/idUS299968+31-Jan-2008+PRN20080131> accessed 6 May 2008.

Richard K. Miller and Associates (2006), 'Sports Online', in *Sports Marketing 2006,* Loganville: Richard K. Miller and Associates.

Richardson, J. (2007), *Analysing Newspapers: an Approach from Critical Discourse Analysis,* Houndsmill: Palgrave Macmillan.

Riewoldt, O., ed. (2002), introduction in *Brandscaping: Worlds of Experience in Retail Design,* Basel: Birkhauser.

Rigauer, B. (1981), *Sport and Work: European Perspectives,* tr. A. Guttmann, New York: Columbia University Press.

Robinson, V. (2004), 'Taking Risks: Identities, Masculinities and Rock Climbing', in B. Wheaton, ed., *Understanding Lifestyle Sports,* London: Routledge.

Rose, G. (2001), *Visual Methodologies,* London: Sage.

Rose, G. (2007), *Visual Methodologies: an Introduction to the Interpretation of Visual Materials* (2nd edn), London: Sage.

Rowe, D. (1998), 'If You Film It, Will They Come?' *Journal of Sport and Social Issues,* 22: 350–9.

Rowe, D. (1999), *Sport, Culture and the Media: the Unholy Trinity,* Buckingham: Open University Press.

Rowe, D. (2004a), *Sport, Culture and the Media: the Unholy Trinity* (2nd edn), Maidenhead: Open University Press.

Rowe, D., ed. (2004b), *Critical Readings: Sport, Culture and the Media,* Maidenhead: Open University Press.

Ryall, T. (1975), 'Scotland v Yugoslavia', in E. Buscombe, ed., *Football on Television,* London: BFI.

Sabey, R., and Bhatia, S. (2004), 'Kelly Does Old Won 2', *News of the World* (29 Aug.).

Sarup, M. (1996), *Identity, Culture and the Postmodern World,* Edinburgh: Edinburgh University Press.

Schneider, S., and Foot, K. (2004), 'The Web as an Object of Study', *New Media and Society,* 6: 114–22.

Seiter, E. (1992), 'Semiotics, Structuralism and Television', in R. Allen, ed., *Channels of Discourse Reassembled,* London: Routledge.

Silverman, K. (1983), *The Subject of Semiotics,* New York: Oxford University Press.

Skeggs, B. (2004), *Class, Self, Culture,* London: Routledge.

Sloan, J. (2008), 'Are Race Punters Sexist? You Bet!', *Daily Mirror* (22 Feb.).

Smith, D. (2004), 'Victory for a Very Modern Heroine', *The Observer* (29 Aug.).

Spancken, J. (2007), 'Time of Nick', *Climber* (Oct.).

Spencer, N. E. (2003), 'America's Sweetheart and "Czech-mate": a Discursive Analysis of the Evert-Navratilova Rivalry', *Journal of Sport and Social Issues,* 27: 18–37.

Spielberg, S. (2007), letter to His Excellency Hu Jintao, President of the People's Republic of China, 2 April, <http://media.npr.org/programs/atc/features/2007/jul/spielberg_letter.pdf> accessed 5 May 2007.

Squire, M., and Redmond, R. (2004), 'Publisher's Letter', *Crush,* 1: 13.

Stam, R., Burgoyne, R., and Flitterman-Lewis, S. (1992), *New Vocabularies in Film Semiotics,* London: Routledge.

Stibbe, A. (2004), 'Health and the Social Construction of Masculinity in Men's Health Magazine', *Men and Masculinities,* 7: 31–51.

Stretch, E. (2004), 'I Wish I Could Hug My Little Girl Again but She Doesn't Want to Know Me', *Sunday Mirror* (29 Aug.).

Thom, R. (1999), 'Designing a Movie for Sound', <http://www.filmsound.org/articles/designing_for_sound.htm> accessed 5 May 2008.

Thomas, J. (1993), *Doing Critical Ethnography,* Newbury Park: Sage.

Tilley, R. (2004), 'Editor's Letter', *Crush,* 1: 13.

Tolvhed, H. (2007), 'Sporting the Nation: Gender, Ethnicity and Whiteness in Swedish Media Coverage of the Olympic Games, 1948–1972', paper presented at ISSA and ISHPES Joint World Congress 'Sport in a Global World: Past, Present and Future', Copenhagen, 31 July–5 August.

Tomlinson, A. (2000), 'Carrying the Torch for Whom? Symbolic Power and Olympic Ceremony', in K. Schaffer and S. Smith, eds, *The Olympics at the Millennium: Power, Politics and the Games,* Piscataway: Rutgers University Press.

Trend, D., ed. (2001), *Reading Digital Culture,* Oxford: Blackwell.

Trujillo, N., and Ekdom, L. R. (1985), 'Sportswriting and American Cultural Values: the 1984 Chicago Cubs', *Critical Studies in Mass Communication,* 2: 261–81.

Tuchman, G. (1978), *Making News: a Study in the Construction of Reality,* New York: Free Press.

Tudor, A. (1975), 'The Panels', in E. Buscombe, ed., *Football on Television,* London: BFI.

Turner, G. (1994), 'Film Languages', in D. Graddol and O. Boyd-Barrett, eds, *Media Texts: Authors and Readers,* Clevedon: Multilingual Matters / Open University Press.

'Using the Brand' (2008), <http://business.london-2012.co.uk/Use-of-Olympic-marks/> accessed 2 May 2008.

Van Dijk, T. (1983), 'Discourse Analysis: Its Development and Application to the Structure of News', *Journal of Communication,* 33: 20–33.

Van Maanen, J. (1988), *Tales of the Field: on Writing Ethnography,* Chicago: University of Chicago Press.

Van Zoonen, L. (1994), *Feminist Media Studies,* London: Sage.

Vecsey, G. (1989), 'Other Shoe Dropping on Johnson', *The New York Times* (3 March).

Wallace, A. C. (1988), 'Drug Testing Programme May Start Quickly', *The New York Times* (29 Nov.).

Walvin, J. (1975), *The People's Game: A Social History of British Football,* London: Allen Lane.

Weisman, L. (2008), 'Flap about Pats' "Spygate" cools off', *USA Today* (1 Feb.).

Wenner, L., ed. (1998), *MediaSport,* London: Routledge.

Wensing, E., and Bruce, T. (2003), 'Bending the Rules: Media Representations of Gender during an International Sporting Event', *International Review for the Sociology of Sport,* 38: 387–96.

Wetherell, R. (2008), 'Patriots' Game Looks Primed for Perfection', *The Observer* (3 Feb.).

Whannel, G. (1992), *Fields in Vision: Television Sport and Cultural Transformation,* London: Routledge.

Whannel, G. (2002), *Media Sport Stars: Masculinities and Moralities,* London: Routledge.

Whannel, G. (2007), 'Mediating Masculinities: the Production of Media Representations in Sport', in C. Aitchison, ed., *Sport and Gender Identities: Masculinities, Femininities and Sexualities,* London: Routledge.

White, G., and Gillett, J. (1994), 'Reading the Muscular Body: a Critical Decoding of Advertisements in Flex Magazine', *Sociology of Sport,* 11: 18–39.

Williams, R. (1974), *Television: Technology and Cultural Form,* London: Fontana.

Williams, R. (1980), 'Advertising the Magic System', in *Problems in Materialism and Culture,* London: Verso.

Williamson, J. (1978), *Decoding Advertisements: Ideology and Meaning in Advertising,* London: Marion Boyars.

'Winking at Steroids in Sports' (1988), *The New York Times* (22 Nov.).

Winter, H. (2003), 'Beckham Now a Real Man', <http://www.theage.com.au/articles/2003/07/02/1056825456225.html> accessed 22 December 2008.

Wissinger, E. (2007), 'Always on Display: Affective Production in the Modelling Industry', in P. Clough, ed., *The Affective Turn: Theorizing the Social,* Durham: Duke University Press.

Index